Bloomsbury Professional's

Guide to the Companies Act 2014

Bloomsbury Professional's

Guide to the Companies Act 2014

General Editor

THOMAS B COURTNEY

Contributors

Nessa Cahill	Thomas B Courtney
William Johnston	Irene Lynch Fannon
Lyndon MacCann	Dáibhí O'Leary

Bloomsbury Professional

Published by
Bloomsbury Professional
Maxwelton House
41–43 Boltro Road
Haywards Heath
West Sussex
RH16 1BJ

Bloomsbury Professional
The Fitzwilliam Business Centre
26 Upper Pembroke Street
Dublin 2

ISBN: 978 178043 834 4
© Bloomsbury Professional Limited 2015
Bloomsbury Professional, an imprint of Bloomsbury Publishing Plc

British Library Cataloguing-in-Publication Data
A catalogue record for this book is available from the British Library

Typeset by Marlex Editorial Services Ltd, Dublin, Ireland
Printed and bound in Great Britain by
CPI Group (UK) Ltd, Croydon, CR0 4YY

Preface

The Companies Bill 2014 passed all stages in the Oireachtas on 10 December 2014 and will, when signed by the President, become the Companies Act 2014. This guide to the Companies Act 2014 is a by-product of *Bloomsbury Professional's Seminar on the Companies Act 2014*, to be held in early 2015.

In recognition of the fact that the Companies Act 2014 is the most significant change in Irish corporate law in two generations, Bloomsbury Professional persuaded its company law authors to agree to speak at a seminar and to contribute a chapter on the papers they present. I was asked to chair the seminar and agreed to deliver three papers. As chairperson of the seminar, the task of editing this book also fell to me. Given the calibre of the authors and their total command of their areas of expertise, however, my role as editor was a very easy one.

This book is a guide to the main changes introduced by the Companies Act 2014. It does not purport to be a comprehensive or complete analysis of the Act, Irish company law or, indeed, all of the changes introduced. For that type of treatment, you will have to await the new editions of Nessa's *Company Law Compliance and Enforcement*, William's *Banking and Security Law in Ireland*, Irene (and Gerard's) *Corporate Insolvency and Rescue*, Lyndon's *Companies Act 2014* and, I suppose, my own (with contributions from Brian and Dáibhí) *Law of Companies*. In persuading us to dip our toes into the new sea of company law, Bloomsbury Professional have whet our interest in writing new editions of our own books as the soundings I have taken from my colleagues in this project suggest that work is afoot.

I do not think a potted summary of each of the chapters, sometimes seen in a guide of this nature, is necessary: I believe that the chapter titles speak for themselves.

As at the time of writing, the Department of Jobs, Enterprise and Innovation has indicated that the Act is likely to be commenced, by statutory instrument, on 1 June 2015.

Dr Thomas B Courtney

General Editor and Contributor

December 2014

General Editor and Contributors

THOMAS B COURTNEY
BA, LLB, LLD, FCIS, Solicitor

Dr Thomas B Courtney is a corporate partner in Arthur Cox where he is head of the firm's Company Compliance and Governance group. He is Chairperson of the *Company Law Review Group* and has been since its establishment in 2000. His publications include *The Law of Companies* (3rd edn, 2012) and *Mareva Injunctions and Related Interlocutory Orders* (1998), *Lending After the Company Law Enforcement Act 2001* (2001 (co-author)) and he is co-general editor with Lyndon MacCann SC of *Companies Acts 1963–2012*. He was editor of the *Commercial Law Practitioner* from 1994 to 2003 and has written numerous legal articles and notes. Tom was awarded the Higher Doctorate in Laws (the LLD) from the NUI in 2004 for his published works including *The Law of Private Companies* (1994) which first introduced and promoted the segregation of the law applicable to private companies limited by shares, the concept which now informs the structure of the Companies Act 2014. He was a member of the McDowell Group on Company Law Compliance and Enforcement (1998) and was a member of the EU Commission's Advisory Group on Corporate Governance and Company Law (2005–2009). In 2014 he was elected a Fellow of the Institute of Chartered Secretaries and Administrators. He is the company law examiner for the Law Society's FE1 examination. Tom was a member of the Arthur Cox team which advised the Irish Government on the legislative response to the financial crisis including the Anglo Irish Bank Corporation Act 2009, the National Asset Management Agency Act 2009 and the Credit Institutions (Stabilisation) Act 2010.

NESSA CAHILL
LLB (TCD, 1996), LLM (Bruges, 1997), BL (King's Inns, 1999)

Nessa Cahill is a practising barrister, having been called to the Irish Bar in 1999, and specialises in the areas of banking, auditing, company law, corporate finance and telecommunications regulation.

She is a graduate of the Law School at University of Dublin, Trinity College, the College of Europe in Bruges, and the Honourable Society of King's Inns. Nessa has worked as a researcher in the Judges' Library, the Law Reform Commission and at the International Criminal Tribunal for Rwanda in Tanzania. In addition to being admitted to practice in Ireland and in Northern Ireland, Nessa is admitted to practice in the State of New York and spent two years working as a capital markets and litigation associate in the New York law firm of Shearman & Sterling.

She has delivered several lectures on company law and company law enforcement, including at the Law Society (Diploma in Corporate Law and Governance and Diploma in Insolvency and Corporate Restructuring) and at the Irish Corporate Law Forum.

Her textbook on Company Law Compliance and Enforcement was published by Bloomsbury Professional in 2008.

WILLIAM JOHNSTON
MA, Solicitor

William Johnston is an economics graduate of Trinity College Dublin, a solicitor and has been a partner in Arthur Cox for 29 years. His experience includes advising on the review of security held by credit institutions for the stress testing of the banking sector, the drafting of the National Asset Management Agency legislation, the preparatory work for the transfer of assets and the preparation of standard financing documents, appropriate bank lending procedures and standard financing and security agreements, deposit protection and the credit union sector. He is regularly ranked in Tier 1 of banking lawyers by Chambers Europe and Chambers World.

He has been a member of the Company Law Review Group since its inception and has chaired sub-committees on creditor protection, registration of charges, charging orders over shares and examinership reform. He was a member of the 1992 Company Law Review Group and a former chair of the Law Society's Business Law Committee.

He is co-chair of the Banking Law Committee of the International Bar Association (IBA), having been chair of the Legal Opinions Committee and the Banking Regulation Committee. He has spoken on banking law at IBA events in Auckland, Prague, Edinburgh, Singapore, Madrid, Dublin and Boston. He is Honorary Secretary of the National Maternity Hospital, Holles Street, Dublin.

His publications include, *Banking and Security Law in Ireland* (1998), *Lending after the Company Law Enforcement Act 2001* (2001 (co-author)), *Arthur Cox Banking Law Handbook* (2007 (co-editor)), *Security over Receivables* (2008 (editor)) and *Set-off Law and Practice* (2006 and 2010, (co-editor)).

IRENE LYNCH FANNON
BCL (NUI), BCL (Oxon), SJD (University of Virginia), Solicitor

Professor Irene Lynch Fannon is a graduate of University College Dublin (BCL, 1982); Oxford University (BCL, 1986, Senior Scholar, Somerville College) and the University of Virginia (Doctor of Juridical Science, 1999). She qualified as a solicitor in 1985. She has published extensively in Irish and EU Corporate Insolvency Law, Corporate Governance and Employment Law. She co-authored the first edition of *Corporate Insolvency and Rescue* (1996) with Jane Marshall and Rory O'Farrell and has co-authored a second edition in 2012 with Gerard Murphy BL. She has written extensively in the area of insolvency law. In 2009 she co-authored a monograph on *IRELAND: Corporations and Partnership Law* for the International Encyclopaedia of Laws which will be updated in 2015. Professor Lynch Fannon maintains an interest in comparative EU and US corporate governance following her work, *Working Within Two Kinds of Capitalism* (2003) and additional chapter and article publications. She was a visiting Professor at Cleveland Marshall College of Law and held the Baker Hostetler Chair during the academic years 2002–2004. She was a member of the Business Regulation Forum and subsequently the High Level Group on Business Regulation 2007–2011, both established by the Irish Government. She was a member of the Audit Review Group established by the Irish Government following the Public Accounts Committee Enquiry into DIRT.

She has been a Professor in the Faculty of Law at University College Cork since 2002 and she is currently a Visiting Academic at Oxford Law Faculty (until December 2014) with scholarship accommodation at Merton College, Oxford.

LYNDON MacCANN
BA (Mod), MLitt, SC

Lyndon MacCann was called to the Bar in 1988 and to the Inner Bar in 2003. He is a Senior Counsel specialising in company and commercial law and has previously lectured in Trinity College Dublin and in Dublin City University. He also lectured for several years on bankruptcy and receiverships in the United Kingdom preparing candidates for the statutory examinations which they must pass to qualify as licensed insolvency practitioners. He is a former external examiner in company law and in insolvency law for the King's Inns and was for several years a nominee of the Bar Council of Ireland on the Rules Committee of the Irish Superior Courts.

Lyndon has written numerous legal articles for both professional and academic publications and is the co-general editor of *Companies Acts 1963–2012* which is now in its fifth edition. He is also the editor of *A Casebook on Company Law* (1991).

DÁIBHÍ O'LEARY
B Comm (Int) and French, M Acc, Solicitor

Dáibhí O'Leary is an associate in the Company Compliance and Governance Group of Arthur Cox, having previously trained and qualified as a chartered accountant with KPMG. Dáibhí has contributed the chapter on Financial Statements, Audit and Annual Return to Courtney, *The Law of Companies*, (3rd edn, 2012) and contributed to MacCann and Courtney, *Companies Acts 1963–2012*. He writes the quarterly update of Irish company law developments for Bloomsbury Professional. Dáibhí has addressed the Annual Conference of Chartered Accountants Ireland in relation to the Companies Act, and has had articles on the Act published in its online journals. He also lectures on the Act on the Law Society of Ireland Professional and Diploma courses. Dáibhí's practice in Arthur Cox primarily involves advising on company law and other legislation, in particular in relation to financial statements and corporate governance matters. Dáibhí was part of the Arthur Cox team which advised on the legislative response to the financial crisis including the Credit Institutions (Stabilisation) Act 2010, Central Bank and Credit Institutions (Resolution) Act 2011 and Irish Bank Resolution Corporation Act 2013.

Contents

Chapter 1 Companies Act 2014: Anatomy of the Act

(*Dr Thomas B Courtney*)

Chapter 2 Changes in the Basics: Constitutions, Share Capital and Governance

(*Dr Thomas B Courtney*)

Chapter 3 Changes to Re-registration, Registers and Filings

(*Dáibhí O'Leary*)

Chapter 4 Changes in the Law of Directors' Duties

(Dr Thomas B Courtney)

Chapter 5 Taking Security, the Summary Approval Procedure and the Registration of Charges

(William Johnston)

Chapter 6 Corporate Restructuring: Schemes, Mergers and Divisions

(Lyndon MacCann SC)

Chapter 7 Insolvency and Rescue

(Professor Irene Lynch Fannon)

Chapter 8 Compliance and Enforcement

(Nessa Cahill BL)

Table of Cases

Table of Legislation

Primary Legislation

Statutory Instruments

European Legislation

Other Jurisdictions

Chapter 1

Companies Act 2014: Anatomy of the Act

by
Dr Thomas B Courtney

Introduction

[1.001] The Companies Act 2014: 25 Parts, 1,448 sections of law and 17 Schedules. The Act repeals in whole some 32 enactments – 17 statutes and 15 statutory instruments – restating much of that law into organised groups as well as amending other provisions, and codifying judicial developments in certain areas. In one enactment we now have a state-of-the-art statement of the law applicable to the creation by registration of separate legal persons, ie companies, from their formation, administration and management to their winding up and dissolution, incorporating the rights and duties of their officers, members and creditors.

[1.002] The Companies Act is, in many respects, innovative and far-reaching but as a massive exercise in consolidation it is not, in fact, unprecedented. If the history[1] of the registered company is taken to begin with the enactment in 1844 of the Joint Stock Companies Act, then company law can be seen to have been through three consolidations already. It seems that every two to three generations company law is subjected to a major make-over: statutory provisions in diverse enactments are consolidated, new or newly nuanced legal principles as developed by the judiciary are codified and new thinking, or reform, is captured in one state-of-the-art enactment.

The Companies Act 1862 which consolidated all previous Joint Stock Companies Acts has been described as the "first great consolidation Act concerning companies [which] was a masterpiece of draughtsmanship and arrangement and, apart therefrom, introduced a number of amendments".[2] Even popular culture picked up on the significance of the 1862 Act, Gilbert and Sullivan incorporating a reference to it in their opera *Utopia Limited*: "*All hail, astonishing Fact!/ All hail, Invention new/ The Joint Stock Company's Act/ The Act of Sixty Two*". Not very catchy, you might think, but given that the opera was

---

[1] For an historical outline of the registered company, see Courtney, *The Law of Companies* (3rd edn, Bloomsbury Professional, 2012) at paras [1.056] to [1.087].

[2] See Schmitthoff (ed), *Palmer's Company Law* (24th edn, Sweet & Maxwell, 1987) at para 2-09.

a lampoon of the concept of limited liability and of the actual or perceived mischiefs to which it gives rise, it can be conceived that it might attract an audience today.

The second great consolidation was the Companies (Consolidation) Act 1908, which contained 296 sections of law, and repealed in their entirety no fewer than 18 statutes spanning a forty-six-year period (between 1862 and 1908).[3] This body of company law saw Ireland through independence, two world wars and a new constitution.

Fast-forward another 55 years to 1963 to the third consolidation and the enactment of the Companies Act 1963. This was at the time conceived as a major innovation and consolidation. What has been until recently the "Principal Act" added over 100 new sections of law and repealed four statutes in their entirety.[4]

Without seeking to downplay the importance and significance of the Act to modern users and practitioners, by placing the Act in an historical context, the truth in the adage *plus ça change, plus c'est la même chose* can be seen. The enactment of the Act has made it the turn of this generation of lawyers, accountants and the users of company law to be the first to work with the fourth, and most recent, consolidating and reforming code of company law.

[1.003] The purpose of this chapter is to provide a mind-map of the Act: a sense of its origins, its innovative design, its focus on the new model company, the private company limited by shares or "LTD", some of the key innovations in the Act, an overview of new obligations on directors and companies as well as newly regulated activities and a brief overview of the structure and key content of each of the Act's 25 Parts. The following structure is followed:

1. Modern Irish company law reform;
2. The CLRG: simplification and consolidation;
3. The architecture of the Act;
4. The "LTD": the new model company;
5. Key innovations introduced by the Act;
6. New obligations and regulations;

---

[3]   The 18 statutes repealed in whole were: the Companies Act 1862, the Companies Seals Act 1864, the Companies Act 1867, the Joint Stock Companies Arrangement Act 1870, the Companies Act 1877, the Companies Act 1879, the Companies Act 1880, the Companies (Colonial Registers) Act 1883, the Companies Act 1886, the Companies (Memorandum of Association) Act 1890, the Companies (Winding up) Act 1890, the Directors Liability Act 1890, the Companies (Winding up) Act 1893, the Preferential Payments in Bankruptcy Amendment Act 1897, the Companies Act 1898, the Companies Act 1900, the Companies Act 1907 and the Companies Act 1908.

[4]   The four statutes repealed in whole were: the Companies (Consolidation) Act 1908, the Companies Act 1913, the Companies (Particulars as to Directors) Act 1917 and the Companies Act 1959.

7. Parts 1 to 15: Overview of the law applicable to the LTD;
8. Parts 16 to 25: Overview of other types of company and miscellaneous.

Modern Irish company law reform

[1.004] The catalyst for modern Irish company law reform was the Working Group on Company Compliance and Enforcement, chaired by Michael McDowell SC, which reported on 30 November 1998. While the McDowell Group is, rightly, primarily remembered for its recommendations which led to the creation of the Office of the Director of Corporate Enforcement, following the enactment of the Company Law Enforcement Act 2001, sight should not be lost of its recommendations on consolidation, codification and simplification.

[1.005] The only serious attempt to review Irish company law since the Arthur Cox Report (which inspired the Companies Act 1963) had been in 1994 when an ad hoc Company Law Review Group was established under the chairmanship of Mr James Gallagher. The group was asked to report, in five months,[5] upon seven discrete aspects of Irish company law:

- examinership,
- investigations,
- financial reporting,
- insider dealing,
- changes for small business,
- restriction of directors, and
- the position of farmer creditors.

While the work programme was described as Phase 1, there never was another phase. The McDowell Group's Report noted that after the Gallagher Group had made their report, the staff of the predecessor to the Department of Jobs, Enterprise and Innovation ('DJEI') had been allocated to implementing its proposals and that the Department felt obliged to deal with the first report before commissioning a second. The McDowell Report noted that the Gallagher Group had been, in effect, "put into a state of suspended animation as soon as it had delivered its report"[6] and said that it considered such a "stop-start procedure entirely unacceptable".[7]

[1.006] The McDowell Group made two specific recommendations which taken together created the environment which incubated the thinking that ultimately

---

[5] For an overview of the Gallagher Group's recommendations, see Courtney, *Company Law Review 1994*, (1995) at 1–13.
[6] *The Report of the Working Group in Company Law Compliance and Enforcement* (1998) at 5.26.
[7] *The Report of the Working Group in Company Law Compliance and Enforcement* (1998) at 5.28.

was translated into the policy of successive Governments and which has resulted in the enactment of the Companies Act 2014. The first of these recommendations was to establish a statutory Company Law Review Group:

"The Group is of the view that a Company Law Review Group composed along similar lines to the CLRG should be established on a statutory basis as soon as possible. This of, course, need not delay its re-establishment, in interim, on a non-statutory basis."[8]

The second seminal reforming recommendation concerned the consolidation and codification of company law. Whereas the first recommendation, when implemented, would provide the forum for reform, the second would set the agenda:

"... the Group is conscious that our company law is now to be found in a lengthening series of statutes and statutory regulations. The Group believes that parallel with the ongoing process of company law reform and renewal, a programme should be undertaken to codify or consolidate company law. The object of the process would be to incorporate the provisions of the existing Companies Acts and the substantive company law now set out in regulations made under the European Communities Act into one single comprehensible companies code."[9]

The McDowell Group's Report's recommendations were approved for implementation on 9 March 1999 by the then Government.

The CLRG: Simplification and consolidation

[1.007] The Company Law Review Group (CLRG) was established, as recommended by the McDowell Group, on an administrative basis on 8 December 1999 under the writer's chairmanship. The original 17 members of the group represented the social partners (ICTU and IBEC), the users of company law (CCABI, Law Society, Bar Council, Courts Service, Irish Stock Exchange, Institute of Directors, Institute of Chartered Secretaries and Administrators and specialist users nominated by the Minister) and regulators and State agencies (Revenue Commissioners, Companies Registration Office, Attorney General's Office, and the predecessor of the DJEI). Even before the CLRG was established on a statutory basis pursuant to s 67 of the Company

---

[8]   *The Report of the Working Group in Company Law Compliance and Enforcement* (1998) at 5.29.

[9]   *The Report of the Working Group in Company Law Compliance and Enforcement* (1998) at 5.41.

Law Enforcement Act 2001, it discharged the following functions, then mandated by s 68(1) of that Act:[10]

"The Review Group shall monitor, review and advise the Minister on matters concerning –

(a) the implementation of the Companies Acts,

(b) the amendment of the Companies Acts,

(c) the consolidation of the Companies Acts,

(d) the introduction of new legislation relating to the operation of companies and commercial practices in Ireland,

(e) the Rules of the Superior Courts and case law judgments insofar as they relate to the Companies Acts,

(f) the approach to issues arising from the State's membership of the European Union, insofar as they affect the operation of the Companies Acts,

(g) international developments in company law, insofar as they may provide lessons for improved State practice, and

(h) other related matters or issues, including issues submitted by the Minister to the Review Group for consideration."

[1.008] The CLRG's first work programme set by the then Tánaiste and Minister for Enterprise, Trade and Employment, Ms Mary Harney, charged the CLRG with making recommendations designed to simplify company law, particularly for small and medium-sized private companies. Building on the consolidation agenda set by the McDowell Group, the first work programme also required the CLRG to make recommendations on consolidation and its sequencing in the context of the major programme of simplification and reform.

[1.009] The CLRG recognised that the simplification of Irish company law was, without doubt, the most daunting of the areas which it was asked to consider and in its first report acknowledged that a body of law that must afford protection to shareholders and creditors and legislate for the orderly administration of solvent and insolvent companies, can never be truly *simple*. The CLRG stated that its approach to simplification involved seven distinct features:

"(i) A primary focus on the simplification of the law applicable to private limited companies.

(ii) Public limited company (plc) simplification to be confined to removing anomalies and uncertainties.

(iii) Simplification to be conducted from the perspective of the generic principles that are the *raison d'être* of our company laws. In the first work programme, those identified and reviewed are creditor protection,

---

[10] Now mandated by s 959(1) of the Act.

shareholder protection, corporate governance, incorporation and registration and the criminalisation of company law transgressions.

(iv) The restructuring of the Companies Acts, the ring-fencing of law that is only applicable to private limited companies and the greater use of defined terms.

(v) Following the *'think small first'* approach when considering new companies legislation.

(vi) The codification of well-established common law and equitable principles of company law.

(vii) The gradual migration of widely adopted provisions, currently contained in Table A, into primary legislation with a view to redefining the articles of association as a document for company specific internal rules."[11]

[1.010] Central to the CLRG's approach was the focus on the private company limited by shares. Since the creation of a distinct type of company, called a private company, was first permitted by the Companies Act 1907, it quickly came to be the most common type of company in Ireland. Ironically, the private company appeared almost as a legislative after-thought, the definition of the private company contained in s 37(1) of the Companies Act 1907 appearing under the heading, "*miscellaneous*". This and other anomalies in the way that some 89 per cent of all companies were treated in company law legislation were described by the CLRG thus:

"That legislative sidelining of the most popular corporate form continues to this day and although the vast bulk of companies are private companies, 'the company' that is envisaged by those Acts is the *public company*. By according the private company a specific definition, s 33(1) of the [Companies Act 1963] presupposes that the average company is the public company of which the private company is but a peculiar variation. Another example of this is provided by the model articles of association contained in Table A of the First Schedule to the 1963 Act. Notwithstanding that most companies registered in Ireland are private companies, Part II of Table A *applies* Part I, with certain modifications, to private companies limited by shares. To the extent that the most popular type of company is treated as if it were a minority variant form of registered company, this is a classic example of the 'tail wagging the dog'. The Group considers that the elevation of the private company, from an apparent afterthought to centre stage in the Companies Acts, is long overdue and recommends accordingly."[12]

Among the CLRG's other recommendations were:

    – "the private company limited by shares should be the primary focus of simplification";[13]

---

[11] See the CLRG's First Report (2001) at para 3.2.9.
[12] CLRG's First Report (2001) at para 3.6.3.
[13] CLRG's First Report (2001) at para 3.2.3.

- "the law should be clear and accessible ... the legislation should be structured in such a way that the provisions that apply to small companies are easily identifiable";[14]
- "the private company limited by shares should be established as the model company";[15]
- "the consolidated Companies Act should be sub-divided into two groups of law: the first group will define the private company and contain all company laws that apply to it and the second group will define the remaining types of company and the provisions that apply to each".[16]

It can be seen, readily, that the recommendations contained in the CLRG's first report provided the blueprint for the structure and approach adopted by the new Companies Act 2014.

The architecture of the Act

[1.011] Whereas other jurisdictions have modernised and consolidated their company laws, no other has flipped the focus from one where the public company is centre stage to one where the private company limited by shares is centre stage.[17] The first 15 Parts of the Act apply exclusively to the private company limited by shares, which shall be referred to in this book as the "LTD".[18] One of the consequences of this approach is to provide for the *physical* simplification of company law by the deliberate separation of its corpus into two distinct groups of parts: Parts 1 to 15 which concern the LTD and Parts 16 to 25 which concern every other type of company. Helpfully, the Government Stationery Office published the Act in two volumes. Users of the LTD (and their advisors) can safely limit their focus on the Act to its first volume.[19] The first 15 Parts, which concern the LTD, are:

- Part 1: Preliminary and general;
- Part 2: Incorporation and registration;
- Part 3: Share capital, shares and certain other instruments;

---

14 CLRG's First Report (2001) at para 3.2.8.
15 CLRG's First Report (2001) at para 3.6.5.
16 CLRG's First Report (2001) at para 3.7.2.
17 See Courtney "Remodelling Irish Company Law: Aspects of the Draft Companies Bill" (2011) Public Affairs Ireland (July/August) at p 8.
18 Initially, the CLRG had thought that the new model company might be known as the company limited by shares, perhaps even its name ending in the suffix, "CLS". When it was realised, however, that this could result in every model company wishing to opt into the new regime being required to changes its name from "LTD" to "CLS", this idea was abandoned. Note, however, that while the private company limited by shares is referred to here as the "LTD", and although the Act stipulates its name must end in "LTD" or "TEO", the company referred to in Parts 1 to 15 is not, unfortunately for shorthand and simplicity of reference, statutorily defined as the "LTD".
19 The only time a visit might be needed to volume 2 is if an LTD wishes to convert to another type of company: see Part 20 Re-Registration.

- Part 4: Corporate governance;
- Part 5: Duties of directors and other officers;
- Part 6: Financial statements, annual return and audit;
- Part 7: Charges and debentures;
- Part 8: Receivers;
- Part 9: Reorganisations, acquisitions, mergers and divisions;
- Part 10: Examinerships;
- Part 11: Winding up;
- Part 12: Strike off and restoration;
- Part 13: Investigations;
- Part 14: Compliance and enforcement;
- Part 15: Functions of Registrar and of regulatory and advisory bodies.

Of these 15 Parts, it is thought that most users of company law (and their advisors) will, ordinarily, be primarily concerned with Parts 1 to 6, some 407 sections of law, since giving security (Part 7) and reorganising (Part 9) will be, at most and for most, occasional events, and insolvency, strike-off, investigations and enforcement (Parts 8, 10–13) will, hopefully, be avoided by most companies.

[1.012] The CLRG recognised the fact that there are many types of company other than LTDs and recommended in favour of continuing to make provision for these other types of company, recognising that each had their own legitimate users.[20] Volume 2 of the Act contains a further 10 Parts, which contain the law governing other types of company, conversion and law relating to public offers of securities:

- Part 16: Designated activity companies;
- Part 17: Public limited companies;
- Part 18: Guarantee companies;
- Part 19: Unlimited companies;
- Part 20: Re-registration;
- Part 21: External companies;
- Part 22: Unregistered companies and joint stock companies;
- Part 23: Public offers of securities, financial reporting by traded companies, prevention of market abuse, etc;
- Part 24: Investment companies;
- Part 25: Miscellaneous;

---

[20] One minor exception to this general principle is that the Act no longer regulates foreign limited companies that come to Ireland and establish only a place of business here (as opposed to a branch) or foreign unlimited companies that establish a place of business or a branch: see Part 21.

[1.013] In addition to the LTD, the Act recognises and legislates for seven other primary types of company:

- the designated activity company or "DAC";[21]
- the public limited company or "PLC";[22]
- the guarantee company without a share capital or "CLG";
- the unlimited company or "UC";[23]
- the investment company;
- external companies; and
- unregistered companies and joint stock companies.

Of these, only the DAC is new and even then, the DAC is only new in the sense of its label, DACs being a sub-set of private company as defined by s 33 of the Companies Act 1963. The rationale for providing for the DAC as a distinct type of company is primarily to provide an option for existing private companies limited by shares which do not want, or are not permitted, to become LTDs. The key distinctions between DACs and LTDs are that DACs will have an objects clause, a distinct memorandum of association and articles of association, can list debt securities and, subject to compliance with Central Bank requirements, may operate as credit institutions or insurance undertakings. All of the other types of company recognised by the Act existed prior to the commencement of the Act.

[1.014] The architecture of the Act is uniform in its approach to how it applies the law to each type of company other than an LTD. In the case of a DAC, the applicable law is the law set out in Parts 1 to 14, save to the extent that it is:

- disapplied,
- modified, or
- supplemented.

by the provisions set out in Part 16. The same architecture applies to PLCs, CLGs and UCs: the law in Parts 1 to 14 apply to each of them, as it does to the LTD, subject to those provisions not being disapplied, modified or supplemented by the provisions in Parts 17, 18 or 19 respectively. One of the key advantages to this approach to legislating for different types of company is that when the legislature proposes to amend the law in future, it must make a conscious decision as to whether what appears to be a good idea for one type of company holds true in relation to each other type of company.

---

[21] The Act recognises two distinct sub-types of DAC: the DAC limited by shares and the DAC limited by guarantee having a share capital.

[22] The Act provides that Part 17 applies, not only to PLCs, but also to *Societas Europaea*.

[23] The Act recognises three distinct sub-types of unlimited company: the private unlimited company or "ULC", the public unlimited company or "PUC" and the public unlimited company without a share capital or "PULC".

[1.015] One of the problems faced by the CLRG has been the tendency of the public and public representatives to label every wrongful act or omission by a company or a director of a company as being capable of being remedied by the amendment of company law. Often, the act or omission complained of could have been perpetrated by a natural person or a body corporate (other than a company registered under the Companies Act) and so is incapable of being comprehensively addressed by company law. The CLRG has since its inception resisted calls to amend the Companies Acts to address real or perceived mischiefs relating to the rights and protections of employees of companies, the taxation and residence of companies or their directors, the administration and regulation of charities, the regulation of commercial contracts, consumer protection or, for that matter, the management of apartment or shopping centre developments. The Act has remained faithful to the philosophy that such matters are not exclusive to companies: a provision in the Companies Act designed to protect the health and safety of employees of companies is all well and good, but the fact the Companies Act does not apply to sole traders, partnerships, industrial and provident societies or, more significantly, perhaps, foreign employers would make it an incomplete and ineffective measure.

The LTD: The new model company

[1.016] In accordance with the CLRG's recommendations, the Act has placed the private company limited by shares centre stage by writing the first 15 Parts from the perspective of the private company limited by shares. It is important to note that not all private companies will be "LTDs": DACs limited by shares and DACS limited by guarantee and ULCs (private unlimited companies) will also continue to be *private* companies. The practical consequences of this is that DACs will be subject to the same ceiling on the number of shareholders, 149, as an LTD and while they may list debt securities within certain parameters, they may not offer for sale to the public, or list, equity securities.

[1.017] It is thought that it will be the LTD which will become the new workhorse of the Irish SME sector. While existing private companies limited by shares (with the exception of those with debt listings or which are credit institutions or insurance undertakings) have a choice in whether to become an LTD or instead to convert to some other type of company, most likely a DAC, the default position at the end of the transition period provided for in Chapter 6 of Part 2 is that such existing companies will become LTDs. Many of the key features of the LTD correspond to the advantages to being an LTD as opposed to another type of company. The key features of an LTD are:

- It may have between one and 149 shareholders;[24]
- It may have just one director;[25]

---

[24] Section 17 of the Act.

- The liability of its members will be limited to the amount, if any, unpaid on the shares taken by them in the LTD;[26]
- It will have a one-document constitution and will not have a separate memorandum and articles of association;[27]
- Its name must end in "Limited" or "LTD" or their Irish equivalent;[28]
- It cannot have an objects clause in its constitution because it has full, unlimited, contractual capacity;[29]
- It cannot invite the public to subscribe for, or offer to the public any shares, debentures or securities, etc, or apply or have to have securities (including debt) admitted to trading on a listed market whether in the State, the EU or anywhere else;[30] and
- The board (including a sole director) and a registered person are each deemed to have the authority to bind the company.[31]

Many of the foregoing features of the LTD will be returned to later in this chapter and elsewhere in this book.

Key innovations introduced by the Act

[1.018] The Companies Act is primarily a consolidating enactment, repealing and restating the provisions contained in 32 Acts and statutory instruments. In this respect, many of the Act's provisions can be described as old wine in a new bottle. The vast majority of the provisions now found in the Act are comparable to provisions that were contained in the old Companies Acts. There are in fact only a limited number of key innovations, but those that are introduced are very far-reaching. The following key innovations are identified here:

(a) The structure of the Act;
(b) Statutory defaults in lieu of Table A;
(c) The summary approval procedure;
(d) Codification of directors' fiduciary duties;
(e) The categorisation of most criminal offences.

While the Act has introduced many other very substantive company law changes for LTDs (for example, abolishing the objects clause, adopting a one-document constitution in lieu of the traditional memorandum and articles of association,

---

[25] Section 128 of the Act. An LTD will still be required to have a company secretary who must be, however, a different person: s 129 of the Act.
[26] Section 17 of the Act.
[27] Section 19 of the Act.
[28] Section 26 of the Act.
[29] Section 38 of the Act.
[30] Section 68 of the Act.
[31] Section 40 of the Act.

permitting one director, permitting merger by administrative procedure) these are not key structural innovations.

(a) The structure of the Act

[1.019] The architecture of the Act has been considered above.[32] It is, however, deserving of special mention in relation to the Act's key innovations. Somewhat unusually in legislation, s 9 of the Act has no substantive purpose other than to act as an statutory signpost. It provides:

> **"Act structured to facilitate its use in relation to most common type of company.**
>
> 9.(1) Subject to *subsections (3)* and *(4)*, all of the law in this Act in relation to private companies limited by shares is to be found in *Parts 1* to *14* (or instruments under them) and *Schedules 1* to *6*.
>
> (2) Subject to *subsection (3)*, all of the law in this Act in relation to other types of company is to be found amongst the provisions of –
>
> (a) *Parts 16* to *25* (or instruments under them) and *Schedules 7* to *17*; and
>
> (b) *Parts 1* to *14* (or instruments under them) and *Schedules 1* to *6* as applied or adapted by *Parts 16* to *25*.
>
> (3) *Part 15* (Functions of Registrar and of regulatory and advisory bodies) applies to both –
>
> (a) private companies limited by shares; and
>
> (b) other types of company,
>
> as well as to certain undertakings to which the European Communities (Accounts) Regulations 1993 (SI No 396 of 1993), as amended, apply.
>
> (4) Exceptionally, provisions either—
>
> (a) of a miscellaneous nature arising out of the relationship between a private company limited by shares and another company type (such as provisions for re-registration); or
>
> (b) which it would not otherwise be practicable to include in *Parts 1* to *14* (such as provisions for a merger between a public limited company and a private company limited by shares),
>
> will be found in *Parts 16* to *25*."

By grouping the legal provisions applicable to particular types of company the structure of the Act is truly innovative in the common law world and provides a far more accessible and understandable code for users and practitioners.

---

[32] See para **[1.014]**.

(b) Statutory defaults in lieu of Table A

[1.020] It was the Joint Stock Companies Act 1956 which – in "Table B" of its Schedule – introduced the concept of standard articles of association applying to companies limited by shares which did not register their own bespoke articles.[33] Over the years many of the provisions concerning the administration of companies – which came to be contained in Table A – have survived re-statements and revisions and have assumed a quasi-official basis in that people have come to expect their adoption by companies. Even PLCs which invariably adopt bespoke articles of association have tended to follow many of the provisions in Table A, verbatim. In its seminal report in 2001, the CLRG recommended:

> "The Group considered that the common modes of internal governance of companies ought to be readable immediately from the main body of the statute, even if certain variations from those common modes of governance are chosen by particular companies. It is thought that notwithstanding existing familiarity with Table A, there is no disadvantage to placing the Table A language in the main body of the statute. Finally, although it is thought that there is some advantage in the removal of Table A in its entirety, it is not possible to consider this in the absence of a consideration of all, rather than part only, of Table A, especially with respect to share capital matters."[34]

Just as the duties of directors as developed by the courts are codified in the Act, so too have many of the provisions contained in Table A been expressed in statute to apply as a statutory default, unless a constitution provides otherwise. Moreover, in the event, the legislature did bite the bullet and has incorporated virtually all of Table A such that there is no Table A provided for in the Act. Of course, private companies limited by shares which become DACs and whose articles of association reference Table A of the 1963 Act (or 1908 Act) can continue to rely on those Tables.[35]

The end result is that the Act has created a series of statutory defaults so that companies will no longer be required to make provision for standard administrative matters in their constitutions as these provisions will apply by default. Importantly, however, the new approach continues to facilitate companies that wish to be governed by bespoke provisions applicable only to them.

---

[33] See Nicholson, *Table A Articles of Association* (1997) at p 1.
[34] Nicholson, *Table A Articles of Association* (1997) at para 4.7.2.
[35] Section 63(10) of the Act.

(c)   The summary approval procedure

[1.021] The summary approval procedure, or SAP, is a good example of the new and the old in the Act. On the one hand, it is an innovation since there was no comparable procedure in the Companies Acts 1963 to 2013, while on the other hand, it is not really novel at all since there were three similar procedures in the old legislation. The SAP has its philosophical origins in the CLRG's first report.[36] The CLRG recognised that there were three distinct procedures providing exceptions to acts which were otherwise prohibited on the grounds that they could prejudice the interests of the two most important stakeholders in company law, namely, creditors and shareholders. These procedures operated on the basis that the interests of creditors and shareholders could be safeguarded whilst at the same time offering companies an exception to the prohibitions. In the case of the provision of financial assistance in connection with the purchase of a company's own shares, the provision of a guarantee or security in connection with a loan, quasi-loan or credit transaction for a director or connected person or the placing of a company into members' voluntary winding up, s 60 of the Companies Act 1963, s 34 of the Companies Act 1990 and s 256 of the Companies Act 1963, respectively, allowed companies to perform those activities where certain conditions were met. The CLRG identified those conditions as being: where the directors made a declaration that the company was solvent, where the members approved of the activity by passing a special resolution and, in two out of the three cases, where an independent person (who could be the company's auditor) opined as to the reasonableness of the directors' declaration of solvency. The CLRG concluded:

> "... there is no justification for having two or more validation procedures and recommends there should be just one validation procedure which is capable of being invoked in the case of a number of specific prohibitions."[37]

The recommendation was that there should be just one procedure which would operate as a sort of universal-wrench, expanding, contracting and adopting to the varied requirements of particular prohibitions, as though they were differently-sized bolts, whilst utilising a common handle. While the CLRG's first report referred only to three prohibitions, over the years as it considered issues arising in other work-programmes, the CLRG identified additional restricted activities which it recommended should be included in a common validation procedure.

What was initially referred to as a validation procedure was, ultimately, rechristened a summary approval procedure and the SAP provided for in s 202 of the Act may be utilised to validate seven activities otherwise restricted by the following provisions:

---

[36]   Nicholson, *Table A Articles of Association* (1997) at para 5.2.
[37]   Nicholson, *Table A Articles of Association* (1997) at para 5.2.6.

- Section 82 (financial assistance for acquisition of shares);
- Section 84 (reduction in company capital);
- Section 91 (variation of company capital on reorganisation);
- Section 118 (prohibition on pre-acquisition profits or losses being treated in holding company's financial statements as profits available for distribution);
- Section 239 (prohibition of loans, etc, to directors and connected persons);
- Section 464 (mergers); and
- Section 579 (members' voluntary winding up).

The operation of the SAP is considered, generally, in Ch 2, in the context of the giving of security in Ch 5, and in the context of mergers in Ch 6.

(d) *Codification of directors' fiduciary duties*

[1.022] At a time when it seems that the dogs on the street are talking about corporate governance, and actual and perceived breaches of duty by directors regularly make the headlines in our daily newspapers, it is hard to believe that until the enactment of the Companies Act 2014, there has never been a statutory statement of the duties owed by directors. The requirement that directors must act in good faith and in the interests of their company as developed in case law may be a tenet dating back over 100 years, but it has never been a statutory requirement for directors. This was recognised by the CLRG in its first report, and recommendation No 146 provided:

> "The fiduciary duties of a director to his company primarily as identified by the Irish courts should be stated in statute law. This statement should be in general rather than specific terms, derived from principles established by the courts and on the basis that the statement of duties is not exhaustive."

Effect has been given to this recommendation in Chapter 2 of Part 5 of the Act and is discussed in some detail in Ch 4.

(e) *The categorisation of most criminal offences*

[1.023] The Companies Acts 1963 to 2013 criminalised several hundred acts or omissions by companies, their officers or members. Compiling a definitive list of all criminal offences under the Companies Acts has always been problematic, a matter that came to the fore upon the imposition of a requirement on the auditors of companies to report their suspicion as to the commission of indictable offences to the Office of the Director of Corporate Enforcement.

[1.024] Although the Act does not interfere with the indictable offences/ summary offences distinction, so central to our general criminal law, it does introduce a readily understandable four-fold classification of all criminal offences created by the Act where category 1 is the most serious and category 4 the most minor. The classification is set out in s 871 of the Act:

- *Category 1* – conviction on indictment may result in imprisonment for a term of up to 10 years and, or in the alternative, to a fine of €500,000;
- *Category 2* – conviction on indictment may result in imprisonment for a term of up to five years and, or in the alternative, to a fine of €50,000;
- *Category 3* – is a summary offence only and may result in imprisonment for a term of up to six months and, or in the alternative, to a Class A fine;
- *Category 4* – is a summary offence only and is punishable by a Class A fine.[38]

A review of the Act discloses that two provisions create category 1 offences, 65 provisions create category 2 offences, 132 provisions create category 3 offences and 49 provisions create category 4 offences. The only offences created by the Act which stand outside the four-fold categorisation are certain market abuse offences[39] (which attract a term of imprisonment of up to 10 years and a fine of up to €10,000,000 or both), prospectus offences[40] (which attract a term of imprisonment of up to five years and a fine of up to €1,000,000 or both) and transparency offences[41] (which attract a term of imprisonment of up to five years and a fine of up to €1,000,000 or both). Offences and sanctions are considered further in Ch 8.

New obligations and regulations

[1.025] Consistent with the earlier observation that many of the Act's provisions represent old wine in a new bottle, in reality for an enactment containing 1,448 sections of law, it introduces remarkably few new obligations and regulations. Here, it is proposed to distinguish between transitional obligations, on-going obligations and new regulations.

(a) Transitional obligations on companies and directors

[1.026] The most significant immediate obligations on companies and directors arise during the transition period and are:

- The directors of an existing private company must prepare a constitution suitable for an LTD and deliver it to the shareholders and the CRO before the end of the transition period *unless* the members have already

---

[38] Note, for the meaning of "Class A Fine" see the Fines Act 2010. A Class A fine is currently a fine of up to €5,000.
[39] As provided for in s 1364 of the Act.
[40] As provided for in s 1352 of the Act.
[41] As provided for in s 1377 of the Act.

adopted a constitution, or the company is required to re-register as a DAC or the company is proceeding to re-register as another type of company (s 60(1));

- An existing private company limited by shares must re-register as a DAC where 25 per cent of the members with voting rights serve a notice requiring this, or as a DAC or some other type of company where it has a debt listing or the company is a credit institution or insurance undertaking (s 56(2) and (3) and s 18(2));

- A company limited by guarantee should, before the end of the transition period, change its name so that its name ends in "company limited by guarantee" or "CLG" instead of "limited" (s 1190(6)) although if the change is not made, then the name will be deemed to have been altered;

- An unlimited company should, before the end of the transition period, change its name so that its name ends in "unlimited" or "UC" (s 1247(5)) although if the change is not made, then the name will be deemed to have been altered.

(b) New on-going obligations on companies and directors

[1.027] The Companies Act imposes a limited number of new on-going obligations on companies and directors which may be summarised as follows:

- Directors of certain companies will be obliged to establish audit committees or else explain why they have not done so (s 167(4));

- Where a company holds its AGM or any EGM outside of Ireland, unless every member entitled to attend and vote so consents, the company has a duty to make, at the company's expense, all necessary arrangements to ensure that the members can by technological means participate in any such meeting without leaving Ireland (s 176(3));

- Directors of certain companies will be obliged to include a compliance statement in their directors' report stating that certain things have been done or else explaining whey they have not been done (s 225(2));

- Where accounting records are not kept by making entries in a bound book, adequate precautions must be taken for guarding against falsification and facilitating discovery of such falsification, should it occur (s 282(2));

- A holding company which has a subsidiary undertaking in relation to which the basic requirements for accounting records in s 282 do not apply is required to take all reasonable steps to secure that the subsidiary keeps such adequate accounting records as will enable the directors of the holding company to ensure that any group financial statements required to be prepared under Irish law comply with Part 6 of the Act and Article 4 of the IAS Regulation (s 282(8));

- Directors must state in their directors' report that so far as each of the directors is aware, there is no relevant audit information of which the company's statutory auditors are unaware and that each director has taken all the steps that he or she ought to have taken as a director in order to be aware of any relevant audit information and to establish that the auditors are aware of that information (s 330(1));

- Directors of insolvent companies must, when requested to do so by the liquidator, cooperate as far as can reasonably be expected in relation to the conduct of the winding up of the company or else the High Court will be obliged to make a declaration, restricting the director (s 819).

(c) Newly regulated activities

[1.028] Companies and their directors need to be aware that there are certain matters which heretofore were unregulated but which are now regulated. These include:

- Companies shall not issue any bearer instrument relating to shares (s 66(9));[42]

- An LTD shall not apply for a debt listing or have debt admitted to trading or listed (s 68(2));

- Shares may not be allotted unless the allotment is authorised (s 69(1)) and cannot be allotted by a committee unless this is authorised by the constitution (s 69(4));

- A person may not be appointed a director unless he or she is 18 years of age (s 131(1)); and

- Loans from directors to their companies and permitted loans from companies to their directors must be in writing or else evidential presumptions adverse to the directors will apply (Chapter 3 of Part 5).

Parts 1 to 15: Overview of the law applicable to the LTD

[1.029] One of the key architectural features of the Act is the physical segregation of the law applicable to the private company limited by shares (LTD) from other types of companies. This section overviews the first 15 Parts of the Act, by identifying the subject matter, identifying the Chapters comprised in each Part and focusing on select new, innovative or otherwise significant sections. While the first 14 Parts apply exclusively to the LTD, Part 15 applies to the LTD and all other types of company.[43]

---

[42] There is a limited power for PLCs to issue certain "permissible letters of allotment" that might otherwise be treated as bearer instruments: s 1019.

[43] Section 9(3) of the Act.

(a) Part 1: Preliminary and general

[1.030] Part 1 contains 14 sections. It provides for the commencement of the Act by statutory instrument, interpretation, repeals, savings and transition and miscellaneous other matters. The most substantive provisions in Part 1 are the *definitions* of various words and terms used throughout the Act as provided for in s 2(2), eg, "company", "constitution", "director", "*de facto* director", "shadow director", etc. Many will have obvious meanings but others, such as "called-up share capital", "company", "deliver", "document", and "sealed" are provided with a particular meaning when used in the Act and will repay careful study. Other important interpretative provisions include the meanings of references to "a company having a sole director" (s 2(8)); "a receiver of the property of a company" (s 2(9)); a company being "related to another company" and to periods of time (s 3).

[1.031] Sections 7 and 8 of the Act provide for the definition of "subsidiary", "holding company", "wholly owned subsidiary" and "group of companies" and make substantive changes to the former law. Prior the Act, the definition of "subsidiary" as set out in s 155 of the Companies Act 1963 for company law purposes and of "subsidiary undertaking" as set out in reg 4 of the European Communities (Companies: Group Accounts) Regulations 1992 for group accounting purposes were separate and distinct.[44] The Companies Act definition was "smaller" than the group accounts definition meaning that more companies would fall to be "subsidiary undertakings" than would fall to be "subsidiaries". Under the Act, there will now be just one definition that will apply for all purposes to bodies corporate.[45]

(b) Part 2: Incorporation and registration

[1.032] Part 2 of the Act is the source of many of the provisions that are key to the identity of the new model private company limited by shares or LTD. Structurally, its 49 sections are divided into six Chapters:

- Chapter 1: Preliminary;
- Chapter 2: Incorporation and consequential matters;
- Chapter 3: Corporate capacity and authority;
- Chapter 4: Contracts and other transactions;

---

[44] See Courtney, *The Law of Companies* (3rd edn, Bloomsbury Professional, 2012) at para [12.008] *et seq* and para [12.030] *et seq*.

[45] Partnerships and unincorporated bodies of persons may still be "subsidiary undertakings" for group accounting purposes. Section 275(1) of the Act provides: "'subsidiary undertaking' has the same meaning as 'subsidiary' in section 7 save that 'company' in section 7 shall, for the purposes of this definition, include, as well as a body corporate – (a) a partnership; and (b) an unincorporated body of persons falling within the definition of 'undertaking' in this section."

- Chapter 5: Company name, registered office and service of documents;
- Chapter 6: Conversion of existing private company to private company limited by shares to which Parts 1 to 15 apply.

Chapter 2 of this book will identify some of the more significant changes introduced in relation to incorporation and registration. This overview will focus on some of the key provisions in Chapters 3 and 6 of the Act.

(i) Chapter 3: Capacity and authority

[1.033] One of the key changes introduced in Chapter 3 of the Act is s 38, the effect of which is to abolish the application of the doctrine of *ultra vires* to the LTD, by providing that an LTD shall have full and unlimited capacity to carry on and undertake any business or activity, to do any act or enter into any transaction and for those purposes shall have full rights, powers and privileges. This is considered further in Ch 5 of this book.

[1.034] The Act will also make it easier for persons to transact business with companies by removing the need to enquire as to the authority of a company's agents in certain circumstances. The board of directors and registered persons will be deemed to have authority to bind the company: in the case of a sole director company, persons dealing with the sole director may rely upon s 40 and will not be required to look into his or her authority. Where the board of directors authorises any person as being a person entitled to bind the company, the company *may* notify the CRO of this fact and the Registrar will register such person as a registered person *unless* the entitlement to bind is expressly or impliedly restricted to a particular transaction or class of transactions. The Bill as initiated had made registration mandatory but at Report Stage in the Seanad "shall" was substituted with "may" and the position of registered persons remains elective as it has been under reg 6(3) of the European Communities (Companies) Regulations 1973 (SI 163/1973).

Where a board of directors authorises, say, a CEO to bind the company generally by conferring on the CEO the power to bind the company without restricting that authority to a particular transaction or class of transaction, then that authorisation of the CEO will mean that the CEO can be registered as a registered person. On the other hand, where a CEO's authority is, for example, restricted to contract up to, say, €250,000 then that would be an authorisation in respect of a particular class of transaction (eg, transactions not exceeding €250,000 in monetary value) which should not be registered. Equally, a check-out operator employed by a company that is a supermarket will not be a registered person for the same reason: his or her authority is restricted to a particular class of transaction (eg, grocery sales). It is important to remember that where persons are given unrestricted authority and are registered they will be deemed by s 40 to have authority to bind the company with third parties. It seems obvious that nobody should be so authorised unless the board of directors is prepared to accept that consequence.

(ii) Chapter 6: Conversion

[1.035] Chapter 6 concerns the conversion of an existing private company to a private company limited by shares to which Parts 1 to 15 apply and will, accordingly, be most people's immediate preoccupation. The default position is that unless it has re-registered as a DAC, an existing private company limited by shares will, at the end of the transition period (18 months post commencement), be deemed to have become an LTD: s 55 of the Act.

[1.036] Chapter 6 imposes obligations on certain existing private companies limited by shares to re-register as DACs[46] or some other type of company in certain circumstances:

- Existing private companies limited by shares which are credit institutions or insurance undertakings may not become LTDs and so must convert to some other type of company;[47]
- Existing private companies limited by shares that have a debt listing must convert to some other type of company;[48]
- The members of existing private companies limited by shares may decide to convert to a DAC by passing an ordinary resolution not later than three months before the end of the transition period;[49]
- Existing private companies limited by shares must re-register as a DAC before the end of the transition period if, not later than three months before its expiry, a notice in writing to do so is served on the company by members holding shares that confer more than 25 per cent of the total voting rights.[50]

Where an existing private company limited by shares does not re-register as a DAC or some other company type, whether it is required to do so in the circumstances outlined above or not, a qualifying member or creditor may apply to the High Court for an order directing it to re-register and the Court shall grant that order unless cause is shown to the contrary. A qualifying member is one who holds not less than 15 per cent in nominal value of the issued share capital or any class thereof or a creditor who holds not less than 15 per cent of the company's debentures provided that the debentures entitle the holders to object to alterations of the company's objects.[51]

---

[46] On re-registration as a DAC, see s 63 of the Act.
[47] Section 18(2) of the Act.
[48] Section 56(3) of the Act.
[49] Section 56(1) of the Act.
[50] Section 56(2) of the Act.
[51] Section 57 of the Act.

[1.037] During the transition period the law applicable to existing private companies limited by shares will be the law set out in Part 16 (ie, the law set out in Parts 1 to 15 save to the extent that it is not disapplied, modified or supplemented by the law in Part 16).[52] However, as soon as an existing private company limited by shares re-registers as an LTD and adopts the requisite one-document constitution, then the law in Parts 1 to 15 will apply to it.[53]

[1.038] Adopting a new constitution is relatively straightforward and is achieved by passing a special resolution.[54] It is to be expected that companies incorporated using "house standard" articles of association from legal and accountancy firms will adopt the new house standard constitutions offered by those firms.

[1.039] The directors of existing private companies limited by shares will have a statutory obligation in certain circumstances to prepare a new constitution, copy it to the company's members and file it in the CRO.[55] These obligations will not arise, however, where the company:

- has already adopted a constitution by the members who have passed a special resolution; or
- is required to re-register as a DAC; or
- is proceeding, in accordance with a resolution passed to re-register as an LTD or as another type of company; or
- is required by a court order to re-register as a DAC, or proceedings are pending.

It is thought that prudent directors will seek to avoid this obligation arising at all, by engaging in early communication of the options to the company's members and encouraging the members to take positive action by resolving to re-register as an LTD, a DAC or some other type of company. Where the members sit on their hands and the obligation does arise, the directors need to be careful to follow, precisely, their statutory obligation lest they over-step their authority concerning the preparation of the constitution. Section 60(3) provides:

> "The provisions of that constitution of the company, to be prepared by the directors as mentioned in *subsection (2)(a)* shall consist solely of –
>
> (a) the provisions of its existing memorandum, other than provisions that –
>> (i) contain its objects; or
>> (ii) provide for, or prohibit, the alteration of all or any of the provisions of its memorandum or articles; and
>
> (b) the provisions of its existing articles,

---

52 Section 58(1) of the Act.
53 Section 58(1) of the Act.
54 Section 59(1) of the Act.
55 Section 60(1) of the Act.

but, despite any exemption of the kind referred to in section 61(3) that had been enjoyed by the company under the prior Companies Acts, nothing in this section shall be read as overriding the requirements of sections 19 and 26(1) relating to a company's name."

[1.040] Section 61 seeks to legislate for the situation where neither the members nor the directors take action and the company defaults to being an LTD at the end of the transition period. In those circumstances, and without prejudice to the fact that the directors will be in breach of their obligations under s 60(1), the existing private company limited by shares:

"… shall be deemed to have, in place of its existing memorandum and articles, a constitution that comprises –

   (i)   the provisions of its existing memorandum, other than provisions that –
        (I)   contain its objects; or
        (II)   provide for, or prohibit, the alteration of all or any of the provisions of its memorandum or articles; and
   (ii) the provisions of its existing articles …"

It is provided that the constitution, as so constituted, is deemed to satisfy the requirements of s 19 as to the form of a company's constitution. The resulting document will make for a far-from-ideal constitution because as a document, it will be virtually indistinguishable from the existing memorandum and articles of association.

(c)   *Part 3: Share capital, shares and certain other instruments*

[1.041] Part 3 concerns the law relating to share capital and its 63 sections are structured into seven Chapters:

- Chapter 1: Preliminary and interpretation;
- Chapter 2: Offers of securities to the public;
- Chapter 3: Allotment of shares;
- Chapter 4: Variation in capital;
- Chapter 5: Transfer of shares;
- Chapter 6: Acquisition of own shares;
- Chapter 7: Distributions.

While share capital is reviewed in Ch 2 of this book, here we will consider briefly some key provisions in Chapters 2 and 4.

(i) Chapter 2: Offers of securities to the public

[1.042] Until relatively recently, in order for a company to list any kind of securities, whether equity or debt, it had to be a PLC. That rule was changed by the Investment Funds, Companies and Miscellaneous Provisions Act 2006 which, by s 7, substituted s 33 of the Companies Act 1963 thereby changing[56] the definition of private company. The result was that a private company was then permitted to have certain debts listed on a stock exchange. One of the key features of the new LTD is that it will not be able to offer (debt or equity) securities to the public or list any securities. Section 68 provides:

"(1) Subject to the provisions of this section, a company shall not –

    (a) make–

        (i)   any invitation to the public to subscribe for; or

        (ii)   any offer to the public of,

        Any shares, debentures or other securities of the company; or

    (b) allot, or agree to allot, (whether for cash or otherwise) any shares in or debentures of the company with a view to all or any of those shares or debentures being offered for sale to the public or being the subject of an invitation to the public to subscribe for them.

(2) A company shall–

    (a) neither apply to have securities (or interests in them) admitted to trading or to be listed on; or

    (b) have securities (or interests in them) admitted to trading or listed on,

any market, whether a regulated market or not, in the State or elsewhere."

It follows that existing private companies limited by shares which availed of the changes introduced by the Investment Funds, Companies and Miscellaneous Provisions Act 2006 will have to convert to a DAC or PLC.

(ii) Chapter 4: Variation in capital

[1.043] The stringent rules on the reduction of share capital in limited companies are being relaxed by the Act.[57] Section 84(1) of the Act now provides that save to the extent that its constitution provides otherwise, an LTD *may* reduce its company capital[58] in any way it thinks expedient, *provided* it complies with ss 84 to 87. The key requirements, set out in s 84(2), are that it may only reduce its company capital by:

"(a) employing the Summary Approval Procedure; or

  (b) passing a special resolution that is confirmed by the court."

Section 84(2)(b) replicates what was the previous law: a company could reduce its share capital by applying to the High Court to confirm a reducing special resolution. The novelty introduced by the Act lies in s 84(2)(a). So, now an LTD may reduce its share capital in reliance upon the SAP: passing a special

---

[56] With effect from 1 July 2005.

[57] See, generally, Courtney, *The Law of Companies* (3rd edn, Bloomsbury Professional, 2012) at para [10.002] *et seq.*

[58] See Ch 2, *Changes in the Basics: Constitutions, Share Capital and Governance* at para **[2.041]**.

resolution, making a declaration of solvency and procuring an independent person's report that the declaration of solvency is not unreasonable.[59]

(d) Part 4: Corporate governance

[1.044] Part 4 sets out the law relating to the governance and administration of companies in 92 sections of law, divided into 10 Chapters:

- Chapter 1: Preliminary;
- Chapter 2: Directors and secretaries;
- Chapter 3: Service contracts and remuneration;
- Chapter 4: Proceedings of directors;
- Chapter 5: Members;
- Chapter 6: General meetings and resolutions;
- Chapter 7: Summary approval procedure;
- Chapter 8: Protection for minorities;
- Chapter 9: Forms of registers, indices and minute books;
- Chapter 10: Inspection of registers, provision of copies of information in them and service of notices.

Part 4 is primarily concerned with the law of meetings of members and directors. Here we will look at key provisions in Chapters 4 and 6. Part 4 is generally considered in Ch 2, *Constitutions, Share Capital and Governance*.

(i) Chapter 4: Proceedings of directors

[1.045] One of the key features of Part 4 is that it contains most of what used to be contained in Table A, the vast bulk of which is expressed to apply to a company *unless its constitution provides otherwise.*

[1.046] Chapter 4 concerns the proceedings of directors, and s 157 begins by stating that each subsequent provision of this Chapter (other than ss 166 and 167) applies "save to the extent that the company's constitution provides otherwise." Section 166 requires minutes to be kept of meetings of directors and committees and is mandatory,[60] and s 167 makes it mandatory for certain LTDs to establish audit committees or explain if they do not. Aside from these two provisions, the other provisions will apply by default or automatically, unless the company's constitution provides otherwise.

[1.047] An example here is s 158 which operates as the new statutory default for what was Regulation 80 of Part I of Table A to the First Schedule of the

---

[59] Sections 202, 204 and 208 of the Act and, further, Ch 2, *Changes in the Basics: Constitutions, Share Capital and Governance*, at para **[2.041]**.

[60] Just as it was by reason of s 145 of the Companies Act 1963.

Companies Act 1963. Regulation 80 might be considered to be the very cornerstone of corporate governance, providing as it did for the members to divest themselves of the powers of management and conferring those powers, for general purposes, on the directors, thereby putting them in charge of the company's affairs and creating a fiduciary relationship. Section 158(1) and (2) provide:

> "(1) The business of a company shall be managed by its directors, who may pay all expenses incurred in promoting and registering the company and may exercise all such powers of the company as are not, by this Act or by the constitution, required to be exercised by the company in general meeting, but subject to –
>
> (a) any regulations contained in the constitution;
>
> (b) the provisions of this Act; and
>
> (c) such directions, not being inconsistent with the foregoing regulations or provisions, as the company in general meeting may (by special resolution) give.
>
> (2) However, no direction given by the company in general meeting under *subsection (1)(c)* shall invalidate any prior act of the directors which would have been valid if that direction had not been given."

Section 158(1)(c) removes one uncertainty associated with Regulation 80 of Table A by making clear that the members may only direct the directors where they pass a special resolution.

(ii) Chapter 6: General meetings and resolutions

[1.048] While further consideration will be given to the changes relating to meetings in Ch 2, *Changes in the Basics: Constitutions, Share Capital and Governance*, it may be noted here that annual general meetings (AGMs) will become optional for all LTDs, even multi-member LTDs as well as all single-member PLCs, DACs, ULCs and UCs. Moreover, for the first time in Irish law, majority written resolutions will be permitted to be used to pass both ordinary resolutions and special resolutions.

(e) Part 5: Duties of directors and other officers

[1.049] Part 5 codifies directors' common law and equitable duties, consolidates directors' existing statutory duties and introduces a limited number of new duties. Its 53 sections of law are divided into six Chapters:

- Chapter 1: Preliminary and definitions;
- Chapter 2: General duties of directors;
- Chapter 3: Evidential provisions concerning loans;
- Chapter 4: Prohibitions and restrictions on loans and other transactions;

- Chapter 5: Disclosure of interests in shares;
- Chapter 6: Responsibilities of officers.

Although a more detailed overview is provided in Ch 4, *Changes in the Law of Directors' Duties*, a number of its key provisions can be mentioned here.

(i) Chapter 2: General duties of directors

[1.050] It is thought that the users of companies will consider that the single greatest imposition on directors and companies is the requirement for directors of certain companies to make a compliance statement. After a false start in 2003, and a comprehensive review by the CLRG in 2005, the directors' compliance statement will finally become a reality upon the commencement of s 225 of the Act which is discussed in Ch 4, *Changes in the Law of Directors' Duties.*[61]

[1.051] One of the ground-breaking changes introduced by the Act is that for the first time, s 227 has codified the duties owed by directors into a statement of eight principal fiduciary duties. These duties are set out in Ch 4, *Changes in the Law of Directors' Duties.*[62]

(ii) Chapter 3: Evidential provisions concerning loans

[1.052] One of the few new restrictions introduced by the Act concerns loans made to directors by their companies and loans made to companies by their directors. Sections 236 and 237 contain a series of presumptions designed to ensure that all such loans are made in writing. These provisions and the means used to incentivise the reduction of such loans into writing are considered further in Ch 4, *Changes in the Law of Directors' Duties.*[63]

(iii) Chapter 5: Disclosure of interests in shares

[1.053] A number of changes have been made to inject some common sense into the law on the disclosure of directors' interests in shares created by Part 4 of the Companies Act 1990, one of the most convoluted regimes in company law. Among the changes are that a *de minimis* limit of 1 per cent is being introduced to the obligation and that interests in shares given by the company to the director are not required to be notified by the director. Further consideration is given to

---

[61] See, generally, Courtney, "Directors' Compliance Statements: Attesting Corporate Compliance on a 'Comply or Explain' Basis", in Keane and O'Neill (eds), *Corporate Governance and Regulation* (Round Hall, 2009) and Ch 4, *Changes in the Law of Directors' Duties* at para **[4.008]**.

[62] See further Ch 4, *Changes in the Law of Directors' Duties* at para **[4.021]**.

[63] See further Ch 4, *Changes in the Law of Directors' Duties* at para **[4.046]**.

these changes in Ch 2, *Changes in the Basics: Constitutions, Share Capital and Governance.*

(f) Part 6: Financial statements, annual return and audit

[1.054] The consolidation of the law relating to financial statements has been needed for some time. The multiple amendments made to the Companies Acts' provisions by the European Communities (International Financial Reporting Standards and Miscellaneous Amendments) Regulation 2005[64] and many other statutory instruments rendered the provisions on accounting virtually unintelligible and were it not for the commercial publication of the consolidated Companies Acts, few would have been able to navigate a safe passage. Part 6 of the Act contains 136 sections and is divided into 23 Chapters, consolidating the law on financial statements, annual return and audit into one place for the first time in over 30 years. The Chapters are:

- Chapter 1: Preliminary;
- Chapter 2: Accounting records;
- Chapter 3: Financial year;
- Chapter 4: Statutory financial statements;
- Chapter 5: Group financial statements: exemptions and exclusions;
- Chapter 6: Disclosure of directors' remuneration and transactions;
- Chapter 7: Disclosures required in notes to financial statements;
- Chapter 8: Approval of statutory financial statements;
- Chapter 9: Directors' report;
- Chapter 10: Obligation to have statutory financial statements audited;
- Chapter 11: Statutory auditors' report;
- Chapter 12: Publication of financial statements;
- Chapter 13: Annual return and the documents annexed to it;
- Chapter 14: Exclusions, exemptions and special arrangements regarding disclosure;
- Chapter 15: Audit exemption;
- Chapter 16: Special audit exemption for dormant companies;
- Chapter 17: Revision of defective statutory financial statements;
- Chapter 18: Appointment of statutory auditors;
- Chapter 19: Rights, obligations and duties of statutory auditors;
- Chapter 20: Removal and resignation of statutory auditors;
- Chapter 21: Notification to supervisory authority of certain matters;
- Chapter 22: False statements – offence;
- Chapter 23: Transitional.

---

[64]   SI 116/2005.

[1.055] Some of the key changes introduced by Part 6 include the following. For the first time, a procedure will be set out which will allow for the revision of defective financial statements.[65] The threshold for medium-sized enterprises has been updated to a turnover of not greater than €20m, a balance sheet not greater than €10m and employees not exceeding 250.[66] In the directors' report, the directors of companies will be required to confirm that, so far as they are aware, there is no relevant audit information of which the auditors are unaware.[67] Auditors' obligations to report their suspicion as to the commission of certain offences will be by reference to category 1 and category 2 offences.[68]

(g) Part 7: Charges and debentures

[1.056] The law relating to charges and debentures has been modernised in 20 sections of law divided into four Chapters:

- Chapter 1: Interpretation;
- Chapter 2: Registration of charges and priority;
- Chapter 3: Provisions as to debentures;
- Chapter 4: Prohibition on registration of certain matters.

The changes introduced in Part 7 are reviewed in Ch 5, *Taking Security, the Summary Approval Procedure and the Registration of Charges*. For present purposes it may be noted that in addition to introducing a new, optional, two-stage registration procedure, there has been a radical departure from the traditional approach that particulars of only certain charges (ie registrable charges) listed in the legislation were required to be delivered to the Registrar of Companies in order to be valid. Section 409 simply requires particulars of every "charge" created by a company over "any property of the company" to be delivered to the Registrar of Companies. Section 408 specifically excludes an interest in:

"(a)   cash;

(b)   money credited to an account of a financial institution, or any other deposits;

(c)   shares, bonds or debt instruments;

(d)   units in collective investment undertakings or money market instruments; or

(e)   claims and rights (such as dividends or interest) in respect of anything referred to in any of paragraphs (b) to (d)."

---

65   Sections 336 to 379 of the Act.
66   Section 350 of the Act.
67   Section 330 of the Act.
68   Section 393 of the Act.

(h) Part 8: Receivers

[1.057] Part 9 contains 21 sections of law and is divided into four Chapters concerning receivers:

- Chapter 1: Interpretation;
- Chapter 2: Appointment of receivers;
- Chapter 3: Powers and duties of receivers;
- Chapter 4: Regulation of receivers and enforcement of their duties.

The law relating to receivers is primarily a restatement of the existing law, but there are a few innovations. For example, s 437 now lists the powers a receiver will have in addition to any powers provided in the order or instrument appointing the receiver.

(i) Part 9: Reorganisations, acquisitions, mergers and divisions

[1.058] Part 9 contains many innovative and new provisions concerning the reorganisation of companies. Its 59 sections of law are divided into four Chapters:

- Chapter 1: Schemes of arrangement;
- Chapter 2: Acquisitions;
- Chapter 3: Mergers;
- Chapter 4: Divisions.

The most significant change here is the provision, in Chapter 3, of a new regime for the merger of two or more Irish companies. Based on the successfully utilised European Communities (Cross-Border Mergers) Regulations 2008[69] (which will, of course, continue to apply to cross-border mergers[70]), Chapter 3 facilitates both judicially-sanctioned merger *and* administrative merger, using the summary approval procedure, for domestic companies. These and other changes to the law in this area are considered in Ch 6, *Corporate Restructuring: Schemes, Mergers and Divisions.*

(j) Part 10: Examinerships

[1.059] Part 10 of the Act sets out the law relating to examinerships, the laws by which an examiner may be appointed to a company and the circumstances in which a company may be granted the protection of the court for a period during which proposals are formulated for saving the company by writing-down

---

69   SI 157/2008.

70   As will the European Communities (Merger and Division of Companies) Regulations 1987 (SI 137/1987) continue to apply to cross-border mergers of PLCs.

particular liabilities. Part 10 contains 51 sections of law, divided into five Chapters:

- Chapter 1: Interpretation;
- Chapter 2: Appointment of examiner;
- Chapter 3: Powers of examiner;
- Chapter 4: Liability of third parties for debts of company;
- Chapter 5: Conclusion of examinership.

The Act consolidates all prior provisions on examinership, including the changes introduced by the Companies (Miscellaneous Provisions) Act 2013 which implemented the CLRG's recommendations, made in September 2012, that all examinership proceedings in relation to small private companies may be brought in the Circuit Court. The changes introduced to the law relating to examinerships are considered in more detail in Ch 7, *Insolvency and Rescue*.

(k) Part 11: Winding up

[1.060] The main corpus of the law relating to the winding up of companies is contained in Part 11 in 166 sections of law, divided into 16 Chapters:

- Chapter 1: Preliminary and interpretation;
- Chapter 2: Winding up by court;
- Chapter 3: Members' voluntary winding up;
- Chapter 4: Creditors' voluntary winding up;
- Chapter 5: Conduct of winding up;
- Chapter 6: Realisation of assets and related matters;
- Chapter 7: Distribution;
- Chapter 8: Liquidators;
- Chapter 9: Contributories;
- Chapter 10: Committee of inspection;
- Chapter 11: Court's powers;
- Chapter 12: Provisions supplemental to conduct of winding up;
- Chapter 13: General rules as to meetings (members, creditors, etc);
- Chapter 14: Completion of winding up;
- Chapter 15: Provisions related to Insolvency Regulation;
- Chapter 16: Offences by officers, etc.

The changes introduced to the law relating to winding up are considered also in more detail in Ch 7, *Insolvency and Rescue*. Perhaps the most significant change introduced is the greater consistency in approach in insolvent liquidations with less recourse to the courts to sanction the exercise of powers by official liquidators through increased utilisation of the sanction of creditors' committees. Some of the other changes introduced include: the requirement for liquidators to be qualified;[71] the power of the Office of the Director of Corporate Enforcement to petition the court to have a company wound up in the public interest;[72] increasing the minimum indebtedness to petition to wind up a company to €10,000;[73] and restricting the powers of provisional liquidators.[74]

(l) Part 12: Strike off and restoration

[1.061] Part 12 contains 21 sections of law, divided into three Chapters, concerning the strike off and restoration of companies:

- Chapter 1: Strike off of company;
- Chapter 2: Restoration of company to register;
- Chapter 3: Miscellaneous.

For the first time, *voluntary strike off* is recognised in statute although, as we know, it has been available on an administrative basis for years, the Registrar of Companies relying on the fact that companies have ceased to trade. The grounds for involuntary strike off are broadly the same as existed previously. As regards restoration, the options of both judicial and administrative restoration are preserved on the same basis as under the former Companies Acts.

(m) Part 13: Investigations

[1.062] The law relating to the investigation of companies through the appointment of inspectors is set out in 51 sections of law, divided into four Chapters in Part 13:

- Chapter 1: Preliminary;
- Chapter 2: Investigations by court appointed inspectors;
- Chapter 3: Investigations initiated by Director;
- Chapter 4: Miscellaneous provisions.

The law is largely a restatement of the previous legal regime applicable to investigations.

(n) Part 14: Compliance and enforcement

[1.063] Part 14 contains 90 sections of law and is divided into nine Chapters:

- Chapter 1: Compliance and protective orders;
- Chapter 2: Disclosure orders;
- Chapter 3: Restriction on directors of insolvent companies;

---

[71] Section 633 of the Act.
[72] Section 569 of the Act.
[73] Section 559 of the Act.
[74] Section 626 of the Act.

- Chapter 4: Disqualification generally;
- Chapter 5: Disqualification and restriction undertakings;
- Chapter 6: Enforcement in relation to disqualification and restriction;
- Chapter 7: Provisions relating to offences generally;
- Chapter 8: Additional general offences;
- Chapter 9: Evidential matters.

While the main changes introduced here are discussed in Ch 8, *Compliance and Enforcement*, the following changes to the law may be noted here: in relation to the restriction of the directors of insolvent companies, it will be no longer sufficient for such a director to show that he or she has acted honestly and responsibly; such directors will also be required to show that they have, when requested to do so by the liquidator, cooperated as far as could reasonably be expected in relation to the conduct of the winding up;[75] disqualification and restriction undertakings are also being introduced.[76] The penalties applicable to those convicted of committing a categorised offence are set out in s 871.[77]

(o) Part 15: Functions of Registrar and regulatory and advisory bodies

[1.064] Whereas Parts 1 to 14 apply exclusively to the LTD, Part 15 is expressed to apply to LTDs and other types of company.[78] Part 15 contains the provisions necessary to administer, regulate and review Irish company law and its 78 sections are divided into four Chapters:

- Chapter 1: Registrar of Companies;
- Chapter 2: Irish Auditing and Accounting Supervisory Authority;
- Chapter 3: Director of Corporate Enforcement;
- Chapter 4: Company Law Review Group.

Parts 16 to 25: Overview of other types of company and miscellaneous

[1.065] Parts 16 to 25 contain 472 sections of law comprising almost one-third of the Act's 1,448 sections. While the provisions in Parts 16 to 25 are only relevant to LTDs that seek to convert to another type of company, other types of companies will have to have regard to the provisions of Parts 1 to 14, most of which apply to them.

---

75 Section 819(2)(b) of the Act.
76 Section 851 and 853 of the Act.
77 See para [1.024].
78 Section 9(3) of the Act.

(a) Part 16: Designated activity companies

[1.066] The designated activity company or DAC is the first-cousin of the LTD. Indeed, the body of law applicable to the DAC most closely resembles the law applicable to existing private companies limited by shares. It is important for practitioners and users to be aware that, initially at least, all existing private companies limited by shares will have to have regard to the law on DACs in Part 16. This is because upon the commencement of the Act, it is Part 16 that will apply to all existing private companies limited by shares and will continue to apply to them until such time as they elect to re-register as LTDs or the transition period ends.[79]

[1.067] Certain existing private companies limited by shares cannot become LTDs and so, if they want to remain as private limited companies, will have to re-register as DACs. These are existing private limited companies:

- which are credit institutions and insurance undertakings;[80]
- which have issued debt securities that are listed on a stock exchange;[81]
- which are required by notice or resolution of its members to become DACs;[82] or
- which are ordered by the High Court to become DACs.[83]

[1.068] The law that is applicable to DACs is the law that is set out in Parts 1 to 14, save to the extent that it is *disapplied*,[84] *modified* or *supplemented* by the provisions contained in Part 16. Part 16 contains 37 sections of law, divided into eight Chapters:

- Chapter 1: Preliminary and definitions;
- Chapter 2: Incorporation and consequential matters;
- Chapter 3: Share capital;
- Chapter 4: Corporate governance;
- Chapter 5: Financial statements, annual return and audit;
- Chapter 6: Liability of contributories in winding up;
- Chapter 7: Examinerships;
- Chapter 8: Public offers of securities, prevention of market abuse, etc.

[1.069] The key features of the DAC which distinguish it from the LTD are:

- It is a private company limited by shares or by guarantee, having a share capital;

---

79   See s 58 of the Act.
80   Section 18(2) of the Act.
81   Section 56(3) of the Act.
82   Section 56(1) and (2) of the Act.
83   Section 57 of the Act.
84   By reason of s 964 of the Act.

- Its name must end in "designated activity company" or "DAC" or the Irish equivalents;
- It will have a memorandum of association and articles of association (although these will be collectively referred to as a constitution);
- It must have an objects clause;
- It must have an authorised share capital;
- It can list qualifying debt securities; and
- It must have at least two directors.

The most obvious features are the mandatory suffix to its name and the format of its constitution, continuing to have a memorandum and articles of association. It will also, however, continue to have an objects clause although the Act attempts to mitigate the effects of the doctrine of *ultra vires*.[85]

(b) Part 17: Public limited companies

[1.070] Whilst economically important, PLCs account for less than 1 per cent of all Irish companies and of these, fewer than 50 have an equity share listing. That ability to list equity securities is the key feature of PLCs which distinguishes them from all other types of company, since no other type of company may offer to the public or list equity securities. Even more scarce are *Societas Europaea* or SEs, of which there are no more than a couple of dozen. The law applicable to both the PLC and the SE is set out in Part 17.

[1.071] The law that is applicable to PLCs and SEs is the law set out in Parts 1 to 14, save to the extent that it is *disapplied*,[86] *modified* or *supplemented* by the provisions contained in Part 17. Part 17 contains 170 sections of law, divided into 18 Chapters:

- Chapter 1: Preliminary and definitions;
- Chapter 2: Incorporation and consequential matters;
- Chapter 3: Share capital;
- Chapter 4: Interests in shares: disclosure of individual and group interests;
- Chapter 5: Acquisition of own shares and certain acquisitions by subsidiaries;
- Chapter 6: Distribution by a PLC;
- Chapter 7: Uncertificated securities;
- Chapter 8: Corporate governance;
- Chapter 9: Duties of directors and other officers;
- Chapter 10: Financial statements, annual return and audit;
- Chapter 11: Debentures;

---

[85]   See s 973 of the Act.
[86]   By reason of s 1002 of the Act.

- Chapter 12: Examinerships;
- Chapter 13: Reorganisations;
- Chapter 14: Strike-off and restoration;
- Chapter 15: Investigations;
- Chapter 16: Mergers;
- Chapter 17: Divisions;
- Chapter 18: Public offers of securities, prevention of market abuse, etc.

Some of the changes introduced by the Act to the law relating to the PLC include: it may be incorporated with just one member;[87] where it has only one member, it may dispense with holding an AGM;[88] and the minimum issued share capital which it must have has been reduced to €25,000.[89]

(c) Part 18: Guarantee companies

[1.072] Under the former Companies Acts, the next most popular company after the private company limited by shares was the public company limited by guarantee without a share capital, accounting for over 8 per cent of all companies. Under the new Act, the public company limited by guarantee without a share capital, or "CLG", is likely to be the third most popular type of company, after the LTD and the DAC. Users of the CLG are:

- Charities,
- Sports and social clubs, and
- Management companies.

Not having a share capital, and instead being owned by non-shareholding members, makes the CLG ideal for use by not-for-profits, being a means whereby people coming together with a view to a social or charitable purpose may incorporate a company that better reflects their purpose. Moreover, the fact that it has no limit on the number of members makes the CLG useful for holding the common areas in apartment buildings and retail complexes where the owners of units will frequently exceed the limit of 149 members now imposed on private companies.

[1.073] The law that is applicable to CLGs is set out in Parts 1 to 14, save to the extent that it is *disapplied,*[90] *modified* or *supplemented* by the provisions contained in Part 18. Part 18 contains 54 sections of law, divided into nine Chapters:

- Chapter 1: Preliminary and definitions;
- Chapter 2: Incorporation and consequential matters;

---

87 Section 1004 of the Act.
88 Section 1089 of the Act.
89 Section 1010 of the Act.
90 By reason of s 1173 of the Act.

- Chapter 3: Share capital;
- Chapter 4: Corporate governance;
- Chapter 5: Financial statements, annual return and audit;
- Chapter 6: Liability of contributories in winding up;
- Chapter 7: Examinerships;
- Chapter 8: Investigations;
- Chapter 9: Public offers of securities, prevention of market abuse, etc.

Some of the changes introduced by the Act to the law relating to the CLG include: it may be incorporated with just one member instead of seven;[91] where it has only one member it may dispense with holding an AGM;[92] its name must end in "company limited by guarantee" or "CLG" or their Irish equivalents;[93] although it will be possible to obtain a dispensation in similar circumstance to those that applied to existing guarantee companies in relation to the use of the suffix "Limited" and for the first time there is a limited audit exemption available to CLGs.[94]

(d) Part 19: Unlimited companies

[1.074] The Act recognises three distinct types of unlimited company:

- The private unlimited company with a share capital (a "ULC");
- The public unlimited company with a share capital (a "PUC"); and
- The public unlimited company without a share capital (a "PULC").

Although Part 19 does use the foregoing three abbreviations, the names of all types of unlimited companies must end in the same suffix: "unlimited company" or "UC", it being sufficient that they are recognisable as simply having members who have unlimited liability for the debts of the company.[95]

[1.075] The law that is applicable to UCs is the law set out in Parts 1 to 14, save to the extent that it is *disapplied*,[96] *modified* or *supplemented* by the provisions contained in Part 19. Part 19 contains 54 sections of law, divided into nine Chapters:

- Chapter 1: Preliminary and definitions;
- Chapter 2: Incorporation and consequential matters;
- Chapter 3: Share capital;

---

[91] Section 1174 of the Act.
[92] Section 1202 of the Act.
[93] Section 1178 of the Act.
[94] Section 334 as modified by s 1218.
[95] Note, though the Minister has power to exempt certain companies, subject to conditions, where he considers this expedient: s 1237(5).
[96] By reason of s 1230 of the Act.

- Chapter 4: Corporate governance;
- Chapter 5: Financial statements, annual return and audit;
- Chapter 6: Winding up;
- Chapter 7: Examinerships;
- Chapter 8: Investigations;
- Chapter 9: Public offers of securities, prevention of market abuse, etc.

One of the most important changes to the law relating to unlimited companies is that the rule requiring that distributions may only be made from distributable profits has been disapplied.[97]

(e) Part 20: Re-registration

[1.076] The principle in Part 20 is that any type of company is capable of changing its status by re-registering as another type of company. Part 20 is comprised of 17 sections in three Chapters:

- Chapter 1: Interpretation;
- Chapter 2: General provisions as to re-registration;
- Chapter 3: Special requirements for re-registration.

Re-registration requires that companies pass a special resolution and lodge an application form with the Registrar of Companies with specified documents which will include a "compliance statement" that the Act's provisions have been complied with. In addition to allowing any type of company to re-register as any other type of company, another change introduced is the removal of the prohibition on private limited companies converting to unlimited where they had previously re-registered as such having been limited. The mischief – namely that a company flip-flops from limited to unlimited, thereby avoiding the requirement to file annual statements whilst retaining limited liability – is addressed in a different, more effective way. So, s 1296 requires that a limited company, seeking to be re-registered as unlimited, must file its financial statements with the other re-registration documentation unless it has within three months from the application, delivered an annual return with financial statements annexed or it was incorporated within three months of the application.

(f) Part 21: External companies

[1.077] Part 21 concerns external companies, and regulates certain foreign companies that establish themselves in Ireland. Part 21 contains 11 sections in five Chapters:

- Chapter 1: Preliminary;
- Chapter 2: Filing obligations of external companies;

---

97 Section 1255 of the Act.

- Chapter 3: Disclosure in certain business documents and translation of documents;
- Chapter 4: Service of documents;
- Chapter 5: Compliance.

[1.078] Under the former Companies Acts, a foreign company that established itself in Ireland had to decide whether either, or any, of two separate registrations applied. So, a foreign company, whether limited or unlimited, that established a *place of business* in Ireland was required to register under Part XI of the Companies Act 1963, whereas a foreign limited company, that established a *branch* in Ireland was required to register under the European Communities (Branch Disclosures) Regulations 1993.[98] The big change introduced by Part 21 is that it is only where a foreign *limited* company establishes a *branch* that registration will be required.[99] Another significant change is the abolition of the so-called *Slavenburg file*.[100]

(g) Part 22: Unregistered companies and joint stock companies

[1.079] Part 22 contains 36 sections divided into five Chapters:

- Chapter 1: Application of Act to unregistered companies;
- Chapter 2: Registration of certain bodies (other than joint stock companies) as companies;
- Chapter 3: Winding up of unregistered company;
- Chapter 4: Provisions concerning companies registered, but not formed, under former Acts and certain other existing companies;
- Chapter 5: Registration of joint stock companies under this Act.

The most significant provisions here are probably in Chapter 1 which applies certain provisions of the Act (those set out in Schedule 14) to certain bodies corporate which are neither companies formed and registered under previous Acts nor statutory corporations, eg chartered bodies, of which The Governor and Company of the Bank of Ireland is the best-known and most economically important.

---

[98] See, generally, Courtney, *The Law of Companies* (3rd edn, Bloomsbury Professional, 2012) at Ch 34.

[99] Section 1302 of the Act.

[100] Section 1301(5) of the Act. On the effect of the *Slavenburg file* see Courtney, *The Law of Companies* (3rd edn, Bloomsbury Professional, 2012) at para [34.020].

(h) Part 23: Public offers of securities, financial reporting by traded companies, prevention of market abuse, etc

[1.080] Part 23 contains 36 sections of law divided into four Chapters:

- Chapter 1: Public offers of securities;
- Chapter 2: Market abuse;
- Chapter 3: Requirement for governance statement and application of certain provisions of Parts 5 and 6 where company is a traded company;
- Chapter 4: Transparency requirements regarding issuers of securities admitted to trading on certain markets.

Chapter 1 re-enacts provisions implementing the Prospectus Directive (Directive 2003/71/EC) first enacted by the Investment Funds, Companies and Miscellaneous Provisions Act 2005 (the 2005 Act); the Prospectus (Directive 3003/71/EC) Regulations 2005 (SI 324/2005) are, however, preserved and references in them to the 2005 Act are substituted with references to the Companies Act 2014.[101] Chapter 2 re-enacts provisions implementing the Market Abuse Directive (Directive 2003/6/EC) first enacted by the 2005 Act, also; again, the Market Abuse (Directive 2003/6/EC) Regulations 2005 (SI 342/2005) are preserved and references in them to the 2005 Act are substituted with references to the Companies Act 2014.[102] Chapter 3 re-enacts provisions in relation to corporate governance statements for traded companies. Chapter 4 re-enacts provisions implementing the Transparency Directive (Directive 2004/109/EC) first enacted by the Investment Funds, Companies and Miscellaneous Provisions Act 2006 (the 2006 Act); the Transparency (Directive 2004/109/EC) Regulations 2007 (SI 277/2007) are also preserved and references in them to the 2006 Act are substituted with references to the Companies Act 2014.[103]

(i) Part 24: Investment companies

[1.081] Part 24 legislates for investment companies, formerly known as "Part XIII" companies, by reference to their origin in the Companies Act 1990. Many provisions of the Companies Act are relaxed in their application to investment companies because they are regulated by the Central Bank.

[1.082] The law that is applicable to investment companies is that set out in Parts 1 to 14, save to the extent that it is *disapplied* to PLCs[104] and to the extent

---

[101] Section 1355(2) of the Act.
[102] Section 1367(2) of the Act.
[103] Section 1381(2) of the Act.
[104] By virtue of s 1004 of the Act.

to which it is *disapplied, modified* or *supplemented* by the provisions contained in Part 24.[105] This Part contains 31 sections of law in nine Chapters:

- Chapter 1: Preliminary and interpretation (Part 24);
- Chapter 2: Incorporation and registration;
- Chapter 3: Share capital;
- Chapter 4: Financial statements;
- Chapter 5: Winding up;
- Chapter 6: Restoration;
- Chapter 7: Public offer of securities, prevention of market abuse, etc;
- Chapter 8: Umbrella funds and sub-funds;
- Chapter 9: Migration of funds.

(j) Part 25: Miscellaneous

[1.083] Part 25 contains 33 sections, divided into two Chapters:

- Chapter 1: Provisions concerning foreign insolvency proceedings (including those covered by the Insolvency Regulation);
- Chapter 2: Other miscellaneous provisions.

Chapter 1 contains provisions related to the Insolvency Regulation (Council Regulation (EC) 1346/2000) such as the registration and enforcement of insolvency judgments and protective measures relating thereto. Chapter 2 contains miscellaneous provisions such as the prohibition on partnerships with more than 20 members, etc.

(k) The Schedules to the Act

[1.084] The Act contains 17 Schedules:

- Schedule 1: Form of constitution of private company limited by shares;
- Schedule 2: Repeals and revocations;
- Schedule 3: Accounting principles, form and content of entity financial statements;
- Schedule 4: Accounting principles, form and content of group financial statements;
- Schedule 5: List of companies for certain purposes of Act (including, in particular, ss 142, 350, 362 and 510);
- Schedule 6: Further savings and transitional provisions;
- Schedule 7: Form of constitution of designated activity company limited by shares;

---

[105] By reason of s 1387 of the Act.

- Schedule 8: Form of constitution of designated activity company limited by guarantee;
- Schedule 9: Form of constitution of public limited company;
- Schedule 10: Form of constitution of company limited by guarantee;
- Schedule 11: Form of constitution of private unlimited company having a share capital;
- Schedule 12: Form of constitution of public unlimited company having a share capital;
- Schedule 13: Form of public unlimited company not having a share capital;
- Schedule 14: Provisions applied to unregistered companies;
- Schedule 15: Repeals and revocations in relation to unregistered companies;
- Schedule 16: Form of constitution of investment company;
- Schedule 17: Conditions to be satisfied for application of segregated liability to sub-funds of investment company trading before 30 June 2005.

Chapter 2

Changes in the Basics: Constitutions, Share Capital and Governance

by
Dr Thomas B Courtney

Introduction

[2.001] The purpose of this chapter is to review the changes made by the Companies Act to company law in relation to the basic matters of constitutions, share capital and governance (ie the administration of companies). The scope of this review is Parts 2, 3 and 4 of the Act and the changes introduced in relation to the following matters:

1. Company constitutions;
2. No requirement for an LTD to have an authorised share capital;
3. Meaning of "company capital";
4. Offers of securities to the public;
5. Allotment of shares;
6. Reduction of share capital;
7. Transfer and transmission of shares;
8. Directors and secretaries;
9. General meetings and resolutions;
10. The summary approval procedure.

Company constitutions

[2.002] One of the most visible changes to company law is the departure from the position that every company had to have a two-document constitution comprised of its memorandum and articles of association.[1] Private companies limited by shares to which Parts 1 to 15 of the Act apply, referred to here as "LTDs", will now have a *one-document constitution* containing both memorandum of association type clauses and articles of association type regulations. DACs, PLCs, CLGs and UCs will also technically have a

---

[1] As to the previous law, see Courtney, *The Law of Companies* (3rd edn, Bloomsbury Professional, 2012) at Ch 3.

"constitution" although in their case it will be in the familiar form of a memorandum of association and articles of association which will continue to fulfil distinct functions and contain distinct provisions. Here, we consider changes in the law relating to the constitutions for each of the following types of company:

(a) LTDs – private companies limited by shares;

(b) DACs – designated activity companies;

(c) PLCs – public limited companies;

(d) CLGs – companies limited by guarantee without a share capital;

(e) UCs – unlimited companies.

(a) LTDs – private companies limited by shares

[2.003] Every private company limited by shares to which Parts 1 to 15 of the Act apply must, by virtue of s 19(1) of the Act, have a constitution which states:

"(a) the company's name;

(b) that it is a private company limited by shares registered under this Part [ie Part 2];

(c) that the liability of its members is limited;

(d) as respects its share capital, either –

  (i) the amount of share capital with which it proposes to be registered ('its authorised share capital'), and the division of that capital into shares of a fixed amount specified in the constitution, or

  (ii) without stating such amount, that the share capital of the company shall, at the time of its registration, stand divided into shares of a fixed amount specified in the constitution;

(e) the number of shares (which shall not be less than one) taken by each subscriber to the constitution; and

(f) if the company adopts supplemental regulations, those regulations."

The constitution of an LTD must be:

* in a form in accordance with the form set out in Schedule 1 of the Act,
* divided into paragraphs numbered consecutively, and
* signed by the subscribers in the presence of at least one attesting witness or authenticated in accordance with s 888 of the Act.[2]

The form of model constitution set out in Schedule 1 displays remarkable brevity which belies the fact that the constitutions of most LTDs will, for reasons that will become apparent,[3] of necessity contain at the very least a dozen

---

2   Section 19(2) of the Act.
3   See para **[4.009]**.

or so supplemental regulations. Once adopted, a constitution cannot be amended except in the manner and to the extent for which express provision is made in the Act;[4] so s 32(1) of the Act provides that a company may, by special resolution, amend its constitution.

A number of key changes in the provisions of constitutions should be noted.

[2.004] First, the constitution of an LTD will not contain an objects clause. This is because s 38 provides that notwithstanding anything in its constitution a company shall have *full and unlimited capacity* to carry on and undertake any business or activity, do any act or enter into any transaction and for that purpose, have full rights, powers and privileges. The abolition of the requirement to have an objects clause is considered further in Ch 5.[5]

[2.005] Second, the constitution of an LTD *need not* prescribe an authorised share capital. An authorised share capital is a "cap" on the number of shares that can be in issue, and in the case of an LTD, whether or not it is to have such a cap is a decision for its members. The only mandatory provision now is that a constitution must state that the share capital is divided into shares of a specified fixed amount, eg "the share capital is divided into ordinary shares of €1 each".

[2.006] Third, the Act does not make provision for a suggested set of supplemental regulations, such that there is no longer a Table A-type list of provisions. The reason for this very significant change in law is because the Act states that most of the provisions which have heretofore been contained in Table A are now applied as statutory defaults which are taken to apply to every company, unless a particular company's constitution provides otherwise. So, for example, s 161(1) now provides:

> "A resolution in writing signed by all the directors of a company, or by all the members of a committee of them, and who are for the time being entitled to receive notice of a meeting of the directors or, as the case may be, or such a committee, shall be as valid as if it has been passed at a meeting of the directors or such a committee duly convened and held."

Previously, model Regulation 109 of Part I of Table A had provided:

> "A resolution in writing signed by all the directors for the time being entitled to receive notice of a meeting of the directors shall be as valid as if it had been passed at a meeting of the directors duly convened and held."

Whereas previously, for such a provision to apply in a company, that company's articles of association had to expressly say so. Over the decades, much of what was contained in Table A became adopted as standard by most companies. In a way that is not dissimilar to the codification of the common law on directors'

---

4   Section 20 of the Act.
5   See Ch 5, *Taking Security, the Summary Approval Procedure and the Registration of Charges* at para **[5.002]** *et seq*.

duties, the Act reflects what has become standard for many companies and so now the directors of companies can pass a resolution in writing without holding a meeting *unless* a company's constitution provides otherwise. In this manner, the Act has created some 151 statutory default provisions applicable to the LTD, of which s 161(1) is just one.

[2.007] While it will no longer be necessary to review a constitution to see whether a particular company allows its directors to pass written resolutions, it will continue to be necessary to review a particular constitution to establish that the statutory default has not been ousted. This is because most of the new statutory default provisions are optional and apply unless a particular constitution provides otherwise. So, for example, a particular company may decide to withhold from its directors the power to pass written directors' resolutions: s 157 provides that s 161 is one of the provisions that "applies save to the extent that the company's constitution provides otherwise".[6] While companies are free to run with the statutory defaults, they are equally free to switch them off or, indeed, provide for a provision that is a modification of the statutory default.

[2.008] Written resolutions of directors is just one example of this; virtually all of the provisions in Table A have been addressed in the Act by the creation of a statutory default or, in a limited number of cases, making mandatory a provision formerly contained in Table A. An example of the latter is the requirement in s 166(1) of the Act that minutes shall record all appointments of officers and the names of the directors present at each meeting of the directors or committees of directors which is not optional; heretofore this requirement was optional in the sense that it was so provided for in Article 89(c) of Part I of Table A and so, in theory, could have been excluded from a company's articles of association. So whilst primarily facilitative, there is an element of reform too; and few could take issue with a requirement that minutes should record the identity of directors present at a meeting or that the appointment of officers must be recorded in minutes.

[2.009] The changes introduced by the Act do not, however, mean that most companies will get away without any supplemental regulations, hence the observation made earlier about the remarkable brevity of the model constitution in Schedule 1 to the Act. There are three primary reasons for this. In the first place, there are certain matters which companies will want to make provision for in their constitution which the legislature cannot anticipate. So, for example, many companies will want to provide for pre-emption rights on the transfer of shares. There is no statutory default in the Act on this point because such is the variety of options open to companies, that a standard default would have been of

---

[6] It can be noted that s 161(1) also extends the use of unanimous written resolutions to committees of directors but, again, this is only a default which can be switched off or modified in a constitution.

limited use. Another example is where there is more than one class of share, the rights attaching may be set out in the constitution. Accordingly, companies which wish to provide for matters not addressed in the Act will have to bespeak a supplemental regulation. In the second place, the Act provides that in order to do certain things, there must be authority to do so either in the constitution or by way of a special resolution. Many companies will elect to hard-wire this authority in their constitutions to avoid the inconvenience of having to pass a special resolution to confer such authority at a later date. Examples here include authorising:

- the having of an official seal for use abroad;[7]
- the allotment of shares;[8]
- the allotment of shares by a committee of directors;[9]
- the disapplication of pre-emption rights;[10]
- the acquisition of own shares,[11] etc.

In the third place, while most of the statutory defaults are defaults because they reflect what companies have tended to adopt over many years, a small number are aspirational and seem intended to drive behaviour: so, for example, requiring companies to expressly disapply pre-emption rights on allotment when the preponderance of practice has been to disapply might be explained by the fact that the State thinks it is a good thing to give shareholders pre-emption rights on allotment and so this is what the default provides.

[2.010] Under the old Companies Acts, where a company adopted Table A or part thereof supplemented by tailored provisions, those provisions formed a statutory contract between the company and its members and the members *inter se*.[12] The substance of this rule is preserved by s 31(1) of the Act which provides:

> "Subject to the provisions of this Act, the constitution shall, when registered, bind the company and the members of it to the same extent as if it has been signed and sealed by each member, and contained covenants by the company and each member to observe all the provisions of the constitution *and any provision of this Act as to the governance of the company*."

---

[7]   Section 44(1) of the Act.
[8]   Section 69(1) of the Act.
[9]   Section 69(4)(a) of the Act.
[10] Section 69(12)(a)(i) and s 69(6) of the Act.
[11] Section 105(4) of the Act.
[12] Section 25 of the Companies Act 1963: see Courtney, *The Law of Companies* (3rd edn, Bloomsbury Professional, 2012) at para [3.092].

The concept of a statutory contract is, therefore, very much retained, so that now, some contractual provisions will be statutory provisions. Further guidance is provided by s 31(2) which states:

"For the avoidance of doubt, in *subsection (1)*, the reference to any provision of this Act as to the governance of the company includes a reference to any provision of this Act that commences with words to the effect that the provision applies save where the company's constitution provides otherwise or otherwise contains a qualification on the provision's application by reference to the company's constitution."

So, where a company's constitution is silent on, for example, unanimous written resolutions of directors such that s 161(1) operates as a statutory default, that provision forms part of the s 31 statutory contract. In contrast, if a particular company's constitution excludes s 161(1), then its provisions will not be a term of the statutory contract for that company.

(b) DACs – designated activity companies

[2.011] There are two types of DAC: a DAC limited by shares and a DAC limited by guarantee (but also having a share capital), although in practice the number of DACs limited by guarantee is likely to be very small. Section 967(1) provides that the constitution of a DAC shall be in the form of a memorandum of association and articles of association which together are referred to collectively in Part 16 as a "constitution". The form of the constitution of a DAC limited by shares must be in accordance with Schedule 7, and that of a DAC limited by guarantee must in accordance with Schedule 8.[13] To all intents and purposes a DAC's constitution will look like an old-style memorandum and articles of association save that it will be one document and the word "constitution" will appear before the start of the memorandum of association.

(i) Memorandum of association of DACs

[2.012] The memorandum of association of a DAC must, by virtue of s 967(2) of the Act, state:

"(a)   its name;

(b)   that it is a designated activity company having the status, as the case may be, of–

   (i)   a private company limited by shares; or

   (ii)   a private company limited by guarantee, and having a share capital, registered under this Part;

(c)   its objects;

(d)   that the liability of its members is limited;

---

13   Section 967(3)(b) of the Act.

(e)   in the case of a DAC limited by shares, the amount of share capital with which the DAC proposes to be registered and the division thereof into shares of a fixed amount;

(f)   in the case of a DAC limited by guarantee – in addition to the matter set out in the preceding paragraph – that each member undertakes that, if the company is wound up while he or she is a member, or within one year after the date on which he or she ceases to be a member, he or she will contribute to the assets of the company such amount as may be required for –

(i)   payment of the debts and liabilities of the company contracted before he or she ceases to be a member;

(ii)   payment of the costs, charges and expenses of winding up; and

(iii) adjustment of the rights of contributories among themselves, not exceeding an amount specified in the memorandum."

In addition, it is provided that the constitution (and so, not necessarily the memorandum of association) must "state the number of shares (which shall not be less than one) taken by each subscriber to the constitution".[14] Amendments to the memorandum of association affecting share capital or any of the other matters provided for in s 967(2) must be updated in the memorandum.[15] The Act also provides that the constitution must be printed in an entire format "that is to say that the memorandum and articles shall be contained in one document" and signed by each subscriber in the presence of at least one attesting witness or authenticated in accordance with s 888 of the Act.

[2.013] So, the memorandum of association of a DAC will contain much the same information as that of an "existing" private company limited by shares or limited by guarantee having a share capital. Unlike an LTD, a DAC *must* prescribe an authorised share capital. In particular, a DAC's memorandum of association must contain an *objects clause* and there is no reason to suspect that people will discontinue the "pernicious practice" described by Lord Wrenbury in *Cotman v Brougham*[16] of registering memoranda of association containing "paragraph after paragraph not specifying or delimiting the proposed trade or purpose". While a DAC will have an objects clause, an attempt is made to oust the doctrine of *ultra vires* and s 973(1) provides that the validity of an act done by a DAC shall not be called into question on the ground of lack of capacity by reason of anything contained in the DAC's objects.[17]

---

[14]   Section 967(3) of the Act.

[15]   Section 967(4) of the Act.

[16]   *Cotman v Brougham* [1918] AC 514.

[17]   See Ch 5, *Taking Security, the Summary Approval Procedure and the Registration of Charges* at para **[5.006]**.

(ii) Articles of association of DACs

[2.014] Section 968(3) provides that the articles of association of a DAC "may contain regulations". This is the licence by which a DAC can include all and any type of regulation that it cares to apply to its governance, save only to the extent that a provision is not prohibited by law or does not negate a mandatory provision imposed by the Act.

Section 968(4) provides that so far as the articles of a DAC do not exclude or modify an *optional provision*, that optional provision shall apply in relation to the DAC. An optional provision is defined to mean:

"... a provision of any of Parts 1 to 14 (as applied by this Part) or this Part that –

(a)   contains a statement to the effect, or is governed by provision elsewhere to the effect, that the provision applies save to the extent that the constitution provides otherwise or unless the constitution states otherwise; or

(b)   is otherwise of such import."

Section 968(5) rather unrealistically provides that articles of association "instead of containing any regulations in relation to the DAC, may consist of a statement to the effect that the provisions of the Companies Act 2014 are adopted and, if the articles consist solely of such a statement, subsection (4) shall apply".

[2.015] Just as in the case of an LTD, there is no Table A that will apply to a DAC. However, where a DAC was incorporated as an existing private company and was governed in whole or in part by the regulations contained in Table A, then it will continue to be so governed unless and until it amends its constitution.[18]

[2.016] By reason of s 964(1), all of the statutory defaults that apply to LTDs will apply to DACs, save to the extent that the DAC's constitution provides otherwise. Section 964(4) specifies a number of provisions contained in Parts 1 to 14 which do not apply to DACs and in consequence of this and other modifications and supplemental provisions in Part 16, circa 152 statutory default provisions will apply to a DAC, save to the extent that its constitution provides otherwise.

(c) PLCs – public limited companies

[2.017] Section 1006(1) provides that the constitution of a PLC shall be in the form of a memorandum of association and articles of association which together are referred to in Part 17 as a "constitution". The form of a PLC's constitution must be in accordance with Schedule 9.[19] To all intents and purposes a PLC's

---

18   Section 63(1) of the Act.
19   Section 1006(3)(b) of the Act.

constitution will look like a memorandum and articles of association save that it will be one document and the word "constitution" will appear before the start of the memorandum of association.

(i) Memorandum of association of PLCs

[2.018] The memorandum of association of a PLC must, by virtue of s 1006(2) of the Act, state:

"(a)   its name;

(b)   that it is a public limited company registered under this Part;

(c)   its objects;

(d)   that the liability of its members is limited;

(e)   its authorised share capital, being the amount of share capital with which the PLC proposes to be registered which shall not be less than the authorised minimum, and the division thereof into shares of a fixed amount."

In addition, it is provided that the constitution (and so, not necessarily the memorandum of association) must "state the number of shares (which shall not be less than one) taken by each subscriber to the constitution".[20] Amendments to the memorandum of association affecting share capital or other matters specified in s 967(2) must be updated in the memorandum.[21] The Act also provides that the constitution must be printed in an entire format "that is to say that the memorandum and articles shall be contained in one document" and signed by each subscriber in the presence of at least one attesting witness or authenticated in accordance with s 888 of the Act.

[2.019] The memorandum of association of a PLC will contain much the same information as that of an "existing" PLC. Unlike an LTD, however, a PLC must prescribe an authorised share capital. In particular, a PLC's memorandum of association must contain an *objects clause*. While a PLC will have an objects clause, an attempt is made to oust the doctrine of *ultra vires* and s 1012(1) provides that the validity of an act done by a PLC shall not be called into question on the ground of lack of capacity by reason of anything contained in the PLC's objects.[22]

(ii) Articles of association of PLCs

[2.020] Section 1007(3) provides that the articles of association of a PLC "may contain regulations". This is the licence by which a PLC can include all and any

---

20   Section 1006(3)(a) of the Act.
21   Section 967(4) of the Act.
22   See Ch 5, *Taking Security, the Summary Approval Procedure and the Registration of Charges* at para **[5.006]**.

type of regulation that it cares to apply to its governance, except a provision that is prohibited by law or a provision that seeks to negate a mandatory provision.

Section 1007(4) provides that so far as the articles of a PLC do not exclude or modify an optional provision, that optional provision shall apply in relation to the PLC. An optional provision is defined to mean:

"… a provision of any of Parts 1 to 14 (as applied by this Part) or this Part that –

(a) contains a statement to the effect, or is governed by provision elsewhere to the effect, that the provision applies save to the extent that the constitution provides otherwise or unless the constitution states otherwise; or

(b) is otherwise of such import."

Again, s 1007(5) rather optimistically provides that articles "instead of containing any regulations in relation to the PLC, may consist of a statement to the effect that the provisions of the Companies Act 2014 are adopted and, if the articles consist solely of such a statement, subsection (4) shall apply".

[2.021] Just as in the case of an LTD, there is no Table A that will apply to a PLC. However, where a PLC formed under the old legislation was governed in whole or in part by the regulations contained in Table A, then it will continue to be so governed until it amends its constitution.[23]

[2.022] By reason of s 1002(1), save to the extent they are disapplied, all of the statutory defaults that apply to LTDs will apply to PLCs, save to the extent that the PLC's constitution provides otherwise. There are, circa, 156 statutory defaults that will apply to a PLC, save to the extent that its constitution provides otherwise. Section 1002(4) identifies a number of provisions contained in Parts 1 to 14 that concern governance which do not apply to PLCs. By way of illustration, s 155 does not apply to PLCs. Section 155 provides, *inter alia*, that unless the constitution provides otherwise, the remuneration of the directors shall be determined by the board of directors: instead, in a PLC, s 1092 provides that the statutory default is that, unless the constitution provides otherwise, the remuneration of the directors shall be determined by the members in general meeting. Section 1090(2) provides, as a statutory default, that unless the constitution provides otherwise, the directors shall retire by rotation; there is no corresponding provision for LTDs (or DACs for that matter).

(d) CLGs – companies limited by guarantee without a share capital

[2.023] Section 1176(1) provides that the constitution of a CLG shall be in the form of a memorandum of association and articles of association which together are referred to in Part 18 as a "constitution". The form of a CLG's constitution

---

23   Section 1007(8) of the Act.

must be in accordance with Schedule 10.[24] To all intents and purposes a CLG's constitution will look like a memorandum and articles of association save that it will be one document and the word "constitution" will appear before the start of the memorandum of association.

(i) Memorandum of association of CLGs

[2.024] The memorandum of association of a CLG must, by virtue of s 1176(2) of the Act, state:

"(a)   its name;

(b)   that it is a public limited company registered under this Part;

(c)   its objects;

(d)   that the liability of its members is limited;

(e)   that each member undertakes that, if the company is wound up while he or she is a member, or within one year after the date on which he or she ceases to be a member, he or she will contribute to the assets of the company such amount as may be required for –

   (i)   payment of the debts and liabilities of the company contracted before he or she ceases to be a member;

   (ii)   payment of the costs, charges and expenses of winding up; and

   (iii)   adjustment of the rights of contributories among themselves,

Not exceeding an amount specified in the memorandum."

Amendments to the memorandum of association affecting matters specified in s 1176(2) must be updated in the memorandum.[25] The Act also provides that the constitution must be printed in an entire format "that is to say that the memorandum and articles shall be contained in one document" and signed by each subscriber in the presence of at least one attesting witness or authenticated in accordance with s 888 of the Act.

[2.025] So, the memorandum of association of a CLG will contain much the same information as that of an "existing" CLG. In particular, a CLG's memorandum of association must contain an *objects clause*. While a CLG will have an objects clause, an attempt is made to oust the doctrine of *ultra vires* and s 1182(1) provides that the validity of an act done by a CLG shall not be called into question on the ground of lack of capacity by reason of anything contained in the CLG's objects.[26]

---

[24]   Section 1176(3)(a) of the Act.

[25]   Section 1176(4) of the Act.

[26]   See Ch 5, *Taking Security, the Summary Approval Procedure, and the Registration of Charges* at para **[5.006]**.

(ii) Articles of association of CLGs

[2.026] Section 1177(3) provides that the articles of association of a CLG "may contain regulations". This is the licence by which a CLG can include all and any type of regulation that it cares to apply to its governance, except a provision that is prohibited by law or a provision which purports to negate a mandatory provision.

Section 1177(4) provides that so far as the articles of a CLG do not exclude or modify an optional provision, that optional provision shall apply in relation to the CLG. An optional provision is defined to mean:

"… a provision of any of Parts 1 to 14 (as applied by this Part) or this Part that –

(a) contains a statement to the effect, or is governed by provision elsewhere to the effect, that the provision applies save to the extent that the constitution provides otherwise or unless the constitution states otherwise; or

(b) is otherwise of such import."

Section 1177(5) provides that subject to compliance with s 1199(3) – articles must state the number of members with which the company proposes to be registered – articles may "consist of a statement to the effect that the provisions of the Companies Act 2014 are adopted and, if the articles consist solely of such a statement, subsection (4) shall apply". It is thought to be most unlikely that this will be availed of.

[2.027] There is no Table C that will apply to a CLG because, as with other types of companies, some 87 statutory defaults will provide for most matters heretofore contained in Table C. The reason there are significantly fewer statutory defaults applying in a CLG is due to the absence of the need to make provision for a share capital. However, where a CLG formed under the old legislation was governed in whole or in part by the regulations contained in Table C, then it will continue to be so governed until it amends its constitution.[27]

[2.028] By reason of s 1173(1), many of the statutory defaults that apply to LTDs will apply to CLGs, save to the extent that the CLG's constitution provides otherwise. Section 1173(4) identifies a number of provisions contained in Parts 1 to 14 that concern governance which do not apply to CLGs. So, for example, s 1196(2) provides, as a statutory default, that unless the constitution provides otherwise, the directors shall retire by rotation and s 1197(1) provides that the remuneration of directors is set by the members in general meeting unless the constitution provides otherwise.[28]

---

[27] Section 1177(8) of the Act.

[28] The failure to disapply s 155 in s 1173(4) (as was done in the case of a PLC) appears an oversight but it is thought that the express provisions of s 1197(1) will prevail.

(e) UCs – unlimited companies

[2.029] Part 19 makes provision for three distinct types of unlimited company: private unlimited companies ("ULCs"), public unlimited companies ("PUCs") and public unlimited companies without a share capital ("PULCs"). When referring to a provision applicable to any type of unlimited company, we will refer to an unlimited company ("UC"). Section 1233(1) provides that the constitution of a ULC and PUC and s 1234(1) provides that the constitution of a PULC shall be in the form of a memorandum of association and articles of association which together are referred to in Part 19 as a "constitution". The form of a ULC's constitution, PUC's constitution and PULC's constitution must be in accordance with Schedule 11, 12 and 13, respectively.[29]

(i) Memorandum of association of UCs

[2.030] The memorandum of association of a ULC and PUC must, by virtue of s 1233(2) of the Act, state:

"(a) its name;

(b) that it is a private unlimited company or public unlimited company registered under this Part;

(c) its objects;

(d) the amount of share capital with which the company proposes to be registered and the division thereof into shares of a fixed amount; and

(e) the fact that its members have unlimited liability."

In the case of a PULC, s 1234(2) provides it must state:

"(a) its name;

(b) that it is a public unlimited company, that has no share capital, registered under this Part;

(c) its objects; and

(d) the fact that its members have unlimited liability."

Amendments to the memorandum of association affecting matters specified in s 1233(2) or s 1234(2) must be updated in the memorandum.[30] The Act also provides that the constitution must be printed in an entire format "that is to say that the memorandum and articles shall be contained in one document" and signed by each subscriber in the presence of at least one attesting witness or authenticated in accordance with s 888 of the Act.

[2.031] So, the memorandum of association of a ULC, PUC and PULC will contain much the same information as that of an "existing" unlimited company. In particular, a UC's memorandum of association must contain an *objects*

---

[29] Section 1233(3)(a)(i) and (ii) and s 1234(3)(a) respectively.

[30] Section 1233(4) and s 1234(4) of the Act.

clause. While a UC will have an objects clause, an attempt is made to oust the doctrine of *ultra vires* and s 1239(1) provides that the validity of an act done by a UC shall not be called into question on the ground of lack of capacity by reason of anything contained in the UC's objects.[31]

(ii) Articles of association of UCs

[2.032] Section 1235(3) provides that the articles of association of a UC "may contain regulations". This is the licence by which a UC can include all and any type of regulation that it cares to apply to its governance, except a provision that is prohibited by law or that purports to negate a mandatory provision.

Section 1235(4) provides that so far as the articles of a UC do not exclude or modify an optional provision, that optional provision shall apply in relation to the UC. An optional provision is defined to mean:

"... a provision of any of Parts 1 to 14 (as applied by this Part) or this Part that –

    (a)   contains a statement to the effect, or is governed by provision elsewhere to the effect, that the provision applies save to the extent that the constitution provides otherwise or unless the constitution states otherwise; or

    (b)   is otherwise of such import."

Section 1235(5) provides that in the case of a ULC or PUC articles may "consist of a statement to the effect that the provisions of the Companies Act 2014 are adopted and, if the articles consist solely of such a statement, subsection (4) shall apply"; s 1235(6) provides the same subject to a PULC's articles being required to state the number of members with which a PULC proposes to be registered.

[2.033] There is no Table E that will apply to a UC because, as with other types of companies, statutory defaults will provide for most matters heretofore contained in Table E. However, where a UC formed under the old legislation was governed in whole or in part by the regulations contained in Table E, then it will continue to be so governed until it amends its constitution.[32]

[2.034] By reason of s 1230(1), save to the extent they are disapplied, all of the statutory defaults that apply to LTDs will apply to UCs, save to the extent that the UC's constitution provides otherwise. Section 1230(5) identifies a number of provisions contained in Parts 1 to 14 that concern governance which do not apply to ULCs; s 1230(6) that do not apply to PUCs; and s 1230(7) that do not apply to PULCs.

---

[31] See Ch 5, *Taking Security, the Summary Approval Procedure and the Registration of Charges* at para **[5.006]**.

[32] Section 1177(8) of the Act.

No requirement for an LTD to have an authorised share capital

[2.035] Section 19(1)(d) of the Act provides that an LTD is not required to state in its constitution the amount of its authorised share capital and may, instead, simply state that the share capital is divided into shares of a fixed amount. It should be noted that this concession applies *only* to the LTD and not to any other type of company. An LTD with an authorised share capital can abandon its authorised share capital by passing a special resolution in accordance with s 32 and in that event must re-register its constitution, thus amended: s 19(3).

Meaning of "company capital"

[2.036] Whereas the former Companies Acts generally referred to share capital, the Act now regulates how companies deal with their *company capital*. "Company capital" is defined by s 64(1) to mean:

> "(a) the aggregate value, expressed as a currency amount, of the consideration received by the company in respect of the allotment of shares of the company; and
>
> (b) that part of the company's undenominated capital constituted by the transfer of sums referred to in sections 106(4) and 108(3)."

"Undenominated capital" is defined also by s 64(1) and means "the amount of the company capital from time to time which is in excess of the nominal value of its issued shares and shall be deemed to include any sum transferred as referred to in ss 106(4)[33] and 108(3)[34]". Section 64(1)(a) means that company capital includes the nominal value of shares and also any premium paid on them and so includes both denominated and undenominated capital. Moreover, s 64(2) provides that the definition of "company capital" also includes:

> "... any amounts standing, immediately before the commencement of this section, to the credit of –
>
> (a) the company's share premium account (within the meaning of the prior Companies Acts);

---

[33] Section 106(4) provides that: "Where the shares are – (a) under section 105, acquired wholly out of the profits available for distribution; or (b) under section 105, acquired wholly or partly out of the proceeds of a fresh issue and the aggregate amount of those proceeds (disregarding any part of those proceeds used to pay any premium on the acquisition is) less than the aggregate nominal value of the share acquired (the 'aggregable difference'), then a sum equal to, in the case of paragraph (a), the nominal value of the shares acquired and, in the case of paragraph (b), the aggregable difference shall be transferred to undenominated capital of the company, other than its share premium account."

[34] Section 108(3) provides: "Where any such shares are redeemed otherwise than out of the proceeds of a fresh issue, there shall, out of profits which would otherwise have been available for distribution be transferred to undenominated capital, other than the share premium account, a sum equal to the nominal amount of the shares redeemed."

(b) its capital redemption reserve fund (within the meaning of those Acts); and

(c) its capital conversion reserve fund."

The concept of a share premium account has not gone away, however, and s 71(5) provides that subject to certain provisions:

"any value received in respect of the allotment of a share in excess of its nominal value shall be credited to and form part of undenominated capital of the company and, for that purpose, shall be transferred to an account which shall be known, and in this Act is referred to, as the 'share premium account'."

Whilst s 64(2) expressly refers to share premium accounts within the meaning of the old legislation, a share premium account within the meaning of the Act is also included in the term "company capital" and will be caught by the definition in s 64(1)(a) being part of the consideration received for shares on their allotment.

Offers of securities to the public

[2.037] A three-fold distinction has been introduced in relation to the making of offers of securities to the public which may best be illustrated in a table:

May offer to the public and list on a market all securities (whether equity securities or debt securities)	PLCs
May list debt securities	DACs, CLGs, PUCs, PULCs
May not offer to the public, or list on a market, any securities (whether equity securities or debt securities)	LTDs, ULCs

Accordingly, whilst all private companies were permitted, subject to adhering to certain conditions, to list debt securities since s 33 of the Companies Act 1963 was amended by s 7 of the Investment Funds, Companies and Miscellaneous Provisions Act 2006 (which had effect from 1 July 2005), it is now the case that only private companies that convert to DACs are permitted to list debt securities.

For the LTD (and a ULC), a tighter more restrictive regime will apply and s 68(1) and (2) provide:

"(1) Subject to the provisions of this section, a company shall not –

(a) make –

(i) any invitation to the public to subscribe for, or

(ii) any offer to the public of,

any shares or debentures or other securities of the company; or

(b)   allot, or agree to allot, (whether for cash or otherwise) any shares in or debentures of the company with a view to all or any of those shares or debentures being offered for sale to the public or being the subject of an invitation to the public to subscribe for them.

(2) A company shall –

(a)   neither apply to have securities (or interest in them) admitted to trading or to be listed on; nor

(b)   have securities (or interests in them) admitted to trading or listed on,

any market whether a regulated market or not, in the State or elsewhere."

In contrast, for DACs, s 981 substitutes for s 68(2) an alternative subsection which permits the admission to trading or listing of debentures.[35]

Section 68 does not apply to PLCs,[36] and s 1020 expressly provides that save where prohibited by its constitution, a PLC has the capacity to offer, allot and issue securities (as defined in Part 3) to the public subject to compliance, where applicable, with Part 23.

Allotment of shares

(a) Statutory defaults and possible tailoring

[2.038] The allotment of shares in LTDs is regulated in Chapter 3 of Part 3. A number of statutory defaults apply, and so *unless the constitution provides otherwise*:

- Where an LTD has an authorised share capital, no shares may be allotted unless comprised in the authorised but unissued share capital;[37]
- Allotment of shares must be authorised, specifically or under a general authority, by an ordinary resolution or by the constitution;[38]
- The authority to allot shares may be limited in duration by the stipulation of a period during which shares can be allotted;[39]
- Shares may only be allotted by the directors;[40]
- Statutory pre-emption rights apply on the allotment of shares.[41]

---

[35] Section 1191 does the same for CLGs as does s 1248 for PUCs and PULCs.
[36] By virtue of s 1002(3) of the Act.
[37] Section 69(2) of the Act.
[38] Section 69(1) of the Act.
[39] Section 69(3) of the Act.
[40] Section 69(4)(a) of the Act.
[41] Section 69(6) of the Act.

It is thought that the shareholders in many LTDs and DACs will wish to displace these defaults and that their constitutions will expressly provide that:

- The LTD has no authorised share capital (note, this is not an option for the DAC);

- The allotment of shares is authorised generally, so that an ordinary resolution is never needed to approve an allotment;

- The general authorisation to allot is not subject to any stipulation as to a period during which shares can be allotted;

- Shares may be allotted by committees of directors and other persons authorised by the directors; and

- The statutory pre-emption regime will not apply.

It should be noted that a different regime applies to the allotment of shares in a PLC and that s 69 is disapplied,[42] s 1021 et seq applying in lieu thereof.

(b) Share premiums and merger relief

[2.039] The general rule remains that shares must be paid up in money or money's worth and may not be allotted at a discount. Moreover, premium on shares must be accounted for in a share premium account which is part of a company's capital, to which the capital maintenance rules apply: s 71(5).

[2.040] One significant change to these general principles is contained in ss 72 to 75, which provide an exception to the rule that value greater than nominal value received is premium and must be treated as part of the company's undenominated company capital in a merger-type arrangement. Before the Act, where an acquiring-company (or "issuing company") issued shares in itself in return for shares in a target company, the value of the shares received by the issuing company in excess of the nominal value of the shares issued was treated as share premium. The effect was to adversely affect the distributable profits of the issuing company ie it could pay less, if any, dividends. This will no longer be the case where the conditions of s 72 are met. So, in an acquisition where shares in the "issuing company" are issued in consideration for shares in another company and the issuing company acquires at least a 90 per cent interest in the other company, s 71(5) – which would require any excess over nominal value to be treated as premium – does not apply. Sections 73 and 74 make supplementary provision for such acquisitions, and s 75 facilitates an Irish company issuing shares in return for all issued shares in a body corporate (which would include a foreign company). It is beyond the scope of this guide to consider these changes in further detail.

---

[42]   Section 1002(3) and the Table thereto.

Reduction and variation of share capital

[2.041] The variation of share capital is addressed in Chapter 4 of Part 3 and there, one of the most significant changes introduced by the Act, is that it is now possible to reduce a company's share capital without always having to apply for a High Court order. Section 84 provides that a company may reduce its share capital by passing a special resolution that is confirmed by the High Court *or* by employing the summary approval procedure contained in Chapter 7 of Part 4.

[2.042] The mechanism for varying share capital in s 91 is also new and of significance. This provides that a company (referred to as the "relevant company") may, for any purpose with the result that the company capital is thereby "reorganised", transfer or dispose of one or more assets, undertaking or part thereof or a combination of assets and liabilities to a body corporate on terms that some or all of the consideration is shares in the body corporate given *to the members* of the relevant company (and not, the relevant company itself). It is obvious that such a reorganisation – whereby a company transfers its assets but its shareholders receive the consideration in the form of shares in another body corporate – could prejudice creditors and so this is only permitted where approved by the *summary approval procedure*. The directors of the relevant company will, *inter alia*, be required to declare that the relevant company will be able to pay its debts and liabilities after the reorganisation, and an independent person must provide a report that the declaration is not unreasonable.[43]

Transfer and transmission of shares

[2.043] Chapter 5 of Part 3 sets out the law in relation to the transfer of shares, re-enacting provisions from the Companies Act 1963 and codifying as statutory defaults a number of provisions from Table A. One of the key changes is that unless the constitution of an LTD, DAC, PLC, ULC or PUC provides otherwise, the directors will have an absolute discretion to decline to register a transfer of a share without assigning any reason (s 95(1)(a)); however, the common law rule that the decision not to register must be communicated within two months has been codified and the power to decline to register will cease to be exercisable on the expiry of two months after the date of delivery to the company of the instrument of transfer of shares. Whereas s 94(2) provides that an instrument of transfer may be signed by the transferor only (except where the shares are partly paid), in the case of a ULC and PUC, it must be signed by the transferee also: s 1253.

In the case of transmission on death, s 96(1) provides that save to the extent that the constitution provides otherwise, the survivor in the case of a joint holding of shares and the personal representatives of a deceased holder shall be

---

[43]   See para **[2.063]**.

the only persons recognised by the company as having any title to the shares. Section 97 confers a power on the Minister for Jobs, Enterprise and Innovation to prescribe procedures whereby the registration of shares may be validly effected in cases of the death of the sole member of a single-member company where that person is also the sole director, and other cases of difficulty. It is interesting that the registration of shares on foot of a merger is recognised as being a form of transmission,[44] and s 92(2) provides that without prejudice to it being provided for in Ministerial procedures, nothing in s 96 prejudices the adoption of alternative procedures to those specified with respect to registration shares transmitted by operation of law in consequence of a merger.

The law relating to directors and secretaries

[2.044] The following changes in the law relating to directors and secretaries are considered next:

(a)   The number of directors in an LTD;

(b)   The age of directors and secretaries;

(c)   Changes to the law of secretaries;

(d)   Details of directors' home addresses;

(e)   Proceedings of directors.

(a)   The number of directors in an LTD

[2.045] One of the more publicised changes is that now an LTD can have just one director.[45] It should be noted, however, that it will be a Category 3 offence for a company *and any officer of it who is in default* where a default is made in complying with the requirement that a company must have one director. This is a rather puzzling provision since it implies that where there is no director, the secretary, being an officer will commit an offence if in default. Given that it is unheard of for a company secretary (or, for that matter, any officer other than the board of directors) to have the power to appoint directors (and so make good the default) it is hard to see how the concept of officer in default can have any relevance to the requirement that a company must have at least one director. It is important to remember that it is only an LTD which is permitted to have just one director and that all other types of companies must have at least two directors.

[2.046] Section 2(8) also provides that a reference in the Act to a company having a sole director "is a reference to its having for the time being and for whatever reason, a single director (and this applies notwithstanding a stipulation in the constitution that there be 2 directors, or a greater number)". Convoluted,

---

[44]   See Courtney, *The Law of Companies* (3rd edn, Bloomsbury Professional, 2012) at para [9.032].

[45]   Section 128(1) of the Act.

yes; but the message is clear – a company will have a sole director when it has in fact only one director.

(b) The age of directors and secretary

[2.047] Another change introduced by the Act is the requirement for all directors and secretaries who are natural persons to be at least 18 years of age.[46] Any purported appointment of a minor will be void: s 131(2). Moreover, no attempt is made to "grandfather" this requirement, and minors who had been lawfully appointed directors before the commencement of the new requirement will cease, on its commencement, to be directors: s 131(3).

(c) Changes to the law of secretaries

[2.048] Companies will still be required to have a company secretary although, as before, the secretary may be one of the directors.[47] It also remains the case that where a provision of the Act, an instrument under it or a company's constitution requires or authorises a thing to be done by or to a director *and* the secretary, such thing shall not be satisfied by its being done by or to the same person acting both as director and as, or in place of, the secretary.[48] Moreover, there is an express prohibition on the sole director of a company also holding the office of secretary of the company: s 129(6).

[2.049] Another change in the law relating to company secretaries is that the directors of LTDs, DACs, CLGs and UCs now have a duty to ensure that the person appointed as secretary "has the skills or resources necessary to discharge his or her statutory and other duties"[49] and this duty applies equally in the case of an appointment of a director as company secretary.[50]

[2.050] In the case of PLCs, s 129(4) is disapplied and, instead, s 1112 provides that a PLC's directors have a duty to ensure that the person appointed as secretary has the skills or resources necessary to discharge his or her statutory and other duties and complies with one or more of the conditions set out in s 1112(2):

> "(a) the person, for at least 3 of the 5 years immediately preceding his or her appointment as secretary, held the office of secretary of a company;
>
> (b) the person is a member of a body for the time being recognised for the purposes of this section by the Minister; or

[46] Section 131(1) of the Act.
[47] Section 129(1) of the Act.
[48] Section 134 of the Act.
[49] Section 129(4) of the Act.
[50] Section 129(5) of the Act.

(c) the person is a person who, by virtue of holding or having held any other position or being a member of any other body, appears to the directors to be capable of discharging his or her statutory and other duties."

(d) Details of directors' home addresses

[2.051] For the directors and other officers of some companies, the provision of their home addresses in CRO returns (eg B10s) or in publically accessible registers (eg the register of directors and secretaries) can pose a security risk. Directors of companies involved in the pharmaceutical sector, for example, have been targeted for attack at their homes by anti-vivisectionists. In response to such security risks, s 150(11) of the Act now empowers the Minister to make regulations providing that any requirement that the usual residential address of an officer appear in a register or be sent to the Registrar of Companies shall not apply to a particular person where certain conditions are met.

(e) Proceedings of directors

[2.052] What can be considered to be the cornerstone of corporate governance – Regulation 80 of Part I of Table A – is now a statutory default in s 158 and will apply to all companies unless their constitution provides otherwise.[51] Section 158 is a hugely important provision of the Act as it is the foundation stone for the directors' powers of management and delegation:

"(1) The business of a company shall be managed by its directors, who may pay all expenses incurred in promoting and registering the company and may exercise all such powers of the company as are not, by this Act or by the constitution, required to be exercised by the company in general meeting, but subject to –

(a) any regulations contained in the constitution;

(b) the provisions of this Act; and

(c) such directions, not being inconsistent with the foregoing regulations or provisions, as the company in general meeting may (by special resolution) give.

(2) However, no direction given by the company in general meeting under *subsection (1)(c)* shall invalidate any prior act of the directors which would have been valid if that direction had not been given.

(3) Without prejudice to the generality of that subsection, subsection (1) operates to enable, subject to a limitation (if any) arising under any of paragraphs (a) to (c) of it, the directors of the company to exercise all powers of the company to

---

[51] Section 157 provides that Chapter 4 (with the exception of ss 166 and 167) shall apply *save to the extent that the company's constitution provides otherwise.*

borrow money and to mortgage or charge its undertaking, property and uncalled capital, or any part thereof.

(4) Without prejudice to *section 40*, the directors may delegate any of their powers to such person or persons as they think fit, including committees; any such committee shall, in the exercise of the powers so delegated, conform to any regulations that may be imposed on it by the directors.

(5) The reference in *subsection (1)* to a power of the company required to be exercised by the company in general meeting includes a reference to a power of the company that, but for the power of the members to pass a written resolution to effect the first-mentioned power's exercise, would be required to be exercised by the company in general meeting."

One change introduced is to clarify that members may only direct the directors to do something by passing a special resolution. This means that if the members wish to override the directors' powers of management, a special resolution must be passed, whether to issue the direction or to amend, generally, their powers by ousting the statutory default in s 158 by inserting a bespoke provision in the constitution.

[2.053] The power of directors to appoint a managing director,[52] the rules governing the holding of directors' meetings and committee meetings[53] (including by conference call[54]) and passing of directors' resolutions (including by written resolution[55]) and alternate directors[56] are all provided as statutory defaults which will apply automatically unless ousted or varied by an express provision in the constitution. By contrast, minutes of meetings (s 166) and the necessity to establish audit committees (for companies in scope) (s 167) are mandatory provisions. It will be noted that now large private companies (balance sheet of €25m or greater and turnover of €50m or greater or which has subsidiaries which in the aggregate meet these criteria) will be obliged to establish an audit committee or if the directors decide not to establish an audit committee, to explain why not.

General meetings and resolutions

[2.054] Chapter 6 of Part 4 of the Act concerns members' meetings. Many of the provisions which previously would have been contained in articles of association are now contained in the Act. The Act has introduced a number of

---

52 Section 159 of the Act.
53 Section 160 of the Act.
54 Section 161(6) of the Act.
55 Section 161(1) to (5) of the Act.
56 Section 165 of the Act.

important changes to the law relating to general meetings of members and resolutions. These changes may be summarised thus:

(a) All single-member companies and multi-member LTDs may dispense with holding an AGM

[2.055] Since 1994 it has been possible for single-member private limited companies to dispense with holding an AGM.[57] Not only does s 175(3) and (4) continue this for LTDs, but this provision is also applied to single-member DACs, PLCs, CLGs and UCs.

[2.056] Section 175(3) of the Act now extends the possibility of dispensing with an AGM to multi-member LTDs where all of the members entitled to attend and vote sign, before the latest date for the holding of the meeting, a written resolution acknowledging receipt of the financial statements that would have been laid at the AGM, resolving all matters as would have been resolved at that meeting and confirming no change is proposed in the appointment of the statutory auditor (where there is a statutory auditor). It is only multi-member LTDs which can dispense with holding an AGM: all other types of company must hold an AGM where they have more than one member.[58]

(b) General meetings held outside of the State

[2.057] Where a company holds its AGM or an extraordinary general meeting outside of the State, then, unless all of the members entitled to attend and vote at the meeting consent in writing to its being held outside of the State, the company has a duty to make, at its expense, all necessary arrangements to ensure that members can by technological means participate in the meeting without leaving the State.[59] The change in the law here is that it is no longer sufficient that an ordinary resolution has been passed at the previous year's AGM.

(c) Members' right to convene general meeting

[2.058] Another change introduced by the Act is that, unless a company's constitution provides otherwise, one or more members holding not less than 50 per cent (or such other percentage as may be specified in the constitution) of the paid up share capital carrying voting rights, may convene an extraordinary general meeting of the company (EGM).[60] This is in addition to the right of qualifying members to requisition the holding of a meeting; the difference is

---

[57] Regulation 9 of SI 275/1994.
[58] See s 988 (DACs), s 1089 (PLCs), s 1202 (CLGs) and s 1262 (UCs).
[59] Section 176(2) and (3) of the Act.
[60] Section 178(1) and (2) of the Act.

that unless the constitution provides otherwise, the members can actually *convene* (as opposed to request that the directors convene) an EGM.

(d) Resolutions

[2.059] Section 191(1) of the Act defines, for the first time, "ordinary resolution" and provides that it means "a resolution passed by a simple majority of the votes cast by members of a company as, being entitled to do so, vote in person or by proxy at a general meeting of the company". Section 191(2) defines "special resolution" as meaning a resolution:

> "(a) that is referred to as such in this Act, or is required (whether by this Act or by a company's constitution or otherwise) to be passed as a special resolution; and
>
> (b) that satisfies the condition specified in subsection (3) [ie that it is passed by not less than 75% of the votes cast]; and
>
> (c) without prejudice to subsections (4) and (5), as respects which notice of the meeting at which the resolution is proposed to be passed has been given in accordance with section 181(1)(a) [ie 21 days' notice of the meeting has been given] and (5) [ie the text or substance of the proposed resolution is specified in the notice]."

Both ordinary and special resolutions can be passed as "written resolutions" in accordance with either s 193 (unanimous written resolutions) or s 194 (majority written resolutions).

(i) Unanimous written resolutions

[2.060] All LTDs can pass unanimous written resolutions irrespective of what their constitutions provide.[61] Section 193 also provides that a written resolution can consist of several signed documents;[62] and is deemed to have been passed on the date it was signed by the last member to sign it.[63] Where a unanimous written resolution is not contemporaneously signed, its signing must be notified to the members within 21 days;[64] it must be delivered (whether by post, hand, email or fax) to the company within 14 days of its being signed;[65] and it shall be retained by the company as if it constituted minutes:[66] however, the failure to do any of the foregoing three things will not invalidate the resolution: s 193(8). As was previously the case, a unanimous written resolution cannot be used to

---

[61] Section 193 of the Act.
[62] Section 193(3) of the Act.
[63] Section 194(4) of the Act.
[64] Section 193(5) of the Act.
[65] Section 193(6) of the Act.
[66] Section 193(7) of the Act.

remove directors or auditors;[67] however, in the case of a single-member company, the member can take a *written decision* to remove a director although this is now expressed to be "without prejudice to the application of the requirements of procedural fairness to the exercise of that power of removal by the sole member" and s 147.[68] A failure by a company, an officer in default or a member to comply with the requirements imposed by this section can in certain circumstances be a category 4 offence.[69]

(ii) Majority written resolutions

[2.061] The concept of a written resolution being passed, not unanimously, but by a majority of those entitled to attend and vote at a meeting is novel in Irish company law. Note, only LTDs and DACs may utilise majority written resolutions. Section 194(1) permits an ordinary resolution to be passed by a majority and provides:

> "Notwithstanding any provision to the contrary in this Act, a resolution in writing –
>
> (a) that is –
>
>   (i)   described as being an ordinary resolution; and
>
>   (ii) signed by the requisite majority of members of the company concerned;
>
>   and
>
> (b) in respect of which the condition specified in *subsection (7)* is satisfied,
>
> shall be as valid and effective for all purposes as if the resolution had been passed at a general meeting of the company duly convened and held."

In the case of an ordinary resolution, the term "requisite majority of members" means members who represent "*more than 50 per cent*" of the total voting rights of all members entitled to attend and vote at a general meeting.[70] Section 194(4) applies the same principle to special resolutions save that there, the term "requisite majority of members", means members who represent at least 75 per cent of the total voting rights.[71]

[2.062] While a unanimous written resolution will take effect upon the last member signing it, there will always be a delay before a majority written

---

67 Section 193(11) of the Act.
68 Section 196(1) of the Act. Section 147 provides a director's removal is without prejudice to any right to be compensated but also confirms the validity of any other power to remove a director other than by resolution.
69 Section 196(9) and (10) of the Act.
70 Section 194(3) of the Act.
71 Section 194(6) of the Act.

resolution takes effect, even after the last person has signed it. So, s 194(9) provides:

> "Without prejudice to *section 195(5)*, a resolution passed –
>
> (a) in accordance with *subsection (1)*, shall be deemed to have been passed, subject to *subsection (10)*, at a meeting held 7 days after the date on which it was signed by the last member to sign; or
>
> (b) in accordance with *subsection (4)*, shall be deemed to have been passed, subject to *subsection (10)*, at a meeting held 21 days after the date on which it was signed by the last member to sign,
>
> and where the resolution states a date as being the date of his or her signature thereof by any member the statement shall be *prima facie* evidence that it was signed by him or her on that date."

This is made expressly subject to s 195(5) which provides that a majority written resolution shall not be valid unless, in accordance with s 195(3), the signatories of a resolution procure delivery (whether by mail, hand, email, fax) to the company of the documents constituting the majority written resolution.

The summary approval procedure

[2.063] As has been noted in Ch 1 of this book,[72] s 202 of the Act provides for a summary approval procedure (SAP) which can be utilised to validate seven activities otherwise restricted by the following provisions:

- Section 82 (financial assistance for acquisition of shares);
- Section 84 (reduction in company capital);
- Section 91 (variation of company capital on reorganisation);
- Section 118 (prohibition on pre-acquisition profits or losses being treated in holding company's financial statements as profits available for distribution);
- Section 239 (prohibition of loans, etc, to directors and connected persons);
- Section 464 (mergers); and
- Section 579 (members' voluntary winding up).

What follows is a brief overview of the SAP; further commentary is contained in Ch 5 on its utilisation in the context of financial assistance and the provision of guarantees and security in connection with loans, etc, to directors and connected persons and in Ch 6 on mergers.

[2.064] The SAP is provided for in Chapter 2 of Part 4. Unusually, s 201 has no substantive purpose other than to purport to explain what the Chapter does. Section 201(1) says that the Chapter sets out the way by which a company can,

---

[72] See Ch 1, *Companies Act 2014: Anatomy of the Act* at para **[1.021]**.

by its members passing a special resolution and its directors making a certain declaration, permit the carrying on of a "restricted activity" that is otherwise prohibited or fulfil the requirement specified in a provision concerned for the restricted activity. While the foregoing is said to describe all restricted activities except merger, s 202(2) says that for merger, the Chapter sets out the way in which each of the merging companies can by unanimous resolution of the members and a certain declaration of their directors authorise the putting into effect of a merger.

(a) The special resolution

[2.065] Section 202(1)(a) requires that the restricted activity, the subject of the SAP, be authorised by the members passing a special resolution or, where merger is the restricted activity, a unanimous resolution of the members of both merging companies. The authorising resolution must be passed not more than 12 months prior to the commencement of the activity.

(b) The declaration

[2.066] In the first place it may be noted that the declaration is no longer required to be a *statutory* declaration and so a statutory declaration made under the Statutory Declarations Act 1938 will not be required and the declaration need not be sworn before a practising solicitor or commissioner for oaths. The declaration required by s 202(1)(b) must be made in writing by the directors at a meeting of the directors held not earlier than 30 days before the date of the meeting to pass the approving resolution or the date of the signing by the last member of the written resolution; by the sole director in a single-director LTD, both of the directors in a two-director company and a majority of the directors where there are more than two directors of the company: s 202(6).

[2.067] The content of the declaration will vary depending upon the nature of the restricted activity. So, declarations for the following restricted activities must comply with the requirements set out in the following provisions:

Restricted activity	Provision to be complied with
Financial assistance *and* transactions with directors	Section 203(1)
Reduction of company capital *and* variation of capital on reorganisation	Section 204(1)
Treatment of pre-acquisition profits	Section 205(1)
Merger	Section 206(1)
Voluntary winding up	Section 207(1)

In all cases, a copy of the declaration must be delivered to the Registrar of Companies not later than 21 days after the date on which the carrying on of the restricted activity concerned is commenced provided that the High Court has the power to declare the carrying on of the restricted activity valid, despite the failure to file within 21 days, when satisfied such would be just and equitable. Section 201(3) provides:

> "The provisions of this Chapter shall be read and shall operate so that a restricted activity may be carried on at a time falling before compliance with the requirement (arising under section 203, 204, 205, 206 or 207 as the case may be) that a copy of the appropriate declaration be delivered to the Registrar; however – should a failure to comply with that requirement occur – that failure then invalidates the carrying on of the activity, but this is without prejudice to the power of validation conferred subsequently by this Chapter on the court."

(c) Independent person's report

[2.068] In the case of four of the restricted activities (reduction of company capital, variation of capital on reorganisation, treatment of pre-acquisition profits and voluntary winding up) a declaration by the directors must be accompanied by a report drawn up in the prescribed form by a person who is qualified to be the statutory auditor of the company which states that in his or her opinion, the declaration is *"not unreasonable"*: s 208. A declaration which is unaccompanied by such a report "shall have no effect".

(d) Extra confirmation in the case of merger

[2.069] A declaration made in connection with a merger shall have no effect unless it is accompanied by a document prepared by the declarant-directors which either confirms that the common draft terms of merger provide for such particular acts of each relevant matter as will enable each of the prescribed effects provisions to operate without difficulty or specifying such particulars of each relevant matter as will enable each of those effects provisions to operate without difficulty in relation to the merger. "Prescribed effects provisions" means the provisions in paras (a) to (i) of s 480(3).

(e) Personal liability

[2.070] Where the a director of a company makes a declaration without having reasonable grounds for the opinion as to solvency, the High Court may declare that the director shall be personally responsible without any limitation of liability for all or any of the debts or other liabilities of the company (or in the case of merger, the successor company): s 210(1). Those with *locus standi* to bring an application to have a director made personally liable are: a liquidator, creditor, member or contributory of the company or, in the case of merger, the successor company, and the Director of Corporate Enforcement. Where the company is wound up insolvent within 12 months, there is a rebuttable presumption that the each director who made the declaration did not have reasonable grounds for their opinion as to solvency: s 210(2).

(f) *Moratorium on executing restricted activity*

[2.071] Where the approving resolution was not unanimous, unless one or more members who hold more than 90 per cent of shares carrying voting rights have voted in favour of the approving resolution the company shall not carry on the restricted activity until the expiry of 30 days after the date the special resolution is passed or, where application is made to court to cancel the special resolution, until after the matter is disposed of by the court: s 211.

Chapter 3

Changes to Re-registration, Registers and Filings

by
Dáibhí O'Leary

Introduction

[3.001] The purpose of this chapter is to review the changes made by the Companies Act 2014 to company law in relation to the re-registration and conversion of companies from one company type to another, the registers required to be maintained by companies, and the corporate filings which companies are obliged to make. This review focuses in particular on provisions set out in Parts 2, 5, 6, 7 and 20 of the Act and the changes introduced in relation to the following matters:

1. Conversion and re-registration;
2. Registers and accounting records;
3. Filings;
4. Annual return and documentation required to be annexed thereto.

Conversion and re-registration

(a) Conversion of existing private companies on commencement of the Act

[3.002] The first consideration that every existing private company limited by shares will face on the commencement of the Act arises under Part 2 of the Act. That is, each such company will have to decide whether it wishes to be a private limited company (referred to here as an LTD) under the new regime set out in Parts 1 to 15 of the Act, or prefers to become a designated activity company (DAC) or, indeed, some other type of company. If such a company is to become some type of company other than an LTD, and avoid becoming subject to the statutory defaults that apply at the end of the transition period, it will be necessary to make a positive election to that effect.[1]

---

[1] The transition period means the period expiring 18 months after the commencement of this section: s 15 of the Act.

The options available for existing private limited companies and the steps in conversion are contained in Chapter 6 of Part 2 of the Act; in summary, an existing private company has the following options under Part 2 of the Act:

(i) it can, within the 18 months following commencement, "opt in" to the new regime and decide to become an LTD;

(ii) it can, during the 15 months following commencement, "opt out" and decide to become a DAC, or some other type of company;

(iii) if it fails either to opt in or opt out it will, at the end of the 18-month period, be deemed to have become an LTD.

During the aforementioned 18-month period, or until it opts to become some type of company other than a DAC, an existing private company will be subject to the law applicable to DACs,[2] with the exception that its name will not be required to end in "designated activity company", "cuideachta ghníomhaíochta ainmnithe" or the appropriate abbreviation, but rather the provisions of the prior Companies Acts shall continue to apply during this period.[3]

(i) Deciding whether to become an LTD or another type of company

[3.003] Section 15 of the Act provides for an 18-month transition period, beginning on the commencement of the Act.[4] There are a number of reasons for believing that most existing private companies will elect to take control of their own fate and will take action before the end of the transition period. The reasons for taking positive action include:

• For companies which want to opt in, it would seem preferable to have the certainty of an early application of the new regime set out in Parts 1 to 15;

• Statutory defaults are generally better avoided, especially when a new bespoke constitution can be adopted so easily;

• Directors can avoid the obligations which would otherwise arise where the members do nothing (as discussed at para **[3.010]** below), by proactively putting a new constitution to the members to adopt;

• Until such time as an existing private company "opts in", the applicable law will be the more complicated law applicable to DACs (ie as contained in Part 16, and Parts 1 to 14 as disapplied, modified or supplemented by Part 16);

• For companies, such as joint ventures, which may want to opt out and retain their objects clauses and avoid re-negotiating their already

---

2 Section 58(1) of the Act.

3 Section 58(3) of the Act; that is, until such a company opts to become some type of company other than an LTD (including a DAC), its name will remain unchanged.

4 The Act is expected to be commenced with effect from 1 June 2015, which would mean that the transition period would run from 1 June 2015 to 30 November 2016.

bespoke articles of association, it is important to take action and opt out to prevent the application of the default form of constitution.

[3.004] A significant proportion of the reforms set out in the Act apply only to the LTD, and therefore it is thought that, save where there is a specific reason for an existing private limited company to become some type of company other than an LTD, that owners and controllers of most such companies will prefer for their company to become an LTD. Some situations in which an existing private limited company might choose not to become an LTD are as follows:

(a)   Where the company is a credit institution or insurance undertaking: an LTD shall not be permitted to carry on the activity of a credit institution or insurance undertaking;[5] accordingly an existing private company that carries on such activity will need to become some other type of company;

(b)   Where the company has, or wishes to have, debentures (or interests in them) admitted to trading or to be listed on a regulated market: an LTD shall not be permitted to carry on such activity;[6] accordingly an existing private company that carries on, or wishes to carry on, such activity will need to become some other type of company;

(c)   Where it is important to the shareholders that the company would retain its objects clause: an LTD will have full and unlimited capacity to carry on and undertake any business or activity, do any act or enter into any transaction; in certain cases, it may be preferable that the company would in fact be restricted in respect of the activities it may undertake (for example in the case of certain joint ventures), and in such cases, it will be necessary that the company would adopt some form other than an LTD.

(ii) The applicable law during the transition period

[3.005] During the transition period (or until an existing private company re-registers as another type of company), the law applicable to an existing private company limited by shares will be that contained in Part 16, and Parts 1 to 14 as disapplied, modified or supplemented by Part 16, ie the law which applies to a DAC.[7] This law adheres relatively closely to the current law applicable to existing private limited companies, with the result that, during this transition period, existing private limited companies will have an opportunity to accustom themselves to the changes proposed by the new regime.

[3.006] This will mean, however, that the advantages that will accrue to the LTD under Parts 1 to 15 will be denied to companies until the end of the transition

---

5   Section 18(2) of the Act.
6   Section 68(2) of the Act.
7   Section 58 of the Act.

period, or unless and until they elect to opt in to the new regime. Existing companies which have adopted regulations contained in Table A of the First Schedule to the Companies Act 1963 will continue during this transition period to be governed by those regulations notwithstanding the repeal of the Companies Act 1963.

(iii) Converting to the new LTD

[3.007] The Act provides for three ways in which an existing private company limited by shares can become an LTD:

(a)   the members may, by special resolution passed in accordance with its existing memorandum and articles of association, adopt a new constitution in the prescribed form (see para **[3.008]** below) and deliver that constitution to the Registrar of Companies (the Registrar) for registration;[8]

(b)   if the members should fail to adopt a constitution, and it is not the case that either the company is proceeding, or is required,[9] to re-register as another type of company, the directors of the company are obliged to draft a one-document constitution in the prescribed form based on the existing memorandum and articles of association, and to deliver a copy of that constitution to each member and to the Registrar for registration;[10] or

(c)   where neither the members nor the directors (in default of their obligations) take any action before the end of the transition period, then on the expiry of that period, the company will (as set out at para **[3.012]** below) *be deemed* to have a one-document constitution comprising its existing memorandum and articles (except its objects clause and any clauses which prevent their alteration).[11]

For most companies, the optimal course of action will be for the directors to initiate a discussion with members on the options open to the company. Otherwise, where the members do nothing, obligations will be imposed on the directors to amend the company's constitutional documents, and they risk having members complain that by doing so, the directors had adversely affected their rights.

---

[8]   Section 59(1) of the Act.
[9]   Whether pursuant to a court order under s 57 of the Act requiring that it re-register as a DAC, or to notice in writing pursuant to s 56 requiring that it so re-register, or because the company has debt securities admitted to trading or listed on a regulated market.
[10]   Section 60 of the Act.
[11]   Section 61 of the Act.

(iv) Adopting a new constitution by special resolution

[3.008] As set out above, the most direct way for an existing private company to convert to an LTD is that the members pass a special resolution to adopt a new constitution in substitution for the existing memorandum and articles of association.

The new constitution is required to comply with s 19 of the Act, ie as discussed at para **[2.003]** above, it must state:

(a)   the company's name;

(b)   that it is a private company limited by shares and registered under Part 2;

(c)   that the liability of the members is limited;

(d)   in respect of its share capital, either:

   (i)   the authorised share capital with which it proposes to be registered, or

   (ii)   that the share capital shall, at the time of its registration, stand divided into shares of a specified fixed amount;

(e)   the number of shares taken by its original subscriber(s); and

(f)   any supplemental regulations which it is adopting.

[3.009] Although most of what was contained in the company's articles of association will now apply by statute unless the constitution otherwise provides, companies would be well advised to review their articles of association and ensure that tailored provisions, such as those dealing with pre-emption on transfer, are included in the new constitution. Upon delivery of the new constitution so passed by special resolution to the Registrar in the Companies Registration Office (the CRO), the company will become the new model private company, a new certificate of incorporation will issue and Parts 1 to 15 of the Act will apply to it.

(v) Obligations on the directors

[3.010] Unless the shareholders have adopted a new constitution, or the company is going to re-register as a DAC or other type of company, the directors of an existing private company are required, before the expiry of the transition period, to prepare a constitution for the company, deliver a copy to each member and deliver a copy of it to the CRO.[12]

The Act prescribes the information to be included in the constitution prepared by the directors, in that the provisions of that constitution must consist solely of the company's existing memorandum of association, excluding its objects clause and any clause that prohibits the alteration of the memorandum and articles of association, and the company's articles of association. If carried

---

[12]   Section 60 of the Act.

out correctly, this will therefore ensure the preserving of shareholders' existing rights.

(vi) Deemed constitution

[3.011] The Act also sets out a default provision to apply in cases where neither the members of a private company limited by shares, nor the directors (in breach of their obligations) take any action – whether to adopt a new constitution or, indeed, to opt out by re-registering as a DAC or some other type of company – and where the company has not has re-registered as some other type of company.

[3.012] In such an event, upon the expiry of the transition period, the existing company shall be deemed to have, instead of its existing memorandum and articles of association, a one-document constitution comprised of its existing memorandum of association (excluding its objects clause and any clause that prohibits the alteration of any provision of its memorandum and articles of association) and its existing articles of association.[13] It will also be deemed to have become a new LTD to which Parts 1 to 15 apply, and the Registrar will be required to issue it with a new certificate of incorporation, attesting to its status as such.

[3.013] While it might seem attractive to avoid taking any active steps and just wait for the statutory default to apply, there are a number of disadvantages to taking such an approach. Firstly, the result will be that the company's publicly-available constitutional documents will on their face include provisions – such as the objects clause – which will be deemed no longer to apply to it. In addition, to the extent that the company has previously adopted any provisions of Table A of the First Schedule to the Companies Act 1963, such provisions will only apply to the extent that they are not inconsistent with any mandatory provision of the new Act, and the deemed constitution is likely to refer to provisions of the previous Companies Acts which will have been repealed by the Act. Finally, as so many of the regulations currently found in Table A of the First Schedule to the Companies Act 1963 (and either adopted by reference or restated in the current articles of association of many private companies) are included in the Act and will apply unless a company's constitution provides otherwise, there are likely to be many provisions in the resulting deemed constitution which duplicate, or overlap with, statutory defaults. In all of the above respects, this will result in a lack of clarity for users of those constitutional documents.

(vii) Electing to re-register as a DAC

[3.014] Alternatively, an existing private company limited by shares may opt out of the new regime and choose to become a DAC. As set out at para **[3.004]**

---

13   Section 55 of the Act.

above, although such an "opt out" will result in the company not benefiting from a number of the reforms proposed under the Act, there are certain limited situations which may either preclude an existing private company from becoming an LTD, or may cause the members of an existing private company to prefer that it would become a company other than an LTD, and in such a situation it may be appropriate that it would re-register as a DAC.

[3.015] Whether an existing company wishes to become a DAC or, indeed, any type of company other than an LTD, that choice is facilitated by Part 2 of the Act. Conversion will be effected by the members passing a special resolution and converting to that other type of company, provided the requirements applicable to such companies (as set out in Part 20 of the Act) are satisfied.[14] Up to three months prior to the expiry of the transition period, there are two re-registration options:

- First, an existing private company may re-register as a DAC by passing an ordinary resolution that the company be so re-registered.[15] Where the directors and members are agreed that conversion to a DAC is the appropriate course, this method of converting to a DAC will be the most convenient.

- Alternatively, where the directors are unwilling to convene an extraordinary general meeting to put an ordinary resolution to this effect to the members, a member or members holding more than 25 per cent of the voting rights in the company can serve a notice in writing on the company requiring it to re-register as a DAC.[16]

[3.016] Additionally, where an existing private company limited by shares does not re-register as a DAC before the end of the transition period (whether it is obliged to do so or not), one or more of its members holding not less than 15 per cent in nominal value of its issued share capital (or of any class thereof), or one or more creditors holding not less than 15 per cent of its debentures entitling them to object to alterations in its objects clause, may apply to court for an order directing the company to re-register as a DAC, and the court shall, unless cause is shown to the contrary, make the order sought or make such other order as seems just.

(viii) The mechanics of re-registration as a DAC

[3.017] Where an ordinary resolution is passed by the members to re-register as a DAC or where the directors resolve to re-register as a DAC (whether because a notice is served by qualifying members, because the company must re-register as a DAC or because such is ordered by the court) the effect is to alter the

---

[14]   Section 56(4) of the Act.
[15]   Section 56 of the Act.
[16]   Section 56(2) of the Act.

company's memorandum of association so that it states that the company is to be a DAC.[17] The most obvious change that will be required is that the name of the company must end with one of the following: "designated activity company", "cuideachta ghníomhaíochta ainmnithe", or some acceptable abbreviation ("d.a.c.", "dac", "c.g.a.", "cga" or any such abbreviation in capitalised form),[18] save where the company is exempted under the Act from the requirement to use such words (or the abbreviation) as part of its name.[19] The company must file the resolution, the new memorandum and articles of association, a declaration of compliance and the prescribed form with the CRO.

(ix) Protecting members and creditors

[3.018] Without limiting the provisions concerning minority shareholder oppression,[20] if any member considers that his rights or obligations have been prejudiced by the exercise or non-exercise of any power under the Chapter dealing with conversion, or its exercise in a particular manner, by the company or its directors, the member may apply to court for an order under s 212,[21] and the court may grant such relief to the applicant(s) as the court thinks just.

(b) Changes in re-registration procedure

[3.019] Until now, the requirements for a company to convert from one company type to another have been scattered across a number of different sections of the former Companies Acts, depending on the type of company from which the company wished to convert, and the type of company to which it wished to convert. In summary, the company was required to file in the CRO:

(a) A form G1 setting out the text of a special resolution passed by the members that it should re-register as the desired type of company and making the necessary changes to its memorandum and articles of association;

(b) A copy of the amended memorandum and articles of association;

(c) The appropriate form stating the company's intention.

[3.020] Under the Act, the basic requirements for re-registration are set out in one section of the Act, being s 1285, which provides that every company which wishes to re-register as a different company type must file in the CRO:

(a) A copy of a special resolution altering the company's constitution (ie the one-document constitution in the case of an LTD, or the memorandum

---

[17] Section 63(2) of the Act.
[18] Section 969 of the Act.
[19] Section 971 of the Act.
[20] Now set out in s 212 of the Act.
[21] Section 62 of the Act.

and articles of association in the case of any other company type) so that it:

    (i)   states that the company is to be of the type as which it wishes to be re-registered;

    (ii)   conforms with the requirements of the Act for the resultant company type; and

    (iii)   meets any other requirements in the circumstances;

(b)   A copy of the constitution, etc, as altered;

(c)   An application in the prescribed form signed by a director or the secretary;

(d)   A compliance statement, signed by a director or the secretary, that the re-registration conditions have been met (the contents will vary depending on the company type involved).

There is no provision for the amendments at (a) above to result in any alteration to the rights and obligations as set out in the company's constitution, etc, and where necessary any replacement constitution or memorandum and articles must include such supplemental regulations as will secure those rights and obligations.

[3.021] Once satisfied that the documentation is in order, the Registrar shall issue a certificate of incorporation that reflects the new company type, states that it has been issued on re-registration and set out the date of its issue. The law applicable to the new company type shall apply to it from the date of the certificate.

(c) With share capital to without (and vice versa)

[3.022] There has until now been no statutory mechanism for a company limited by shares to re-register as a company limited by guarantee, or vice versa. The Act allows such re-registration. Section 1286 provides for the re-registration of a company without a share capital as one having a share capital (requiring that the re-registration application shall include a statement of the shareholdings and of the share capital with which the company is to be re-registered), and s 1299 provides for the re-registration of a company with a share capital as a DAC limited by guarantee (the requirement being that a prescribed assent form signed by all the members of the company be delivered to the Registrar, together with a statement signed by a director or secretary confirming that those who signed the form constitute the whole membership).

(d) Limited company to unlimited and back to limited

[3.023] The Companies (Amendment) Act 1983 had precluded a company from repeatedly changing from being a private limited company to an unlimited company. That is, where a private limited company had re-registered as unlimited under s 52 of the Companies (Amendment) Act 1983, it was barred from re-registering as limited under s 53 of that Act; and where an unlimited company had re-registered as a private limited company under s 53 of that Act, it was barred from re-registering as unlimited under s 52. The concern was that a limited company might re-register as unlimited shortly before it was due to file its annual return – thereby avoiding the obligation to file financial statements – and then change back once that return had been filed, to continue to avail of limited status. The Act removes this prohibition by addressing the underlying issue.

[3.024] The Act achieves this by requiring that, unless the limited company has filed an annual return, with financial statements, within the period of three months preceding the date of the re-registration application, it must file, with the re-registration application, financial statements covering a period of at least 12 months, ending not earlier than three months before the date of that application.[22] Save where the limited company can avail of the audit exemption, those financial statements must be audited.

Registers and accounting records

[3.025] Key changes proposed by the Act in respect of the obligations on companies to maintain registers and accounting records include the following:

(a) Structural change in relation to provisions concerning the inspection of registers, etc;

(b) Increased clarity regarding requirement to keep accounting records;

(c) Possible exemption from stating director's home address in register;

(d) *De minimis* threshold for disclosure of interests in shares and debentures;

(e) Written records to be kept of loans to and from directors;

(f) Disclosure of interest in shares in a PLC.

(a) Structural change in relation to inspection of registers, etc

[3.026] An important structural innovation arises in the architecture of the Act in that, for the first time, provisions relating to the inspection of registers, the place where such registers must be kept and the provision of copies of information in them are set out in one place. Previously such provisions were scattered across a number of sections of the Companies Acts. Chapter 10 of Part 4 of the Act therefore covers registers relating to all of the following:[23]

(a) the copies of directors' service contracts and memoranda;

(b) the copies of instruments creating charges;

---

22 Section 1296 of the Act.
23 Section 216 of the Act.

(c)   the directors' and secretaries' register;

(d)   the disclosable interests' register;

(e)   the members' register; and

(f)   the minutes of meetings.

[3.027] The Act requires[24] that each of the above registers or documents be kept at *either*:

(a)   the company's registered office;

(b)   its principal place of business within Ireland; or

(c)   another place within Ireland.

The Act makes clear that any such register or document may be kept by another person on behalf of the company, but must be kept by them at a place within Ireland.[25] If a register is kept at a place other than the company's registered office, the company must notify the Registrar of that place, and of any change in that place.[26] If the company keeps several of these registers or documents at a place other than that referred to at (a) or (b), those registers or documents must be kept by it at a single place.[27]

[3.028] In relation to inspection rights, the Act provides[28] that each of the registers or documents above (save for the members' register, when it is closed under s 174) shall be open to the inspection of any member without charge, and a member of the company shall be entitled (on payment of the relevant fee) to a copy of all or part of:

(a)   the directors' and secretaries' register;

(b)   the disclosable interests register;

(c)   the members' register; and

(d)   the minutes of meetings.

The term "minutes of meetings" is defined by s 215(a) to mean the books kept by the company under s 199, including records referred to in s 196(6) and any written resolutions kept under s 193(7) and s 195(4). These obligations refer, exclusively, to meetings of members, not directors. Minutes of directors' meetings are only disclosable to the Director of Corporate Enforcement.[29]

[3.029] The Act further provides[30] that any other person shall be entitled, on payment of the relevant fee, to inspect any of the following registers or

---

24   Section 216(3) of the Act.

25   Section 216(2) and (4) of the Act.

26   Section 216(6) of the Act.

27   Section 216(5) of the Act.

28   Section 216(7), (8), (11) and (13) of the Act.

29   Section 166(5) of the Act.

30   Section 216(7), (9), (12) and (13) of the Act.

documents (save for the members' register, when it is closed under s 174), or to obtain a copy of all or part thereof:

(a)   the directors' and secretaries' register;

(b)   the disclosable interests register; or

(c)   the members' register.

In addition, the copies of instruments creating charges shall be open to the inspection of any creditor of the company without charge.[31]

(b) Increased clarity regarding requirement to keep accounting records

[3.030] The Act adopts new terminology in respect of the requirement on a company to keep accounting information and to prepare statutory financial accounts. Firstly, the Act requires that a company keep (or cause to be kept) *"adequate accounting records"*.[32] This effectively replaces the requirement under the previous Companies Acts that the company cause to be kept "proper books of account".[33] Secondly, the Act uses the term *"financial statements"*[34] rather than (as previously[35]) "accounts" to refer to the statutory financial statements which a company is required to prepare. It is hoped that this will avoid any confusion that may have previously arisen where the term "accounts" was employed to refer to both the statutory financial statements and the company's underlying accounting records.

(c) Possible exemption from stating director's home address in register

[3.031] A company's register of directors and secretaries is open to inspection by any person (on payment of a minimal fee)[36] and so the obligation on a director to disclose his usual residential address in the company's register of directors and secretaries has caused some concern among the directors of certain companies, as noted at para **[2.051]** above. While this obligation is restated in the Act, there is a new provision whereby the Minister for Jobs, Enterprise and Innovation may make regulations to provide that the requirement to record the usual residential address of an officer in the register maintained by the company will not apply where it is determined that circumstances concerning the personal safety or security of the person warrant the application

---

31   Section 216(10) of the Act.
32   Section 281 of the Act.
33   Section 202(1) of the Companies Act 1990.
34   Section 274 of the Act.
35   Section 2(1) of the Companies Act 1963.
36   Section 216 of the Act restates s 195 of the Companies Act 1963 in this regard.

of the exemption, or where such other conditions as are specified in the regulations are specified.[37] Any such regulations may also provide that the obligation to notify the Registrar of any changes in residential address will not apply, as addressed at para **[3.040]** below.

(d) De minimis threshold for disclosure of interests in shares and debentures

[3.032] A very welcome reform relates to the disclosure of interests in shares and share options so that *de minimis* interests are not required to be notified. That is, where the interest of a director or secretary, aggregated with their spouse (or civil partner) and children, is in shares representing 1 per cent or less, in nominal value, of the shares carrying rights to vote in all circumstances at general meetings of the body corporate, this will not constitute a disclosable interest, such that it would require to be notified to the directors and recorded in a register of interests.[38] This will clearly be particularly relevant in the context of large companies.

(e) Written records to be kept of loans to and from directors

[3.033] As discussed in detail at para **[4.046]**, the Act sets out new evidential provisions which will apply where it is claimed in civil proceedings:

(a) that a company has made a loan or quasi-loan[39] to a director of a company or of its holding company, or a person connected with such a director[40] (a "relevant person");[41] or

(b) that a transaction or arrangement entered into, or alleged to have been entered into, by a director (or a connected person) with the company or its holding company constitutes a loan or quasi-loan by that person to that company.[42]

[3.034] In the first case, there will be a rebuttable presumption that the loan or quasi-loan is repayable on demand and bears interest at a specified rate, while in the latter case the presumption will be, unless the contrary is clearly stated:

(a) that the transaction or arrangement is neither a loan nor a quasi-loan, but rather is in the nature of a gift to the relevant company;

(b) that (if it is a loan or a quasi-loan) it does not bear interest;

---

37 Section 150(11) of the Act.
38 Section 260(f) of the Act.
39 Section 219(2) of the Act.
40 Section 220 of the Act.
41 Section 236 of the Act.
42 Section 237 of the Act.

(c)   that (if it is a loan or a quasi-loan) it is not secured; and

(d)   that (if it is a loan or a quasi-loan) it is subordinated to all other creditors.

[3.035] Therefore it will be in the interests of directors that any loan or quasi-loan between the director of a company (or a connected person) and the company or its holding company be fully documented and a copy of that documentation retained. While there is no express requirement to maintain a register of such documentation, it would seem to be good practice – and in the interests of directors entering into such transactions – to ensure that such documentation is carefully maintained.

(f)   Disclosure of interest in shares in a PLC

[3.036] Currently, a shareholder of an Irish public limited company (PLC) the shares of which are listed on a regulated market (ie a main securities market in an EEA Member State) is required to disclose interests of 3 per cent.[43] However where the securities of the PLC are not listed on a regulated market, the minimum disclosure threshold is 5 per cent.[44] The Act aligns the disclosure threshold obligations for shareholders in all Irish PLCs and provides for greater consistency by requiring notification in all cases of interests of 3 per cent,[45] whether or not the PLC has securities listed on a regulated market.

Filings

[3.037] The Act proposes a number of important reforms in respect of the filings made by companies; the following changes are addressed below:

(a)   Two-stage procedure for registration of charges;

(b)   Rectification of filing in respect of a defective allotment;

(c)   Possible exemption for making public director's home address.

(a)   Two-stage procedure for registration of charges

[3.038] The Act now introduces a new two-stage procedure for the registration of charges, as an alternative to the existing one-stage procedure; this change, and the reasoning behind it, are discussed in detail at para **[5.070]**, but in summary it should ensure that a creditor proposing to make finance available can have greater certainty that when credit is advanced, security taken will have priority not only over other charges created subsequently but also over any

---

[43]   Regulation 81 of the Transparency (Directive 2004/109/EC) Regulations 2007, and rule 7.1 of the Transparency Rules issued by the Central Bank of Ireland.

[44]   Sections 67 and 70 of the Companies Act 1990.

[45]   Section 1052(1)(a) of the Act; or such other rate as may be specified by order made by the Minister for Jobs, Enterprise and Innovation pursuant to s 1052(2).

charges previously created but unfiled at the date of the advance. The two-stage procedure will require that the following steps be taken:[46]

(a)   a notice (being a notice in the prescribed form and containing the prescribed particulars of the charge) is filed with the Registrar stating the company's intention to create a charge; and

(b)   not later than 21 days after the date of the Registrar's receipt of the notice under (a) (the "first notice"), the Registrar receives a notice, in the prescribed form, stating that the charge referred to in the first notice has been created.

It is envisaged that the first filing would contain all the required details other than the date of the charge, while the second filing would confirm the creation of the specified charge and indicate its date. Therefore it is anticipated that completion of the second filing would not be time consuming or cumbersome. If the requirement under (b) above is not complied with, within 21 days, the notice received under (a) in relation to the charge shall be deemed to have lapsed and to have been removed from the register.

(b) *Rectification of filing in respect of a defective allotment*

[3.039] Where a company allots shares, it must make a return to notify the Registrar of the allotment. Currently, where issued share capital is accidentally overstated in this return, the view of the Registrar – shared by the High Court[47] – is that a refiling setting the correct (lower) amount might amount to a reduction in share capital, which under the former Companies Acts would require a court order. Therefore the Registrar will not permit a correctional refiling, and will instead require a court order directing the Registrar to show the lower amount of issued share capital. This is now addressed under the Act. The existing provision[48] whereby a company may, without application to the court, at any time rectify any error or omission in the register (provided that any person who is adversely affected must have agreed to the rectification) and whereby the company shall give notice of the rectification to the Registrar if the error or omission also occurs in any document forwarded by the company to the Registrar, is restated in the Act;[49] however, the Act also now provides expressly that the rectification that may be so effected includes that of an error or omission that relates to the amount of the company's issued share capital (whether it consists of an overstatement or understatement of it), and that this also extends to the notification of the rectification to the Registrar where

---

[46]   Section 409(4) of the Act.
[47]   *Air France Aircraft Leasing v Registrar of Companies* (30 April 2007, unreported) HC, Laffoy J.
[48]   Section 122(5) of the Companies Act 1963.
[49]   Section 173(5) and (6) of the Act.

applicable.[50] Therefore it will now be possible, where a company has incorrectly overstated its issued share capital in a return of allotments filed with the Registrar, to correct that return without recourse to the courts.

(c) Possible exemption from making public director's home address

[3.040] As set out at para **[3.031]** above, the obligation on a director to disclose his usual residential address in the company's register of directors and secretaries has caused some concern among directors; the obligation to notify the Registrar of changes in that register (the result being that that information is publicly available) has caused even greater concern, again as considered at para **[2.051]** above. While this obligation is again restated in the Act, the new provision whereby the Minister for Jobs, Enterprise and Innovation may make regulations to provide that the requirement to record the usual residential address of an officer in the register maintained by the company will not apply in certain circumstances will also extend to the register maintained by the Registrar. Accordingly, this obligation will not apply where it is determined that circumstances concerning the personal safety or security of the person warrant the application of the exemption, or where such other conditions as are specified in the regulations are met.[51]

Annual return and documentation required to be annexed thereto

[3.041] Although the Act has not made any significant changes in respect of the requirement to make an annual return to the Registrar (save that a new prescribed form will replace the current form B1), there are a number of changes in respect of the documents required to be annexed to the annual return. These are addressed below under the following headings:

(a) Extension of filing exemptions;

(b) Extension of audit exemption;

(c) Revision of defective financial statements;

(d) Disclosure requirements in financial statements;

(e) Summary financial statements for PLCs.

---

[50] Section 173(7) of the Act.
[51] Section 150(11) of the Act.

(a) Extension of filing exemptions

(i) Increase in size thresholds for medium-sized companies

[3.042] The Act updates the thresholds for the definition of medium-sized companies for the purpose of availing of certain exemptions from filing accounting information. The turnover threshold is raised from approximately €15.2m to €20m and the balance sheet from approximately €7.6m to €10m.[52] These figures are being increased to reflect inflation, and should also be easier to remember. It had been proposed that the thresholds for small companies would also be increased; however, this was pre-empted by the European Union (Accounts) Regulations 2012 (SI 304/2012) and so no additional increase is now proposed. Just as is the case at present, these definitions are only relevant for private companies, since PLCs,[53] PUCs (public unlimited companies) and PULCs (public unlimited companies having no share capital)[54] will not be able to avail of an exemption on the basis of size.

(ii) Increase in size thresholds for group

[3.043] In addition, a holding company will be exempt from the requirement to prepare group financial statements for a financial year if the holding company and all of its subsidiary undertakings taken as a whole satisfy (for that financial year and the preceding financial year) two out of three qualifying conditions. These conditions are that:

(a) the balance sheet total of the company and its subsidiary undertakings taken as a whole does not exceed €10m;

(b) the turnover of the company and its subsidiary undertakings taken as a whole does not exceed €20m; and

(c) the average number of persons employed by the holding company and its subsidiary undertakings taken as a whole does not exceed 250.[55]

While both the availability of this exemption and the nature of the conditions reflects the existing law, the Act updates and increases the threshold figures for balance sheet total and turnover, from approximately €7.6m to €10m as regards the balance sheet total and from approximately €15.2m to €20m in respect of turnover (just as was the case for the filing exemptions in respect of individual companies at para **[3.042]** above). It should be noted that this is an exemption from consolidation rather than an exemption from filing per se, although the effect is the same.

---

[52] Section 350(6) of the Act.
[53] Section 1002 of the Act.
[54] Section 1230 of the Act.
[55] Sections 297 and 298 of the Act.

(iii) Group exempted where every subsidiary could be excluded from consolidation

[3.044] The Act states that where every subsidiary of a holding company would be exempt from consolidation in Companies Act group financial statements, the holding company will be exempt from preparing consolidated accounts.[56] A subsidiary may be excluded from consolidation in Companies Act group financial statements if:[57]

(a) its inclusion is not material for the purposes of giving a true and fair view (and subject to the caveat that two or more undertakings may be excluded only if they are not material when taken together);

(b) severe long-term restrictions substantially hinder the exercise of the rights of the holding company over the assets or management of the subsidiary undertaking;

(c) the information necessary for the preparation of group financial statements in accordance with Part 6 cannot be obtained without disproportionate expense or undue delay; or

(d) the interest of the holding company is held exclusively with a view to subsequent resale.

The above provisions whereby a subsidiary might be excluded from consolidation were previously set out in the European Communities (Companies: Group Accounts) Regulations 1992; however, this is the first occasion on which it is expressly set out in statute that the holding company might, as a result, be exempt from preparing consolidated accounts.

(iv) Requirement does not apply where company is being wound up or struck off

[3.045] The Act provides for the first time that the obligation to deliver an annual return to the CRO within 28 days of the annual return date will not apply where that date falls in a period when the company is being wound up;[58] the disapplication of this obligation in that situation can be justified on the basis that during that time the liquidator will be required to file returns relevant to the winding up and the annual return will be superfluous. The obligation is also disapplied where a company is in the course of being voluntarily struck off the register[59] (ie on the Registrar publishing a notice in the *CRO Gazette* of the Registrar's intention to strike the company off the register[60]), although should it not ultimately be dissolved, or subsequently be restored to the register, it will be

---

56   Section 301 of the Act.
57   Section 303(2) and (3) of the Act.
58   Section 343(8) of the Act.
59   Section 343(9) of the Act.
60   Section 343(10) of the Act.

required to file all outstanding returns; the latter provision is intended to prevent companies abusing the voluntary strike-off regime to avoid filing its annual return in respect of a particular year.

(b) Extension of audit exemption

(i) Less stringent requirements

[3.046] A company may avail of an exemption from audit under the Act in respect of its financial statements for a particular financial year if it qualifies as a small company for that financial year;[61] that is, if it meets at least two of the following requirements:[62]

(a)   the amount of the turnover of the company does not exceed €8.8m;

(b)   the balance sheet total of the company does not exceed €4.4m;

(c)   the average number of employees of the company does not exceed 50.

These threshold figures match those set out previously under the Companies Acts for availing of the exemption from audit.[63]

[3.047] However the Act is different in two key respects from the previous regime in respect of the availability of the audit exemption. Firstly, under the Act, it is only necessary that the company meet two of the three requirements set out above; under the previous regime, it was necessary that the company meet all three requirements. Secondly, under the Act, it is only necessary that the company meet those requirements for the financial year for which it is seeking the exemption; under the previous regime, it was necessary that it meet those conditions both in respect of that financial year *and* (unless the financial year was the first financial year of the company) in respect of the previous financial year.

(ii) Group companies

[3.048] In addition, under the previous regime, even if a company met all three requirements for both the financial year in question and the preceding financial year, it was barred from availing of an exemption from having its financial statements audited if, *inter alia*, it was either a parent undertaking or subsidiary undertaking.[64] The Act extends the availability of the audit exemption by allowing that it will be available to a holding company and its subsidiaries,

---

[61]   Section 358 of the Act.

[62]   Section 350 of the Act.

[63]   The thresholds in the Companies (Amendment) (No 2) Act 1999 had been increased by the Companies (Amendment) (No 2) Act 1999 (Section 32) Order 2012 (SI 308/2012) to match the updated thresholds proposed in the Act.

[64]   Section 32 of the Companies (Amendment) (No 2) Act 1999; the terms "parent undertaking" and "subsidiary undertaking" have the meaning given to them in the European Communities (Companies: Group Accounts) Regulations 1992.

where the holding and subsidiary companies taken as a whole do not exceed two of the three thresholds for the financial year in question and (unless the year in question is the company's first financial year) its preceding financial year.[65]

(iii) Company limited by guarantee

[3.049] Under the previous regime, the audit exemption was only available to a private company,[66] and therefore was not available to a company limited by guarantee and not having a share capital.[67] The Act extends the availability of the audit exemption to a company limited by guarantee (CLG), although it seeks to achieve a balance by providing that if any one member[68] of the CLG serves notice in writing on the company to the effect that that member does not wish the audit exemption to be available to the company in that financial year, the CLG will not be entitled to avail of the audit exemption in that financial year.[69]

(iv) Dormant companies

[3.050] In addition, the Act introduces a new "special" audit exemption, whereby a "dormant" company (a company which has no significant accounting transactions during the year, and has only intra-group assets and liabilities) may avail of a "special" audit exemption.[70] This is an entirely separate exemption to the standard audit exemption referred to in paras **[3.046]** to **[3.049]** above.[71] Accordingly, even if an LTD, a DAC, a UC or a CLG[72] is part of a group of companies which does not qualify for the standard audit exemption, it will be able to avail of the dormant company exemption if it meets the relevant tests. The provision whereby a minority of members can prevent a company from availing of the standard audit exemption will not apply to the dormant company exemption.

---

[65] Section 39 of the Act.
[66] Section 32(1) Companies (Amendment) (No 2) Act 1999.
[67] As s 33 of the Companies Act 1963 provides that a private company "means a company which has a share capital", a company not having a share capital must by definition be a public company.
[68] For a company limited by shares, the requirement is that a member or members of the company holding shares that confer at least 10 per cent of the voting rights in the company would serve such notice.
[69] Sections 334 (as amended by s 1218) and 361 of the Act.
[70] Section 365 of the Act.
[71] As set out in Chapter 15 of Part 6 of the Act.
[72] As is currently the case, the exemption does not extend to PLCs, public unlimited companies (PUCs and PULCs), or companies with securities listed on a regulated market in an EEA State.

(c) Revision of defective financial statements

(i) Preparation of revised financial statements

[3.051] A major innovation is that the Act permits, for the first time in Irish company law, the revision of defective statutory financial statements. At present, where financial statements have been finalised and filed with the CRO, and those financial statements are then found to be defective, there is no provision for their correction. The Act proposes to address this gap by setting out a clear procedure which if followed will allow the preparation, approval, audit and filing of revised financial statements or a revised directors' report in respect of a prior year.

[3.052] The procedure is that, if it appears to the directors that any financial statements of the company (the "original financial statements") or directors' report (the "original directors' report") for a financial year did not comply with the requirements of the Act or, where applicable, the IAS Regulation, the directors may prepare revised financial statements or a revised directors' report in respect of that year.[73] This is the case even where copies of the original financial statements or report have been laid before the company in general meeting and delivered to the CRO. In such cases, the revisions shall be confined to necessary corrections and any necessary consequential alterations.[74]

[3.053] Where the reason for the revision is that information that should have been included by way of note to the financial statements was not so included, or was incorrect or incomplete, and the profit and loss account, balance sheet or other required statements are not affected, the revision may be effected by supplementary note. In all other cases revised financial statements shall be prepared. Similarly, where information that should have been included in a directors' report was omitted, incorrect or incomplete, and the revision of the directors' report does not affect other information in the report, the revision may be effected by supplementary note; otherwise a revised report shall be prepared.[75]

[3.054] Where financial statements are revised, the fact of the revision and particulars of it, its effect and the reasons for it shall be set out in a note to the next financial statements prepared.[76]

[3.055] The revised financial statements must be prepared under the provisions of the Act as were in force at the date of approval of the original statements. In particular, the revised statements must give a true and fair view as viewed at the date of the original statements.[77]

---

[73] Section 366(1) of the Act.
[74] Section 366(2) of the Act.
[75] Section 366(3) and (4) of the Act.
[76] Section 366(5) of the Act.

(ii) Approval and signing by the directors

[3.056] The revised financial statements (or where the revision is by supplementary note, that note) must be approved and signed,[78] save that, where the original financial statements have already been sent to, or laid before, the members, or delivered to the Registrar, the directors shall, prior to approval, cause the date on which the approval is given to be stated, and cause the following statements to be made prominently in the revised financial statements (or in the note if applicable):[79]

    (a)   where the revision is effected by replacement, a statement clearly identifying the replacement financial statements as being revised financial statements, and statements:

        (i)   that the revised financial statements replace the original statements for a specified financial year and are now the statutory financial statements for that financial year;

        (ii)   that they have been prepared at the date of the original statements and not at the date of revision and so do not deal with events and transactions between those dates;

        (iii)   as to the respects in which the original financial statements did not comply with the requirements of the Act or, where applicable, of Article 4 of the IAS Regulation; and

        (iv)   as to any significant amendments made consequential to remedying those defects;

    (b)   where the revision is effected by supplementary note, statements:

        (i)   that the note revises in certain respects the company's original financial statements and is to be treated as forming part of those original financial statements; and

        (ii)   that the financial statements have been revised as at the date of the original financial statements and not as at the date of the revision and so do not deal with events and transactions between those dates.

Similar provisions apply in relation to the approval and signing of a revised directors' report[80] (or of a supplementary note to such a report).[81]

---

[77]   Section 367 of the Act.

[78]   Following the rules in s 324, as it applied when the original financial statements were approved.

[79]   Section 368 of the Act.

[80]   Save that the relevant rules in relation to approval and signing of that report are as set out in s 332.

[81]   Section 369 of the Act.

(iii) Requirement for auditors' report

[3.057] The company's current statutory auditors must make a report (or a further report) in the form required on any revised financial statements to the company's members. Where the auditors' report on the original financial statements was not made by the company's current statutory auditors, the directors may resolve that the report on the revised financial statements be made by the former statutory auditor(s) who made the first report, provided that they agree to do so and would be qualified for appointment as statutory auditors of the company.[82] The statutory auditors' report shall state whether, in their opinion:

(a)   the revised financial statements have been properly prepared in accordance with the relevant financial reporting framework and the provisions of the Act (or, where applicable, of the IAS Regulation) and, where the IAS Regulation applies, whether the revised financial statements give a true and fair view as at the date of approval of the original financial statements;

(b)   the original financial statements failed to comply with the relevant requirements in the respects identified by the directors.

[3.058] The auditors shall also consider whether the information contained in the directors' report (or revised directors' report) is consistent with those financial statements, and shall state that fact in their report. The statutory requirements regarding the signature of a statutory auditor's report[83] shall apply (with necessary modifications) to the above report, and it shall be the auditors' report on the company's financial statements in place of the report on the original statements. Where the directors' report has been revised, and not the financial statements, corresponding provisions to the above apply to the auditors' report (or further report) on the directors' report.[84]

[3.059] Where a company is entitled to, and avails itself of, the audit exemption, the above audit report shall not be required.[85] An audit report shall also not be required where an entitlement to avail of the exemption arises or is apparent following the revision, even if the time taken in revising the financial statements meant that the directors were not able to make the decision to avail of the exemption at the time of the original financial statements.[86] However where, following revision, a company is no longer entitled to the audit exemption, an auditors' report on the revised statements must be prepared, and delivered to the Registrar within two months after the date of revision.[87]

---

[82]   Section 370 of the Act.
[83]   Section 337 of the Act.
[84]   Section 372 of the Act.
[85]   Section 371(1) of the Act.
[86]   Section 378 of the Act.

[3.060] Upon the directors approving revised financial statements or a revised directors' report, the provisions of the Act shall have effect as if the revised statements or report were, from the date of their approval, the company's financial statements or directors' report, in place of the original. In particular, the revised statements or report shall be the relevant financial statements or report as regards the right to demand copies of financial statements and reports, the publication of financial statements, and if such steps have not yet been carried out, in relation to the circulation, laying before the members and annexing to the annual return of financial statements.[88]

[3.061] Where the directors have prepared revised financial statements or a revised directors' report and copies of the original statements or report have previously been sent to any person, the directors shall, not more than 28 days after the date of revision, send to any such person, and to any other person who (although not entitled to receive a copy of the financial statements) is a member or debenture-holder of the company, or a person entitled to receive notice of general meetings, a copy of (as applicable) the revised financial statements or report, or supplementary note, together with a copy of the auditors' report on the revised statements or report.[89]

[3.062] Where the directors have prepared revised financial statements or a revised directors' report and copies of the original statements or report have been laid before a general meeting of the company, a copy of the revised statements or revised report, and a copy of the auditors' report on those financial statements or report, shall be laid before the company's next general meeting after the date of revision at which any statutory financial statements are laid.[90]

[3.063] Where revised financial statements or a revised directors' report are prepared, and a copy of the original statements or report has been delivered to the Registrar (with the company's annual return), the directors shall, within 28 days after the date of revision, deliver to the Registrar a copy of (as applicable) the revised financial statements, revised directors' report or supplementary note, with a copy of the auditors' report on the revised financial statements or report. The original financial statements shall also remain on the public record.[91]

(iv) Small and medium companies

[3.064] Where a company has, prior to the date of revision, delivered to the Registrar abridged financial statements, pursuant to the exemption for a small or medium company, and the company would not qualify as such a company in light of the revised financial statements, or those statements affect the content of the abridged financial statements, the directors must cause the company to

---

[87] Section 371(2) of the Act.
[88] Section 373 of the Act.
[89] Section 374 of the Act.
[90] Section 375 of the Act.
[91] Section 376 of the Act.

deliver to the Registrar, within 28 days after the date of revision, a copy of the revised financial statements (or if it is permitted to do so on the basis of the revised statements, abridged revised financial statements), together with a copy of the directors' and auditors' reports.[92]

[3.065] Where the abridged financial statements would, if they had been prepared by reference to the matters taken account of in the revised financial statements, comply with the requirements of the Act (or of the IAS Regulation), the directors of the company must cause the company to deliver to the Registrar, within 28 days after the date of revision, a note stating that the financial statements for the specified financial year have been revised in a respect which has no bearing on the abridged financial statements delivered, and a copy of the statutory auditors' report on the revised statements.[93]

(d) Disclosure requirements in financial statements

(i) Directors' compliance statement

[3.066] The Act requires[94] that directors of LTDs, DACs and CLGs which have both a balance sheet total exceeding €12.5m and a turnover exceeding €25m, and all PLCs (except for investment companies) include a "directors' compliance statement" in the directors' report set out with their financial statements; this obligation is addressed in detail at para **[4.008]** below. The directors' compliance statement must:

    (a)   acknowledge that the directors are responsible for securing the company's compliance with its relevant obligations;[95] and

    (b)   with respect to each of the following three things, confirm that it has been done, or specify the reasons why it has not been done:

        (i)   the drawing up of a compliance policy statement, setting out the company's policies (that in the directors' opinion, are appropriate to the company) respecting compliance by the company with its relevant obligations;

---

[92]   Section 377(1) to (3) of the Act.

[93]   Section 377(4) to (6) of the Act.

[94]   Section 225(1) of the Act.

[95]   Meaning obligations under tax law (which includes the Customs Acts, statutes relating to excise duties, the Tax Acts, the Capital Gains Tax Acts, the VAT Acts, the Capital Acquisitions Tax Consolidation Act 2003, the Stamp Duties Consolidation Act 1999 and instruments made under these Acts or otherwise relating to tax); obligations where a failure to comply would be a category 1 or category 2 offence, a serious market abuse offence or a serious prospectus offence; and, where the company has shares or debentures admitted to trading on a regulated market of an EEA State, obligations where a failure to comply would be a serious transparency offence.

(ii)   the putting in place of appropriate arrangements or structures that are, in the directors' opinion, designed to secure material compliance with the company's relevant obligations; and

(iii)   the conducting of a review, during the financial year to which the directors' report in which the compliance statement is contained relates, of any arrangements or structures referred to in (ii) above that have been put in place.

[3.067] Arrangements or structures will be regarded as being designed to secure material compliance with relevant obligations (as at (ii) above) if they provide a reasonable assurance of compliance in all material respects with those obligations. Those arrangements or structures may, if the directors so decide, include reliance on the advice of persons employed by the company or retained by the company under a contract for services, being persons who appear to the directors to have the requisite knowledge and experience to advise the company on compliance with its relevant obligations.

(ii) Remuneration of directors and connected persons

[3.068] The Act requires that a company disclose, in the notes to its statutory financial statements, remuneration amounts – for both the current and the preceding financial year – in respect of persons who were, at any time during the financial year concerned, directors of the company.[96] While this provision largely restates the existing law,[97] there is now an express obligation to disclose the aggregate amount of the gains by the directors on the exercise of share options during the financial year.

[3.069] In addition, the Act provides for broader disclosure requirements than is currently the case by requiring that the remuneration amounts to be shown shall include all amounts paid or payable by a company to a person connected with a director of that company.[98] "Connected person" is defined[99] as meaning:

(a)   a spouse, civil partner, parent, brother, sister or child of a director;

(b)   a body corporate controlled by a director (ie in which the directors or persons connected to them are interested in 50 per cent or more of the equity share capital, or in which those persons are entitled to control the exercise of 50 per cent or more of the voting power);

(c)   a person acting as trustee of a trust, the principal beneficiaries of which are the director or their spouse, civil partner, children, or any body corporate controlled by the director; or

(d)   a person acting in partnership with that director.

---

96   Section 305 of the Act.
97   As set out in s 191 of the Companies Act 1963.
98   Section 306(1) of the Act.
99   Section 220 of the Act.

Children, spouses and other family of directors who work in a company may find their earnings made public as a result of this.

(iii) Statement regarding provision of information to auditors

[3.070] A new obligation is proposed whereby a company's directors will be required to include a statement in their report (which forms part of the financial statements) that so far as each director is aware, there is no relevant audit information of which the statutory auditors are unaware, and the director has taken all the steps that he ought to have taken as a director to make himself aware of relevant audit information and to establish that the auditors are aware of that information.[100] It had previously been the case that the auditors had a right of access at all reasonable times to the books of the company, and to require from the officers of the company such information and explanations that were within their knowledge or could be procured by them; and the auditors were required to state in their report whether they had obtained all the information and explanations which to the best of their knowledge and belief were necessary for the purpose of their audit.[101] These provisions, in combination with the ongoing communications that would typically take place between the directors and auditors in the course of the audit, mean that the requirement on directors to take all the steps referred to above is not likely to constitute a significant substantive change. However the inclusion of the statement in the directors' report may further focus directors' attention on their responsibilities in this regard.

(e) Summary financial statements for PLCs

[3.071] Section 1119 is a new provision, which allows the directors of a PLC to prepare a summary financial statement for the company in relation to a particular financial year, for the purpose of its being sent to members in lieu of the full statutory financial statements, directors' report and auditors' report[102]. The summary financial statement must give a fair and accurate summary account of the PLC's financial development during the financial year and of its financial position at the end of the financial year, and it must include a statement of the auditors' opinion as to its consistency with the statutory financial statements and the directors' report, and as to its conformity with the requirements of s 1119. The intention of this section, which is modelled on s 79 of the Building Societies Act 1989, is to allow PLCs just to circulate a summary

---

[100] Section 331 of the Act.

[101] Section 193 of the Companies Act 1990.

[102] If the auditors' report on the statutory financial statements includes a qualification, this report must also be sent to the members with the summary financial statements.

financial statement; this may be particularly useful where the PLC has a large shareholder base, and where the full annual financial statements are of considerable size. Copies of the full financial statements will be available to shareholders on request.

Chapter 4

Changes in the Law of Directors' Duties

by
Dr Thomas B Courtney

Introduction

[4.001] Part 5 of the Act consolidates and adds to the law relating to the duties and responsibilities of directors and other officers.[1] This chapter will identify and analyse the changes introduced to this ever-increasingly important area of company law, and will do so as follows:

1. De facto directors, shadow directors, connected persons and officers in default;
2. The directors' compliance statement;
3. The codified duties of directors;
4. Disclosure of interests in contracts;
5. The consequences of breach of duty;
6. Directors' indemnities;
7. Changes to the law relating to loans, etc, to directors;
8. Changes to the law requiring disclosure of interests in shares.

The focus of this chapter is on the changes to the law relating to directors' duties introduced by the Act.

De facto directors, shadow directors, connected persons and officers in default

[4.002] Chapter 1 of Part 5 contains a number of provisions which, while properly clustered under the heading "preliminary and definition", should be recognised as the source of substantive duties and liabilities, some of which are being introduced by the Act. We begin with Chapters 1 and 6 of Part 5: Chapter 1 identifies three types of persons who will be subject to some or all of the duties owed by directors and who are also subject to the same restrictions in

---

[1] For a statement of the law as applied prior to the commencement of the Act, see Courtney, *The Law of Companies* (3rd edn, Bloomsbury Professional, 2012) at Ch 15, Duties of Directors and Other Officers and Ch 16, Statutory Regulation of Directors' Transactions.

their dealings with companies as directors are subject; Chapter 6 of Part 5 identifies which directors and other officers will be criminally responsible for their, or their companies' transgressions. Here we consider:

(a) Shadow directors;

(b) *De facto* directors;

(c) Connected persons;

(d) Officers in default.

(a) Shadow directors

[4.003] One of the important changes introduced in Part 5 is the express extension of the duties imposed on legally appointed *de jure* directors to both shadow directors and *de facto* directors. The definition of shadow director remains as before, *a person in accordance with whose directions or instructions the directors of a company are accustomed to act*.[2] One new provision here is that it is now the case that a body corporate is not to be regarded as a shadow director of any of its subsidiaries;[3] this is thought to be more of a clarification than a change of law since the directions or instructions of holding companies, like those of receivers or the directors of holding companies, are given in the context of a particular relationship and not of a sort ever intended to amount to the maker of the direction becoming a shadow director.[4]

Shadow directors must, like *de jure* directors, disclose their interests in contracts in accordance with s 231 save that instead of declaring their interests at a meeting of directors, they must do so by notice in writing: s 221(3) of the Act.

A significant change in law is that, now, a shadow director will be treated for the purposes of Part 5 as a director of the company and so the general duties of directors set out in Chapter 2, and considered below, apply to a shadow director just as they do to a *de jure* director. Heretofore, although shadow directors could be made personally responsible for a company's debts and liabilities for reckless and fraudulent trading and could not obtain loans, etc, from their companies, they owed no positive duties to companies. Now, however, shadow directors are required to act in good faith in the company's interests, act honestly and responsibly in relation to the conduct of its affairs, and in accordance with the other requirements of s 228. When we consider the substantive detail of

---

[2] Section 221(1) of the Act.

[3] Section 221(2) of the Act.

[4] So in *Lynrowan Enterprises Ltd* [2002] IEHC 90, O'Neill J noted that a person may not be found to be a *de facto* director where there is evidence that the role of the person is explicable by the exercise of a role other than director, a distinction also noted in *Revenue and Customs Commissioners v Holland* [2011] 1 All ER 430. Although both were made in the context of *de facto* directors, it is thought that the same distinction holds good in the context of shadow directors.

directors' duties later in this chapter, it should be borne in mind that those provisions apply equally to shadow directors.

(b) De facto directors

[4.004] The concept of *de facto* director is not a new one since "director" has for some time been defined to include a person occupying the position of director;[5] and the Act restates this in s 2(1). While such persons came to be referred to as *de facto* directors, they were not so named by the old Companies Acts. This has now been changed and s 222(3) of the Act expressly provides that such a person is referred to in the Act as a *de facto* director.

Another significant difference is that s 222 expressly extends the statutory duties of directors in Part 5 to *de facto* directors, s 222(1) providing:

> "Without limiting the manner in which the expression "director" is to be read by virtue of *section 2(1)*, a person who occupies the position of director of a company but who has not been formally appointed as such director shall, subject to *subsection (4)*, be treated, for the purposes of this Part, as a director of the company."

As Patrick Ussher memorably observed, statute is not required to repeat itself for emphasis,[6] yet despite just providing that a *de facto* director shall be treated "for the purposes of this Part, as a director of the company" s 222(2) goes on to say that, in particular, s 231, which concerns the disclosure of interests in contracts, "shall apply to such a director as it applies in relation to directors generally."

Section 222(4) provides a defence to a person who gives advice in a professional capacity to the company or any of its directors and such a person shall not be a *de facto* director by reason only of that fact. Being a professional adviser does not mean a person will not be found to be a *de facto* director, but that fact alone will not in and of itself be sufficient.

(c) Connected persons

[4.005] The concept of a person being connected with a director of a company has become part of the company law landscape since the commencement of Part III of the Companies Act 1990 which regulated loans, etc, to directors of companies, their holding companies and persons connected with them. The general principle set out in s 220 remains – a person is connected with a director if, but only if, the person (not being himself or herself a director) is:

   (a)   that director's spouse, civil partner, parent, brother, sister or child;

   (b)   a person acting in his or her capacity as the trustee of any trust, the principal beneficiaries of which are that director, the spouse (or civil

---

5   Section 2(1) of the Companies Act 1963.
6   Ussher, *Company Law in Ireland* (1986) at p 315.

partner) or any children of that director or any body corporate which the director controls;

(c) in partnership with that director,

(d) a body corporate controlled by that director or by another body corporate that is controlled by that director.

The key changes introduced here are as follows:

- For the purposes of (a) and (b) above, "child" includes the child of a director's civil partner who is ordinarily resident with the director and the civil partner.[7]

- It is now expressly provided that a body corporate will be connected with a director if it is controlled by that director *or by another body corporate that is controlled by that director.*[8] While this was previously considered to be the case it was in reliance upon what is now s 220(6)(b); the new formulation is clearer.

- It is now stated that references to "voting power" in s 220(5) and (6) and the test for determining whether a director controls a body corporate do not include any power to vote which arises only in specified circumstances.[9]

(d) Officers in default

[4.006] Chapter 6 of Part 5 defines the concept of *officer in default*, a key concept in the context of imposing criminal liability on directors, secretaries and other officers for corporate wrongdoing. There have been a number of significant changes in the meaning of officer in default. Many of the criminal offences created by the Act are expressed to apply to the company and any officer in default or, in some cases, just to any officer in default. The basic concept is set out in s 270(1) which provides that an officer in default is:

> "... any officer who authorises or who, in breach of his or her duty as such officer, permits the default."

Moreover, "default" is defined to include "a refusal to do a thing or a contravention of a provision".

[4.007] The key change relates to the presumption as to when a default is permitted. Section 383(2) of the Companies Act 1963 had said that an officer shall be presumed to have permitted a default by the company "unless the officer can establish that he took all reasonable steps to prevent it or that, by reason of circumstances beyond his control, was unable to do so". This has been

---

7   Section 220(2) of the Act. Note, "child" includes a step-child and an adopted child: s 2(1) of the Act.

8   Section 220(3) of the Act.

9   Section 220(7) of the Act.

changed significantly and now, s 271(2) – following an amendment in Report Stage of the Seanad – provides:

> "In relevant proceedings, where it is proved that the defendant was aware of the basic facts concerning the default concerned, it shall be presumed that the defendant permitted the default unless the defendant shows that he or she took all reasonable steps to prevent it or that, by reason of circumstances beyond the defendant's control, was unable to do so."

The presumption relies heavily on defined terms and so *"relevant proceedings"* is defined by s 271(1)(c) to mean proceedings for an offence under a provision of the Act, being a provision which provides that an officer of a company who is in default shall be guilty of an offence. Relevant proceedings will always be criminal proceedings and the defendant in those proceedings is defined to mean the defendant or each of them alleged to be in default (except the company) being a person who was an officer of the company: s 271(1)(d).

Moreover, *"basic facts concerning the default"* is defined by s 271(1)(a) to mean such of the facts, relating to the one or more acts or omissions that constituted the default, as can reasonably be regarded as indicating, at the relevant time, the general character of those acts or omissions. Even the meaning of the word "permitted" is not left its ordinary, everyday, meaning and s 271(1)(b) provides that *"permitted"* in relation to the default, means permitted in breach of the defendant's duty as an officer of the company concerned.

The directors' compliance statement

[4.008] The requirement that the directors of certain companies include a statement in their Directors' Report that the company complies with certain obligations was first mooted by the Review Group on Auditing in its Report made in July 2000.[10] Although s 45 of the Companies (Auditing and Accounting) Act 2003 introduced a directors' compliance statement by inserting ss 205E and 205F into the Companies Act 1990, those sections were never commenced. In response to concerns from many quarters that the cost of compliance was disproportionately high to any benefit to be derived from a mechanism seemingly intended to prove commitment to compliance, the question of their commencement was referred to the Company Law Review Group which, in 2005, recommended that the provisions should not be commenced. A majority of the CLRG recommended against proceeding with any form of compliance statement but an even stronger majority recommended a compromise statement, if the then Minister was determined to proceed with a

---

[10] The Review Group on Auditing was established following the Comptroller and Auditor General's Report on the evasion of deposit investment retention tax and the subsequent Public Accounts Committee's Report: see generally, Courtney, "Directors' Compliance Statements: Attesting Corporate Compliance on a 'Comply or Explain' Basis", in Keane and O'Neill (eds), *Corporate Governance and Regulation* (Round Hall, 2009).

compliance statement. Section 225 of the Act now introduces the form of compliance statement recommended by the CLRG. The new requirement for the directors of certain companies to include in their Directors' Report a compliance statement is considered under the following headings:

(a) Companies in scope;

(b) The nature of the obligation on directors of companies in scope;

(c) The meaning of "relevant obligations";

(d) Compliance policy statements;

(e) Having in place "appropriate arrangements or structures", etc;

(f) The annual review of the arrangements or structures; and

(g) The "comply or explain" alternative.

(a) Companies in scope

[4.009] Only directors of the following companies must comply with s 225 of the Act:

- All PLCs[11] (except PLCs that are Part 24 investment companies);[12] and

- LTDs,[13] DACs[14] and CLGs[15] where, in respect of the financial year to which the Directors' Report relates, their balance sheet total for the year exceeds €12.5m *and* the amount of its turnover for the year exceeds €25m.

In addition to LTDs, DACs and CLGs that do not meet the thresholds specified above, the directors of all unlimited companies[16] (ULCs, PUCs and PULCs) are excluded from the requirement.

(b) The nature of the obligation on directors of companies in scope

[4.010] The obligations imposed on the directors of companies in scope are four-fold:

- To acknowledge, in the Directors' Report, that the directors are responsible for securing the company's compliance with its relevant obligations;[17]

- To confirm that a compliance policy statement setting out the company's policies (that, in the directors' opinion are appropriate to the

---

11 Section 1002(4) of the Act.
12 Section 1387(4) exempts investment companies from the application of s 225.
13 Section 225(7) of the Act.
14 Section 964(1) of the Act.
15 Section 1173(1) of the Act.
16 Section 1230(5), (6) and (7) of the Act.
17 Section 225(2)(a) of the Act.

company) respecting compliance by the company with its relevant obligations has been drawn up or, if this has not been done, specifying the reasons why it has not been done;[18]

- To confirm that there are in place appropriate arrangements or structures that are, in the directors' opinion, designed to secure material compliance with the company's relevant obligations or, if this has not been done, specifying the reasons why it has not been done;[19] and
- To confirm that a review has been conducted, during the financial year to which that Directors' Report relates, of any arrangements or structures, referred to above, that have been put in place or, if this has not been done, specifying the reasons why it has not been done.[20]

Each of these shall now be considered after first considering the meaning of "relevant obligations".

(c)   The meaning of "relevant obligations"

[4.011] "Relevant obligations" is defined by s 225(1) to mean a company's obligations under:

- the Companies Act where a failure to comply with any such obligation would (were it to occur) be a category 1 or category 2 offence or a serious market abuse offence[21] or a serious prospectus offence[22], or, in the case of a traded company, a serious transparency offence;[23] and
- tax law.

The references to a serious market abuse offence and a serious prospectus offence will not be relevant to LTDs but may be relevant to other types of company that have listed securities. So, for most LTDs the relevant Companies Act provisions that are the subject of the compliance policy statements are *category 1* and *category 2* offences.

[4.012] "Relevant obligations" are defined as follows:

"… in relation to a company, means the company's obligations under (a) this Act, where a failure to comply with any such obligation would (were it to occur) be –
(i) a category 1 offence or a category 2 offence …"

The Act provides that there are, in total, 11 category 1 offences (created by just two sections) and 96 category 2 offences (created by 65 sections). The first question is whether all category 1 and category 2 offences constitute relevant

---

[18]   Section 225(2)(b) and s 225(3)(a) of the Act.
[19]   Section 225(2)(b) and s 225(3)(b) of the Act.
[20]   Section 225(2)(b) and s 225(3)(c) of the Act.
[21]   As defined in s 1368 of the Act.
[22]   As defined in s 1356 of the Act.
[23]   As required by s 1374 of the Act and as defined by s 1382 of the Act.

obligations of companies? It is thought that the answer to this is "no": an offence will not be a relevant offence where it does not impose obligations on a company. So, for example, the category 2 offence created by s 642 of the Act, which provides that it is a category 2 offence for a person to act as a liquidator of a company when he or she is not qualified to so act, does not impose an obligation on a company.

On the other hand, a company may have an obligation under the Act, the contravention of which will not mean that the company has committed that offence. So s 248 provides that where a company contravenes s 239 (by making a loan, etc, to a director) any officer of the company who is in default will be guilty of a category 2 offence. In such an event, the company will not commit an offence, only its officers in default. However, the focus of the compliance statement is on a company's *obligations,* and not on offences which may be committed by a company. The definition of "relevant obligations" does not say that the category 1 or 2 offence must be committed by the company, only that the failure to comply with the company's obligations would be a category 1 or 2 offence. In this case, s 239 imposes a clear obligation on a company not to make a loan, etc, to a director, etc, and so although the company will not commit an offence where s 239 is breached, it is thought that s 239 is a relevant obligation of the company.

[4.013] In addition, certain tax enactments also comprise a company's "relevant obligations" and "tax law" has been defined to mean:

- the Customs Acts;
- the statutes relating to the duties of excise and to the management of those duties;
- the Tax Acts;
- the Capital Gains Tax Acts;
- the Value-Added Tax Acts;
- the Capital Acquisitions Tax Consolidation Act 2003 and the enactments amending or extending that Act;
- the Stamp Duties Consolidation Act 1999 and the enactments amending or extending that Act; and
- any statutory instruments made under an enactment referred to above or any other enactment relating to tax.

(d) Responsible for securing compliance with relevant obligations

[4.014] Ever since s 383 of the Companies Act 1963 was amended by s 100 of the Company Law Enforcement Act 2001, every director has had an express statutory duty to ensure that the requirements of the Companies Acts were complied with by the company. The obligation in s 225(2)(a) of the Act to acknowledge in the Directors' Report that the directors are responsible for securing the company's compliance with "relevant obligations" is, therefore, not new at least as far as relevant obligations refer to company law obligations. As is noted above, however, "relevant obligations" also includes tax law and, in this respect, this acknowledgement imposes a new duty on directors.[24]

It is suggested, however, that this acknowledgement does not impose any new liabilities on directors and simply states the obvious: being an artificial legal person, a company can only act through others and where s 158 of the Act applies, it is the directors who are charged with the management of the company and so accountable for ensuring that it complies with the Act. So, if a company breaches a provision of the Act, unless that provision expressly imposes penalties or liabilities on the directors, or any of them, in consequence of the breach, the acknowledgement in s 225(2)(a) will not of itself impose an additional penalty or liability on them. It is opined that the same applies in relation to any breach of tax law: unless the tax enactment imposes a penalty or liability on directors in consequences of its breach, s 225(2)(a) does not impose a new penalty or liability on the directors.

(e) *Drawing up a compliance policy statement*

[4.015] Directors of companies which are in scope will have to confirm that a compliance policy statement setting out the company's policies respecting compliance by the company with its relevant obligations has been drawn up or else explain why not. It is important to note that it is acknowledged that the directors have a role in determining what policies are appropriate to their company. Since no statutory definition of "policies" is provided it is appropriate to consider the ordinary meaning of the word. In practice, many people refer to "policies and procedures" in the same breath. In fact, they refer to two very different matters. A "*policy*" is defined as:

> "a course or principle of action adopted or proposed by an organisation or individual."[25]

In contrast, a "*procedure*" is:

> "an established or official way of doing something. A series of actions conducted in a certain order or manner."[26]

In its report on the originally enacted, but not commenced, directors' compliance statement, the CLRG was satisfied that one of the chief factors giving rise to the high costs of evidencing compliance was the specificity and prescription surrounding the requirement to have "*procedures*" designed to ensure compliance with a company's relevant obligations. It is important to recognise the distinction between "policies" and "procedures", and in drawing

---

[24] As to the meaning of "relevant obligations" see para **[4.011]**.
[25] *Concise Oxford English Dictionary* (11th edn, 2004).
[26] *Concise Oxford English Dictionary* (11th edn, 2004).

up a *compliance policy statement* companies should state the company's policies as regards compliance with its relevant obligations.

[4.016] It is to be expected that the compliance policy statement will be a short, concise document which will express the company's commitment to complying with its relevant obligations as an express policy of the company. It is expected, also, that there will be little by way of variation in the terms of most companies' compliance policy statements; there are only so many ways that a company can commit to complying with the relevant obligations it shares with every other company in scope.

As a company policy, it is to be expected, also, that it will be disseminated throughout the company so that its employees are familiar with its content and understand that in discharging their functions in the company, they must always do so having regard to the company's policies on compliance.

(f) Having in place appropriate arrangements or structures, etc

[4.017] The most onerous aspect of the directors' compliance statement obligation is the requirement to confirm that there are in place appropriate arrangements or structures that are, in the directors' opinion, designed to secure material compliance with the company's relevant obligations. The original form of directors' compliance statement, however, was very much more Draconian and proposed requiring confirmation that a company has "internal financial and other procedures in place designed to secure compliance". As alluded to above, the reference to "procedures" in particular was highly prescriptive and would have created an industry in documenting, recording and prescribing all manner of means in executing activities in return for considerable cost without adding appreciable value.

[4.018] Instead of "procedures" the requirement is now that the directors confirm that the company has in place *appropriate arrangements or structures*. Section 225(4) provides assistance in understanding this requirement, providing:

> "The arrangements or structures referred to in *subsection (3)(b)* may, if the directors of the company in their discretion so decide, include reliance on the advice of one or more than one person employed by the company or retained by it under a contract for services, being a person who appears to the directors to have the requisite knowledge and experience to advice the company on compliance with its relevant obligations."

While it will be for each company's directors to determine what are appropriate arrangements and structures for their company, one could imagine that a policy requiring, for example, all transactions to be approved by the company's finance director coupled with he or she being a tax professional could comply with the requirement to have a *policy* and *appropriate arrangements or structures* to secure material compliance with the company's relevant obligations under tax law.

(g) The annual review of the arrangements or structures

[4.019] The Directors' Report must also confirm that a review has been conducted, during the financial year to which that Directors' Report relates, of the arrangements or structures that have been put in place. This might be included as part of the company's statutory audit or the statutory auditors might rely upon the company's own compliance unit to carry out such a review.

(h) The "comply or explain" alternative

[4.020] There is no absolute requirement to provide the confirmations at (e), (f) and (g), above, and the directors of a company in scope can elect to decline to provide each of the confirmations and instead specify the reasons why any or all of them have not been done.

The codified duties of directors

[4.021] One of the more far-reaching reforms introduced by the Act is the codification of the duties of directors. Surprising though it may be, the Companies Acts have never before attempted to state the fiduciary duties owed by the directors of an Irish company. In its seminal 2001 Report, the Company Law Review Group recommended that "the fiduciary duties of a director to his company should be stated in general rather than specific terms, and on the basis that the statement of duties is not exhaustive".[27]

[4.022] While the duties are set out in s 228, it is s 227(1) of the Act that imposes and contextualises the duties listed in s 228. First and foremost is the statement in s 227(1) that the duties are owed to the company, *and to the company alone*:

> "Without prejudice to the provisions of any enactment (including this Act), a director of a company shall owe the duties set out in section 228 (the 'relevant duties') to the company (and the company alone)."

This confirms the position established in cases such as *Pervical v Wright*[28] that directors' duties are owed to the company and not to its individual shareholders or, for that matter, anybody else. The Act goes on to clarify further that a breach of duty by a director is, as a general rule, a matter between the company and the director and cannot, for example, be relied upon to invalidate a contract entered into by the company. So, s 227(2) provides:

> "The breach by a director of the relevant duties shall not of itself affect –
>
> (a)   the validity of any contract or other transaction; of

---

27   First Report (2001) at p 239.
28   *Pervical v Wright* [1902] 2 Ch 421. See generally, Courtney, *The Law of Companies* (3rd edn, Bloomsbury Professional, 2012) at para [15.004] *et seq*.

(b)   the enforceability, other than by the director in breach of that duty, of any contract or other transaction by any person,

but nothing in this subsection affects the principles of liability of a third party where he or she has been an accessory to a breach or duty or has knowingly received a benefit therefrom."

Accordingly, a third party cannot seek to avoid a contract entered into with a company on the grounds that the directors had caused the company to enter into the contract in breach of their duties to the company. Equally important is the fact that the general rule is that a company cannot seek to avoid a contract entered into with a third party on the grounds that its directors caused it to enter into the contract in breach of their duties: were it otherwise, a hornets' nest could have been opened up by the Act as third parties might have considered that they had a new duty to enquire in transacting with companies and might have sought new assurances that contracts were being entered into in compliance with the directors' duties. The Act makes clear that the compliance with directors' duties is a matter of internal governance of which outsiders need not be concerned. Of course it would be manifestly wrong if third parties could connive with directors, knowing that the directors were abusing their powers, and could enforce such contracts or transactions against the company. For this reason, there is a carve-out from the general rule just stated and nothing in the general rule will affect the principles of liability of a third party who is an accessory to a breach of duty or has knowingly received a benefit therefrom. No doubt, the meaning of being an "accessory to a breach of duty" and of "knowingly received a benefit therefrom" will be, in time, the subject of judicial interpretation.

[4.023] Section 227(4) and (5) provide very useful guidance as to the nature of the relevant duties. These provide:

"(4) The relevant duties (other than those set out in *section 228(1)(b)* and *(h)*) are based on certain common law rules and equitable principles as they apply in relation to the directors of companies and shall have effect in place of those rules and principles as regards the duties owed to a company by a director.

(5) The relevant duties (other than those set out in *section 228(1)(b)* and *(h)*) shall be interpreted, and the provisions concerned of section 228 shall be applied, in the same way as common law rules or equitable principles; regard shall be had to the corresponding common law rules and equitable principles in interpreting those duties and applying those provisions."

The carve-outs in s 227(4) and (5) for the duties to act honestly and responsibly and to have regard to the interests of members, reflect the fact that the relevant duties are not in fact all based on common law rules. The duty to act honestly and responsibly in relation to the affairs of the company is in fact drawn from s 150 of the Companies Act 1990, being the test required to be proved if a director of an insolvent company is to avoid being restricted.

[4.024] The eight relevant duties of directors as set out in s 228(1) are next considered. An important point to remember is that the relevant duties described in s 228 apply not only to *de jure* or legally appointed directors who are registered as such in the Companies Registration Office but also to *de facto* directors and shadow directors.[29]

(a) In good faith and in the interests of the company (s 228(1)(a))

[4.025] The first duty is that a director must act in good faith in what the director considers to be the interests of the company. This imposes a subjective test on a director to act in what he or she believes to be the interests of the company and implicitly recognises that two directors can, legitimately, have different opinions as to what is in a company's best interests. This relevant duty is based on an established fiduciary duty of directors[30] recognised in cases such as *Clark v Workman*,[31] *G&S Doherty Ltd v Doherty*,[32] *Re Hafner*[33] and *Re North City Milling Company Ltd*.[34]

[4.026] This will, therefore, restate the existing legal position which is that two individual directors may hold diametrically opposing views as to which course of action is in the best interests of their company and both be acting in accordance with their duty. This is in recognition of the fact that there is rarely one right answer and that people can genuinely hold opposing views as to what course is in the best interests of someone else. Recognition of this is entirely appropriate: just as a mother and a father can truly believe they are acting in the best interests of their child when one wants him to practice rugby and the other wants him to practice piano, so too can directors have different views on what is in their company's best interests.

(b) Honestly and responsibly in relation to the conduct of the affairs of the company (s 228(1)(b))

[4.027] Although perhaps a first-cousin of the duty to act in good faith and of the duty to exercise skill, care and diligence, the duty to act honestly and responsibly in relation to the conduct of the affairs of the company was not in fact a common law or equitable duty but a defence available to directors of insolvent companies in response to an application to have them restricted under s 150 of the Companies Act 1990. On the recommendation of the CLRG in its

---

[29] See ss 221 and 222 and paras **[4.003]** and **[4.004]**.
[30] See Courtney, *The Law of Companies* (3rd edn, Bloomsbury Professional, 2012) at para [15.027] *et seq*.
[31] *Clark v Workman* [1920] IR 107.
[32] *G&S Doherty Ltd v Doherty* (19 June 1969, unreported) HC *per* Henchy J.
[33] *Re Hafner* [1943] IR 426.
[34] *Re North City Milling Company Ltd* [1909] 1 IR 179.

Report on General Scheme of Companies Consolidation and Reform Bill (2007) this was added to the list of duties previously proposed as a positive statement of that defence. One of the reasons why the CLRG recommended that this be set out as a positive duty was because the words "honestly and responsibly" have received more judicial consideration and elaboration as to what they mean in the context of a director's obligations than probably any other three words in Irish company law. Guidance as to the meaning of this duty can be obtained from decisions such as *Re La Moselle Clothing Ltd and Rosegem Ltd*,[35] *Re Squash (Ireland) Ltd*,[36] *Mitek Ltd; Grace v Kachkar*,[37] *Re 360Atlantic (Ireland) Ltd; O'Ferral v Coughlan*,[38] and many others.[39]

(c)   In accordance with the constitution and exercise of powers only for the purposes allowed by law (s 228(1)(c))

[4.028] Directors have an existing common law duty to act in accordance with the company's memorandum and articles of association. As officers of a company the directors have always been bound to observe the provisions of the company's memorandum and articles of association which is a statutory contract between the members and the company and the members *inter se*.[40] Where directors are conferred with powers, whether under the Act or a company's constitution, they have a duty to exercise those powers only for the purposes allowed by law. This duty would, it is thought, extend to exercising powers only for their proper purpose, a duty recognised in cases such as *Nash v Lancegaye Safety Glass (Ireland) Ltd*,[41] *Howard Smith Ltd v Ampol Petroleum Ltd*,[42] and *Hogg v Cramphorn Ltd*.[43]

This duty is especially relevant to DACs and other companies with an objects clause. In the case of a DAC, for example, s 973(3) provides that notwithstanding that the validity of an Act done by a DAC shall not be called into question on the ground of lack of capacity, "it remains the duty of the directors to observe any limitations on their powers flowing from the DAC's objects".

---

[35] *Re La Moselle Clothing Ltd and Rosegem Ltd* [1998] 2 ILRM 345.
[36] *Re Squash (Ireland) Ltd* [2001] 3 IR 35.
[37] *Mitek Ltd; Grace v Kachkar* [2010] IESC 31.
[38] *Re 360Atlantic (Ireland) Ltd; O'Ferral v Coughlan* [2004] 4 IR 266.
[39] See Courtney, *The Law of Companies* (3rd edn, Bloomsbury Professional, 2012) at para [28.097] *et seq*.
[40] Section 31(1) of the Act. See further, Ch 2, *Changes in the Basics: Constitutions, Share Capital and Governance* at para **[2.010]**.
[41] *Nash v Lancegaye Safety Glass (Ireland) Ltd* [1947] IR 426.
[42] *Howard Smith Ltd v Ampol Petroleum Ltd* [1974] AC 821.
[43] *Hogg v Cramphorn Ltd* [1967] Ch 254.

(d) Not to misuse the company's property, information or opportunities (s 228(1)(d))

[4.029] Section 228(1)(d) provides that a director shall:

"Not use the company's property, information or opportunities for his or her own or anyone else's benefit unless –

(i)   this is expressly permitted by the company's constitution; or

(ii)   the use has been approved by a resolution of the company in general meeting."

The duty not to use company property, information or opportunities for anyone else's benefit but the company's is not an absolute duty: directors can be relieved by means of a provision in the constitution or by resolution in general meeting. It is thought it would be highly unusual for the constitution to give a blanket blessing to directors using the company's property and that transaction specific blessings by way of special resolution and tailored constitutional exemption for reasonable or de minimis use of company cars, phones, etc are more likely to be appropriate. While s 228 is silent on the point, it is thought that there has to be a limit on the extent to which members can release directors from their duties to the company and that the tipping point will arise where the effect of the release is to harm the interests of the company's creditors by affecting the company's solvency. It is entirely reasonable that members can release directors from their strict duties where the only persons who will be affected will be the shareholders, in the sense that there will be less profit available for distribution to them. Equally, it would seem unreasonable to expect that shareholders could release directors from their duties to the detriment of creditors.

[4.030] The duty not to misuse property, etc, reflects the common law position that directors are similar to trustees and control property owned by someone else (ie the company).[44] Directors cannot use or benefit from company property or gain from their fiduciary position: *Regal (Hastings) v Gulliver*;[45] neither can directors divert business opportunities away from the company to themselves or companies controlled by them or other third parties.[46]

The unauthorised disclosure of confidential information resulting from a breach of the duty of confidentiality owed by a director to a company and

---

[44]   See Courtney, *The Law of Companies* (3rd edn, Bloomsbury Professional, 2012) at para [15.055] *et seq*; see generally *Bray v Ford* [1896] AC 44, *Aberdeen Rly Company v Blaikie Bros* [1854] 1 Macq 461 and *Bhullar et al v Bhullar and Anor* [2003] 2 BCLC 241.

[45]   *Regal (Hastings) v Gulliver* [1942] 1 All ER 378; see also *Daniels v Daniels* [1878] Ch 406.

[46]   *Peso Silver Mines Ltd v Cropper* (1966) 58 DLR 1, *Gencor ACP Ltd et al v Dalby et al* [200] 2 BCLC 734, *Parolen Ltd v Doherty and Lindat Ltd* [2010] IEHC 71, *Hunter Kane Ltd v Watkins* [2003] EWHC 186.

recognised in many Irish cases,[47] can be seen as another manifestation of the duty now set out in s 228(1)(d).

(e) Not to fetter independent judgment (s 228(1)(e))

[4.031] Section 228(1)(e) provides that a director shall:

> "Not agree to restrict the director's power to exercise an independent judgment unless–
>
> (i) this is expressly permitted by the company's constitution;
>
> (ii) the case concerned falls within subsection (2); or
>
> (iii) the director's agreeing to such has been approved by a resolution of the company in general meeting."

This reflects the common law rule that a fiduciary cannot enter into an agreement as to how he or she will act or refrain from acting in the future because, as a fiduciary, the director needs to be able to act in whatever manner the director will believe will be in the company's best interests at that future time: *Clark v Workman*.[48] It is thought that by "independent judgment" is meant consideration of all relevant matters without being obliged or compelled to give preference to any factor.

[4.032] The statutory duty recognises, however, the two common law exceptions to the general rule.[49] So, it is noted that it may be expressly permitted by the company's constitution or by a resolution passed at a general meeting. This reflects the position at common law that the members can release directors from the strict application of this duty as seen in *Boulting v Association of Cinematography, Television and Allied Technicians*.[50] It is thought that few companies' constitutions will contain a blanket provision permitting directors to restrict the exercise of an independent judgment without a context and that it is more likely that directors will be released by resolution in particular situations.

This is particularly so when the most likely form a relieving provision in a constitution would have taken (ie to provide that directors could fetter their discretion where they believe this to be in the company's best interests) is the subject of an express statutory provision. So, s 228(2) supplements s 228(1)(e) by acknowledging the existing common law rule that a director *may* fetter his or her independent judgment where to do so is in the best interests of the company

---

47 See, eg, *Cremin and Oxyvent Ltd v Ecoplus Ltd et al* [2012] IEHC 82 and *Spring Grove Services (Ireland) Ltd v O'Callaghan* [2000] IEHC 62.

48 *Clark v Workman* [1920] 1 IR 107. See generally, Courtney, *The Law of Companies* (3rd edn, Bloomsbury Professional, 2012) at para [15.035] *et seq*.

49 See, generally, Courtney, *The Law of Companies* (3rd edn, Bloomsbury Professional, 2012) at paras [15.035]–[15.041].

50 *Boulting v Association of Cinematography, Television and Allied Technicians* [1963] 2 QB 606.

and is done in good faith: *Fulham Football Club Ltd v Cabra Estates plc.*[51] Section 228(2) provides:

"If a director of a company considers in good faith that it is in the interests of the company for a transaction or engagement to be entered into and carried into effect, a director may restrict the director's power to exercise an independent judgment in the future by agreeing to act in a particular way to achieve this."

So, aside from where released by the constitution or by ordinary resolution from the strict application of this duty, the directors can themselves decide that it is in the company's best interests to agree, for example, not to institute legal proceedings in the future in respect of a contingent matter, as part of a present settlement.

(f)   Avoid conflicts of interest (s 228(1)(f))

[4.033] Section 228(1)(f) requires that a director shall:

"Avoid any conflict between the director's duties to the company and the director's other (including personal) interests unless the director is released from his or her duty to the company in relation to the matter concerned, whether in accordance with provisions of the company's constitution in that behalf or by a resolution of it in general meeting."

Avoiding a conflict between a director's duty as director and his or her other interests precludes a director from participating in a board decision concerning, for example, the company's entering into of a contract with that director.

Section 228(1)(f) expressly acknowledges that a director can be released from the duty to avoid conflicts of interest in accordance with a provision in the company's constitution. In this regard it may be noted that s 162(2) and (3) are statutory defaults which will apply unless excluded. These provide:

"(2) No director of a company or intending such director shall be disqualified by his or her office from contracting with the company either with regard to his or her tenure of any such other office or place or profit or as vendor, purchaser or otherwise.

(3) In particular, neither shall –

(a)   any contract with respect to any of the matters referred to in subsection (2), nor any contract or agreement entered into by or on behalf of the company in which a director is in any way interested, be liable to be avoided; nor

(b)   a director so contracting or being so interested be liable to account to the company for any profit realised by any such contract or arrangement,

by reason of such director holding that office or of the fiduciary relation thereby established."

---

[51]   *Fulham Football Club Ltd v Cabra Estates plc* [1994] 1 BCLC 363.

Other relevant statutory defaults, which will apply in the case of an LTD unless its constitution provides otherwise, are:

- a director may vote in respect of any contract, appointment or arrangement in which he or she is interested and shall be counted in the quorum present at the meeting (s 161(7));

- a director may hold any other office or place of profit under the company (except auditor) (eg executive director, CEO, CFO, etc) on such terms as the directors think fit (s 162(1)); and

- a director may be counted, notwithstanding his interest, in the quorum at a meeting at which he is appointed to hold office or place or profit, etc, and may vote on but that he may not vote on his own appointment or its terms (s 163).

These are not exceptions to the duty in s 228(1)(f) which applies subject to the exceptions contained in its own terms.

[4.034] Also relevant here is s 229. This provides that, save to the extent that a company's constitution provides otherwise, a director may become a director or officer of, or otherwise interested in (eg a shareholder in) any company promoted by the company or in which the company may be interested as shareholder or otherwise, but this is subject to the provisions of s 228. This would permit, for example, a director to be a shareholder in a joint-venture company where the other party was the company. Where this provision applies, a director will not be accountable to the company for any remuneration or benefits received by him as a director or officer of the company or from his interest in the other company.

[4.035] Section 230(1) is also relevant to conflicts of interest. This provides that, save to the extent that a company's constitution provides otherwise:

"(a) any director may act by himself or herself, or his or her firm, in a professional capacity for the company of which he or she is a director; and

(b) any director, in such a case, or his or her firm, shall be entitled to remuneration for professional services as if he or she were not a director."

The one exception to this concerns a director (or his firm) acting as statutory auditor, which is prohibited: s 230(2).

(g) Exercise the care, skill and diligence (s 228(1)(g))

[4.036] Section 228(1)(g) of the Act provides that a director shall:

"Exercise the care, skill and diligence which would be exercised in the same circumstances by a reasonable person having both –

(i) the knowledge and experience that may reasonably be expected of a person in the same position as the director; and

(ii) the knowledge and experience which the director has."

This requires directors to perform their functions with care, skill and diligence. The standard by which a director is to be judged in relation to this duty is a quasi-objective-subjective standard. While the test is that a director must exercise the same care, skill and diligence *as a reasonable person* would exercise, that reasonable person is to be taken to be someone with that director's knowledge and experience. Therefore, a director who is an accountant will be expected to exercise the same skill as a reasonable person who is a chartered accountant; a volunteer director of a charity who is, say, a tradesman will be judged as against a reasonable person who is a tradesman.

(h) Have regard to members' interests (s 228(1)(h))

[4.037] Section 224 provides that directors must have regard to the interests of employees; however, like its predecessor, the duty under s 52 of the Companies Act 1990, this duty is owed to the company and enforceable only by the company. Section 228(1)(h) provides that in addition to the duty under s 224, a director shall have regard to the interests of a company's members. While this could be seen as a new duty, it is thought that it is more accurate to view it as a manifestation of the duty to act in the best interests of the company (the duty now specified in s 228(1)(a)) since "company" as used in that context has been interpreted as meaning the members as a whole.

[4.038] The duty in s 288(1)(h) is to have regard to the interests of the company's members *as a whole* and in this respect differs from the *right* of directors who have been appointed or nominated for appointment by a member, to have regard to the interests of that particular member: s 228(3).

[4.039] It is important to make the distinction, therefore, between *acting in* the company's interests and *having regard to* the interests of others, be they the members as a whole, employees or a particular member with a right to nominate or appoint a director. Having regard to a third party's interest means understanding what they would like by way of outcome from a corporate act or omission and, to the extent it is possible, harmonising that with the outcome that is in the company's best interests. So if Option A is in the interests of the company's employees and Option A and Option B are both, unequivocally and indisputably, in the best interests of the company, then in choosing Option A the directors will have discharged their duties under both s 224 and s 228(1)(a). Were the directors of the subjective and *bona fide* belief that Option A was in any way less beneficial to the company, then they would be compelled to choose Option B.

Disclosure of interests in contracts

[4.040] There have been some important changes to the law relating to the duty of directors to disclose their interest in contracts made with the company. The basic requirement remains: it is the duty of a director who is in any way, directly or indirectly, interested in a contract or proposed contract with the company to declare the nature of his or her interest at a meeting of the directors of the company: s 231(1).

The first major change is set out in s 231(10)(a) which operates to define what contracts the duty applies to, and so references to "contract" shall be read as excluding a reference to a contract, the decision as to whether to enter into it is taken, or falls to be taken, other than by the board of directors or a committee of which the first-mentioned director in s 231(1) is a member. The purpose of the duty to disclose is to ensure that when directors meet as a board to discuss a contract, each of the directors is aware of any interests the others have in that contract. This type of provision was never intended to require a director to disclose to the board of directors *every* contract entered into by him with the company. Were it otherwise, a director of a company that operated a supermarket would have to disclose to his board his weekly contract to buy groceries! It should be a matter of indifference to the board that one of their number contracts with the company at arm's length. Such contracts are irrelevant to the other directors because they are not contracts made by the board involving a director. Accordingly, while it was always implied that the predecessor to s 231(1) only applied to contracts entered into by the board or a committee of which the contracting director is a member, s 231(10)(a) makes express that which had been implied.

The other major change is contained in s 231(2) which provides that the requirement to disclose does not apply in relation to an interest that cannot reasonably be regarded as likely to give rise to a conflict of interest.

The consequences of breach of duty

[4.041] The basic rule as regards the breach of directors' relevant duties – namely, the codified duties set out in s 228(1) – is that set out in s 227(3) and is that it is enforceable "in the same way as any other fiduciary duty owed to a company by its directors". In general, therefore, the company may sue for damages, seek an indemnity for losses or seek an account for profits. In addition, however, s 232 provides for a statutory right to indemnity and account in relation to the breach of certain duties.

(a) Indemnity and account for breach of certain relevant duties

[4.042] Section 232(1) provides that where a director acts in breach of the directors' relevant duties except s 228(1)(b) (to act honestly and responsibly) and s 228(1)(h) (to have regard to the interests of members) he shall be liable to do either or both (as the corresponding common law rule or equitable principle with respect to the matter would have required) of the following things, namely:

"(a)   account to the company for any gain which he or she makes directly or indirectly from the breach of duty;

(b)   indemnity the company for any loss or damage resulting from that breach."

The omission of the duties at (b) and (h) is most likely because these were not common law duties to which the common law remedy to account for gain and indemnity for losses applied.

It should be noted that s 232(3) provides that this right is expressed to be without prejudice to:

"(a)   the company's right at common law to claim damages for breach of duty; or

(b)   the company's right to make an application seeking the grant of equitable relief,

but the provisions of this section shall not be read as having the combined effect of enabling the company to be afforded more compensation for any damage or injury, or more protection of any proprietary right, that is just and equitable in the circumstances."

(b)   Indemnity and account for unlawful loans and substantial property transactions

[4.043] The statutory right of a company to be indemnified or to seek an account from directors where the company has made an unlawful loan, quasi-loan, credit transaction or has entered into an unlawful guarantee or provided security in connection with such or has entered unto an unlawful substantial property transaction as provided in s 232(2) is not new.[52] Neither is the carve-out for transactions or arrangements with connected persons where a director can show that he or she took all reasonable steps to secure the company's compliance, as provided for in s 232(6).

(c)   Indemnity and account for unlawful payments for loss of office, etc

[4.044] There is a new statutory right for companies to seek an indemnity and an account from directors where there has been a breach of ss 251 or 252. Section 251 provides that certain payments to directors by way of compensation for loss of office must be approved by the members in general meeting who must receive particulars of the proposed payments; this is not new and a similar provision was

---

[52]   Such existed in the case of substantial property transactions by virtue of s 29(4), and in the case of loans, etc, s 38 of the Companies Act 1990.

contained in the Companies Act 1963.[53] Similarly, the necessity for approval of a payment to a director in connection with a transfer of property is also not new.[54] While it is thought that it has always been open to companies to seek an indemnity and account where such unlawful payments were made, this is now an express statutory remedy, and where a company makes a payment to a director in breach of ss 251 or 252 that director shall be liable:

> "(a)   to account to the company for any gain which he or she makes directly or indirectly from the payment;
>
> (b)   to indemnity the company for any loss or damage resulting from the payment, or
>
> (c)   to do both of those things as the circumstances may require
>
> and in the case of section 252, this is without prejudice to subsection (3) of that section."

The right of a company to damages and equitable relief is also confirmed in respect of this statutory right to indemnity and account on the same terms as outlined above. [55]

Directors' indemnities

[4.045] The key point to note is that it remains the law that a provision will be void where:

> "(a)   purporting to exempt any officer of a company from; or
>
> (b)   purporting to indemnify such an officer against,
>
> any liability which by virtue of any enactment or rule of law would otherwise attach to him or her in respect of any negligence, default, breach of duty or breach of trust of which he or she may be guilty in relation to the company."

The same exception to this as before applies: *viz* a company may enter into a binding contract to indemnify any officer against any liability incurred in defending proceedings, whether civil or criminal, in which judgment is given in the officer's favour or in which the officer is acquitted or in connection with any proceedings under ss 233 or 234 in which relief is granted by the High Court. [56] One change has been introduced, however, in relation to companies that were previously incorporated in a jurisdiction which permitted such indemnities for directors and which migrate to Ireland and come to be re-registered here, provided certain conditions are met.[57] Of course, only certain investment

---

[53]   Section 186 of the Companies Act 1963.
[54]   Section 187 of the Companies Act 1963.
[55]   See para **[4.042]**.
[56]   Section 235(3) of the Act.
[57]   Section 235(6) of the Act.

companies and *societas europae* can move their registered office from one member state to another, so this change will be of very limited application.

Changes to the law relating to loans, etc, involving directors

[4.046] The most significant change to the law relating to loans concerns the introduction of new evidential provisions concerning loans from companies to their directors *and* loans from directors to their companies.

(a) Evidential provisions concerning loans to directors

[4.047] If a company makes a loan or a quasi-loan to a director of the company, its holding company or a person connected with either, then s 236(2) provides that if the terms are not in writing it will be presumed until the contrary is proved that:

(a) the loan or quasi-loan is repayable on demand; and

(b) for any period before repayment of the amount of the loan or quasi-loan (or for any period before repayment of part of that amount) the amount or part has borne interest at the appropriate rate.

The first point to note is that the presumption only applies in "relevant proceedings" which are defined as civil proceedings in which it is claimed that a company has made a loan or quasi-loan to a director of the company, or its holding company or a person connected with any such director. The second point is that the reference to "appropriate rate" means 5 per cent or such other rate as may be specified by order of the Minister under s 2(7). Where in relevant proceedings the terms of a loan or quasi-loan are in writing or partially in writing but the terms are ambiguous on either the repayment date or interest rate, the same presumptions shall apply: s 236(3).

(b) Evidential provisions concerning loans by directors

[4.048] It may seem strange that the legislature has deigned to interfere in cases where directors make loans to their companies. Surely, such a practice is to be encouraged and does not require to be regulated? In fact, the opposite is the case and this change was made on the recommendation of the CLRG who found that there was evidence that unscrupulous directors of insolvent companies were claiming that they had made loans to their companies and were therefore entitled to be repaid and to share *pari passu* with the other unsecured creditors of the company and as such had the right to vote in the creditors' meeting on the company's winding up; in some cases no loans had been made at all and in other cases while advances may have been made they were not intended to be loans. This is the rationale for encouraging loans to companies from their directors to be evidenced in writing.

[4.049] Section 237(2) provides that in relevant proceedings, if the terms of a transaction or arrangement:

"(a) are not in writing; or

(b) are in writing, or partially in writing, but are ambiguous as to whether the transaction or arrangement constitutes a loan or quasi-loan or not (or as to whether it constitutes a quasi-loan as distinct from a loan),

then it shall be presumed, until the contrary is proved, that the transaction or arrangement constitutes neither a loan nor a quasi-loan to the company or its holding company, as the case may be."

The presumption is that there is no loan, the implication being that it was a gift or an advance. Here, "relevant proceedings" means civil proceedings in which it is claimed that a transaction or arrangement entered into, or alleged to have been entered into by a director of the company, its holding company or a person connected with such a director, constitutes a loan or quasi-loan by the director or connected person to the company or its holding company.

[4.050] There is a second series of presumptions. Section 237(3) provides that in relevant proceedings where it is proved that an advance was indeed a loan or quasi-loan from the director to the company (whether the terms of the loan or quasi-loan are in writing, partially in writing or wholly oral) then if:

(a) the case is one in which those terms are ambiguous with respect to whether, or the extent to which, the loan or quasi-loan bears interest, it shall be presumed, until the contrary is proved, that the loan or quasi-loan bears no interest;

(b) the case is one in which those terms are ambiguous with respect to whether, or the extent to which the loan or quasi-loan is secured, it shall be presumed, until the contrary is proved, that the loan or quasi-loan is not secured; or

(c) in the event that the loan or quasi-loan is proved to be secured and the case is one in which those terms are ambiguous with respect to the priority that the security concerned is to have as against other indebtedness of the company, it shall be presumed, until the contrary is proved, that the loan or quasi-loan is subordinate to all other indebtedness of the company.

[4.051] Since loans made to persons connected with directors are caught by s 237 (ie they are included in "relevant proceedings") and since bodies corporate controlled by directors will be connected persons, care should be taken to enquire as to whether a particular corporate loan is within scope. A loan made by a company to another company in the same group will be caught by s 237 where the other company is a person connected with a director of the company making the loan, etc, even if the loan comes within the group exemption in s 243 to the prohibition in s 239.

(c) Substantial property transactions and loans, quasi-loans, credit transactions, etc

[4.052] No significant material changes have been made to the provisions on substantial property transactions between directors and their companies although s 238 does make a number of minor changes. Again, in relation to loans, quasi-loans, credit transactions and guarantees and security in connection with loans, quasi-loans and credit transactions, the law now contained in s 239 is broadly as it was before the enactment of the new legislation. One change is that there is no longer a stand-alone validation procedure and instead, a transaction or arrangement prohibited by s 239 may be validated in accordance with the summary approval procedure (SAP) in Chapter 7 of Part 4. In that regard it will be noted that a report from an independent person on the reasonableness of the directors' declaration of solvency is no longer required and does not form part of the SAP in its application to s 239. Other changes to the law include:

- Where an arrangement entered into in reliance of the less than 10 per cent comes to fall outside that exemption because of a reduction in relevant assets, it is now expressly provided that if the arrangement is not amended within two months, it becomes voidable at the instance of the company subject to the savers in s 246: s 241(6);

- In the exemption dealing with inter-group transactions, it has been made express that it will apply to where the holding company or subsidiary is not an Irish company (although it is thought for reasons given elsewhere, that this was always implied)[58]: s 243(1) and (2);

- The business transactions exemption has been extended and may now be invoked to exempt guarantees and the provision of security: s 245(1)(c).

Changes to the law requiring disclosure of interests in shares

[4.053] Part IV of the Companies Act 1990 created a minefield for the unwary as it required directors and secretaries to disclose their interest in shares to their company without any *de minimis* exception and even if the company itself granted the shares to them! The new law set out in Chapter 5 of Part 5 of the Act is every bit as horrible as the old law but a number of small changes have been made which will make its provisions somewhat easier to navigate.

---

[58] See Courtney, *The Law of Companies* (3rd edn, Bloomsbury Professional, 2012) at para [16.089].

[4.054] The first and most significant change is the introduction of a new exemption in s 260(f) which states that the following interests shall not constitute *disclosable interests* for the purposes of the Chapter:

"Any interest in shares in, or debentures of, a body corporate where the aggregate interest of the director or secretary and spouse or civil partner and children or such director or secretary is in:

(i) shares representing 1 per cent or less, in nominal value, of the body corporate's issued share capital of a class carrying rights to vote in all circumstances at general meetings of the body corporate (provided that the temporary suspension of voting rights in respect of shares comprised in issued share capital of a body corporate of any such class shall be disregarded); or

(ii) shares or debentures not carrying the right to vote at general meetings of the body corporate, save a right to vote which arises only in specified circumstances."

So, if a director and his kin hold 1 per cent or less in nominal value of shares carrying voting rights, this need not be disclosed; and no amount of shares which do not carry voting rights need be disclosed.

[4.055] The 1 per cent threshold will also apply to where directors and secretaries acquire options in the nature of a right to subscribe. So, where the aggregate interest of the director, etc, in shares in the body corporate is less than 1 per cent, then no duty to notify the acquisition of options under s 263(2) will arise: s 263(5).

[4.056] Another highly sensible change recommended by the CLRG and now contained in the Act is that where a director or secretary is granted an option to subscribe for shares in that company, nothing in ss 261, 262 or 263 shall impose an obligation to make any notification to that company in respect of such grant: s 264(3).

[4.057] A failure to notify a disclosable interest will, as before, mean that no right or interest of any kind whatsoever in respect of the shares or debentures concerned shall be enforceable by the person: s 266(2). Heretofore, the only way in which to have the rights to the shares or options reinstated was to apply to the High Court. Now, two provisions mean that it may not be necessary to go to the expense of obtaining a High Court order. In the first place, a failure to notify a disclosable interest will not render the rights attaching to the shares or debentures unenforceable where:

"... the identity of the director or secretary and his or her holding, acquisition and disposal (as the case may be) of the shares or debentures in question and the consideration paid or payable therefor has, from not later than 30 days after the date the duty arose, been apparent on the face or all or any of the following registers or documents of the company concerned (including some or all of them when consulted together) namely –

(a)   the register of members;

(b)   the register of directors and secretaries;

(c)   the register of interests under section 267;

(d)   documents made available by that company which those registers."

Section 266(5) will be helpful where the failure relates to a disclosure of shares in the company in which the shares are held but will not save shares held in its holding company from the fate described in s 266(2) since it is unlikely that a register of a subsidiary would contain such matters.

[4.058] In the second place, unsaleable restricted shares resulting from the operation of s 266(2) can be made saleable again through complying with the procedure in s 266(6). This provides:

> "If a company in general meeting passes a special resolution providing that the following protection shall apply in favour of a third party having the following dealing in relation to shares in, or debentures or, the company specified in the resolution then, upon production of a copy of such resolution by the secretary of the company to the third party, a third party having any dealing with the company or the registered holder of the shares or debentures in question shall be entitled to presume, without further enquiry, that –
>
> (a)   the provisions of this Chapter have been complied with in relation to the shares or debentures; and
>
> (b)   the registered holder is entitled to deal with the shares or debentures registered in his or her name."

[4.059] Another significant change is that the contravention of ss 261, 262 or 263 is now a category 3 offence. Previously, it was an indictable offence and where auditors suspected it had been committed, they were obliged to report their suspicions to the ODCE. This is no longer the case.

Chapter 5

Taking Security, the Summary Approval Procedure and the Registration of Charges

by
William Johnston

Introduction

[5.001] In this chapter, the following matters concerning security and the registration of charges are considered:

1. Capacity of a company;
2. Corporate authority;
3. Matters relating to security;
4. Financial assistance given for own share purchase;
5. Summary approval procedure;
6. Registration of charges.

Capacity of a company

[5.002] One of the first tasks of a lender's solicitor is to ensure that the corporate borrower and each corporate guarantor and security provider have the power to borrow, guarantee and/or provide security in pursuance of their principal objects.

(a) Private company limited by shares

[5.003] Eighty-six per cent of companies in Ireland are private companies limited by shares.[1] Apart from the companies which are set up for a specific purpose and which become designated activity companies, the objects and powers clause of these companies will become redundant.[2] A company, being a private company limited by shares that is registered under Part 2 of the Act (an "LTD"), will have full and unlimited capacity to carry on and undertake any

---

[1] On 31 December 2013, there were 187,139 companies registered in Ireland; see Annual Report of Companies Registration Office.

[2] For a review of the demise of *ultra vires*, see Ahern, "Unlimited corporate capacity – Plotting the slow demise of *ultra vires*" (2004) CLP 17; for further reading see Anderson, "The Evolution of the Ultra Vires Rule in Irish Company Law" (2003) Ir Jur Vol 1 263.

business or activity, do any act or enter into any transaction as though it is a natural person.[3] Accordingly, the lender's solicitor will have no objects clause to review when considering the constitution of a private company limited by shares (which has not otherwise opted to become a DAC).

(b) DACs, PLCs, guarantee companies and unlimited companies

[5.004] However, the capacity of any other type of company to enter into and be bound by its obligations under a contract continues to be dependant upon its objects and powers as set out in its memorandum of association.[4] An agreement entered into by a company involving rights or obligations not permitted by the company's memorandum of association remains *ultra vires* and unenforceable against the company (unless clearly incidental to the objects as set out).[5] However, this is subject to a saving provision as set out in para **[5.006]** below.

[5.005] A company's objects must be set out in its memorandum of association.[6] However, "one cannot have an object to do every mortal thing one wants because that is to have no object at all".[7] In practice as before, a company's objects clause will be sub-divided into numerous paragraphs, the first few of which will set out the objects (or principal activity) of the company, for example, the sale and distribution of law books. Subsequent to these objects will be the paragraphs denoting the powers of the company.[8] Such powers can be carried out only for the purpose of fulfilling the objects and cannot be carried

---

3   Section 38 of the Act.
4   See s 972(1) of the Act for DACs, s 1011(1) for PLCs, s 1182(1) for guarantee companies, s 1239(1) for unlimited companies; for the background to the reform of the *ultra vires* principle for the private company limited by shares, see ch 10 of the First Report of the Company Law Review Group (2001).
5   Buckley LJ in *Re Horsley & Weight Ltd* [1982] 3 All ER 1045 at 1050; Slade LJ in *Rolled Steel Products (Holdings) Ltd v British Steel Corp* [1984] BCLC 466 at 500; for a thorough review of the case law on the doctrine of *ultra vires* see MacCann, "The Capacity of the Company" (1992) ILT 79; see also Smith, "The Constitution of a Company" (1984) 5 Co Law 78 and 123; for further reading see Courtney, *The Law of Companies* (3rd edn, Bloomsbury Professional, 2012), Ch 3; see also Ussher, *Company Law in Ireland* (1986) Ch 4.
6   Section 967(2)(c) of the Act for DACs, s 1006(2)(c) for PLCs, s 1176(2)(c) for guarantee companies, ss 1233 and 1234 for unlimited companies.
7   *Per* Harman LJ in *Re Introductions Ltd, Introductions Ltd v National Provincial Bank Ltd* [1969] 1 All ER 887 at 888.
8   See s 972(2)(a) for DACs, s 1011(2)(a) for PLCs, s 1182(2)(a) for guarantee companies and s 1239(2)(a) for unlimited companies; for the distinction between objects and powers see Keane, *Company Law* (4th edn, Bloomsbury Professional, 2007) at para [5.31]; see also Instone, "Powers and Objects" (1978) NLJ 948.

out (save where specifically provided otherwise[9]) as ends in themselves.[10] As before, the objects clause may be amended by special resolution.[11]

(c) Capacity not limited by constitution

[5.006] Having abolished the *ultra vires* principle from the standard private company limited by shares, and retaining it for DACs and other companies, for the very valid reason that the promoters of these companies may wish to limit such companies' activities, it is somewhat counterintuitive to provide that those dealing with such companies can ignore any act of such company outside its powers even where such incapacity was known or ought to have been known. The counterparty to a transaction which is *ultra vires* a company no longer has to act in good faith, as formerly required by reg 6 of the European Communities (Companies) Regulations 1973[12] or effectively by s 8 of the Companies Act 1963,[13] both of which have been replaced by the Act.

[5.007] Section 973(1) of the Companies Act 2014 provides:[14]

> "The validity of an act done by a DAC shall not be called into question on the grounds of lack of capacity by reason of anything contained in the DAC's objects."

A measure of protection against directors' abuse of power is granted to a shareholder by subs (2) of s 975 which provides:

> "a member of a DAC may bring proceedings to restrain the doing of an act which, but for subsection (1), would be beyond the DAC's capacity but no such proceedings shall lie in respect of any act to be done in fulfilment of a legal obligation arising from a previous act of the DAC."

However, the protection may be illusory as if the company is already committed to a third party on foot of an *ultra vires* agreement, the shareholder cannot prevent the company from fulfilling what is in effect an unlawful agreement.

---

[9] See eg *Re Horsley & Weight Ltd* [1982] 3 All ER 1045.
[10] See Buckley J in *Re David Payne & Company Ltd, Young v David Payne & Company Ltd* [1904] 2 Ch 608 at 612.
[11] Section 974 for DACs, s 1013 for PLCs, s 1184 for guarantee companies and s 1241 for unlimited companies.
[12] SI 163/1973.
[13] This section exempted a counterparty who was "not shown to have been actually aware" of the incapacity.
[14] The same provisions apply for PLCs (s 1012(13)), guarantee companies (s 1183(1)) and unlimited companies (s 1240(1)).

[5.008] There is also new law in that an act committed by a company outside its capacity can be ratified by special resolution.[15] This upsets the established law that an act *ultra vires* the company cannot be ratified.[16]

(d) Whether to review objects clause

[5.009] The new statutory provision raises the question as to whether it is preferable, for a lender, to make finance available and obtain security without reviewing the borrower's/guarantor's/chargor's memorandum of association for fear of failing to understand that the company was incapable of entering into the proposed transaction, or that it was being entered into for an *ultra vires* purpose.[17] This is a question which bankers not unreasonably may ask their advisers.[18] Can a lender who ignores reviewing a company's memorandum or articles of association, a document publicly filed, obtain the benefit of ignorance of incapacity? It may be doubtful where the prudent practice is to review the memorandum and articles of association.[19] Accordingly, in practice, for significant financing, these sections may be ignored as lenders will want to avoid any actions against the company or its directors by shareholders and in the case of companies other than the new private company limited by shares, lenders are likely to continue to make certain basic enquiries as to the company's capacity and to review the information provided from such enquiries when completing a financing transaction.

---

[15]   Section 973(3) and (4) of the Act for DACs; s 1012(3) and (4) for PLCs; s 1183(3) and (4) for guarantee companies; and s 1240(3) and (4) for unlimited companies.

[16]   See *Northern Bank Finance Corporation Ltd v Quinn and Achates Investment Company* [1979] ILRM 221 following *Re MJ Cummins Ltd, Barton v The Governor and Company of the Bank of Ireland* [1939] IR 60 where Johnston J stated (at 69): "it is almost unnecessary to say that a company cannot ratify an act of its own or an act of its directors which is outside and beyond the constitutional powers of the company"; see also *The Ashbury Railway Carriage & Iron Company v Riche* (1875) LR 7 HL 653 and Overend J in *National Agricultural and Industrial Development Association v The Federation of Irish Manufacturers Ltd* [1947] IR 159 at 203; see also Sir Barnes Peacock in *Irvine v The Union Bank of Australia* (1877) 2 App Cas 366 at 374: "A ratification is in law treated in law as equivalent to a previous authority, and it follows that, as a general rule, a person or body of persons, not competent to authorise an act, cannot give it validity by ratifying it."

[17]   Ussher, *Company Law in Ireland* (1986) p 126 states: "indeed it may be arguable that an agent such as a solicitor in a conveyancing transaction, acting for an outsider might be under a duty to his principal not to investigate the company's capacity to enter into the proposed transaction, since his consequent awareness of lack of capacity might put into jeopardy what would otherwise have been an advantageous transaction."

[18]   "It would appear to be wiser not to look at the objects clause at all": MacCann, "The Capacity of the Company" (1992) ILT 151 at 152.

[19]   See the duty on a solicitor imposed by the Supreme Court in *Roche and Roche v Peilow and Peilow* [1986] ILRM 189.

[5.010] For the practitioner to be safe, the memorandum of association of a corporate guarantor which is not an LTD should still be reviewed to establish whether the guarantor has the capacity to give a guarantee and to understand the purpose for which the guarantee is being given in order to establish whether the power being exercised is in furtherance of one of the company's principal objects.[20] The same principle applies to a company borrowing money or creating security over its present or future assets or undertaking.

Corporate authority

(a) Authority of directors and other persons to bind company

[5.011] A company operates through its board of directors who are deemed to have been granted authority by the company's constitution (unless it provides otherwise) to manage the company's business, exercise the company's powers to borrow money, to guarantee and to create security and approve documentation on behalf of the company.[21] The acts of a director are valid notwithstanding any defect subsequently discovered in the director's qualification or appointment.[22] A directors' meeting may take effect by way of conference call.[23] A written resolution (which may consist of more than one document) signed by all the directors is valid as it if had been passed at a meeting of the board of directors.[24]

Under the Companies Act 2014, the minimum number of directors for an LTD is to be reduced from two to one which effectively means there will be no requirement to have a board meeting should a company have only one director.[25] In addition, persons who are not directors may be authorised to bind the company and details of such authorisation may be filed in the Companies Registration Office.[26] Any such registered person and the board of directors have authority to exercise any power of the company and to authorise others to do so.[27] A company may also appoint, under hand or under seal, a person to act as its attorney.[28]

Many companies are still likely to have two or more directors and have a quorum of two so that in such cases a meeting of the directors should take place

---

[20]   See also Keane, *Company Law* (4th edn, Bloomsbury Professional, 2007) at para [12.06].
[21]   Section 158(1) of the Act; this provision is similar to Regulation 80 of Part I of Table A to the Companies Act 1963.
[22]   Section 135 of the Act.
[23]   Section 161(6) of the Act.
[24]   Section 161(1) and (5) of the Act.
[25]   Section 128(1) of the Act.
[26]   Section 39(1) of the Act.
[27]   Section 40(1) of the Act.
[28]   Section 41(1) of the Act; the Bill as initiated required an attorney to be appointed under seal, but this requirement was removed as the Bill passed through the Oireachtas.

to approve the borrowing and guaranteeing and/or, as the case may be, giving security. It might be anticipated that SMEs are more likely to operate through one director and thus in the case of SME lending there may be no need to have approved board minutes.

(b) Articles of association

[5.012] All companies, other than the LTD, will have an identifiable articles of association, although most of the provisions of what was Table A will apply as statutory defaults unless the articles of association provide otherwise.[29] The articles of association will continue to set out the rules by which a company is managed internally, although, as just noted are likely to be considerably shorter due to the existence of statutory defaults. The practice of lenders to review the company's articles of association is likely to remain. The LTD may have regulations as part of its constitution which could set out any variation of its rules from that set out in the Companies Act.[30]

[5.013] The persons who decide on behalf of the company whether to implement a banking transaction and approve the underlying documentation remain the board of directors, or where only one director that director, or where a person is registered to bind the company that person. Nothing has changed here.[31] Revocation of a registered person's authority to act will not be effective unless and until the company notifies the Registrar of Companies of the revocation in the prescribed form.[32]

(c) Rule in Turquand's case

[5.014] This rule emanates from the decision in *The Royal British Bank v Turquand*[33] and is given specific mention in the Companies Act 2014[34] as applying with regard to persons authorised to bind the company. Under this rule persons dealing with a company are assumed to have read the company's constitution, as filed in the Companies Registration Office, and to have ascertained that a proposed transaction is not inconsistent with it.[35] The rule

---

[29] For DACs see s 967(3) and Schedule 7 or 8, for PLCs see s 1006(3) and Schedule 9, for guarantee companies see s 1176 and Schedule 10, and for unlimited companies see s 1223(3) and Schedule 11 or 12.

[30] Section 19(2) and Schedule 1.

[31] The European Communities (Companies) Regulations 1973 (SI 163/1973) enabled persons to be registered with the Companies Registration Office to bind the company.

[32] Section 39(3) of the Act.

[33] *The Royal British Bank v Turquand* (1856) 6 El & Bl 327.

[34] Section 40(11).

[35] For further reading on this rule and its scope see Courtney, *The Law of Companies* (3rd edn, Bloomsbury Professional, 2012) at para 7.123 to 7.126; see also McCormack, "The Indoor Management Rule in Ireland" (1935) ILSI 17.

does not require the person to enquire into the regularity as to how the transaction was entered into.[36]

[5.015] This rule was successfully relied upon in *Ulster Investment Bank Ltd v Euro Estates Ltd and Drumkill Ltd.*[37] In that case, Carroll J held that the bank could rely on the rule in *Turquand's case*; the bank was not obliged to call for copies of the board resolutions or make specific enquiries but was entitled to assume that such authorisations had been properly dealt with in accordance with the company's articles of association. In that case, as in most financing transactions, it was a condition precedent to the advance of funds that copies of the appropriate board resolutions would be furnished to the bank's legal advisers. The question arose as to whether this requirement disentitled the bank from relying on the rule in *Turquand's case*. Carroll J found the bank acted *bona fide* throughout and had no reason to believe that the resolution furnished to it had not been validly passed at a meeting with a quorum present. Furthermore, it was entitled to assume that the affixing of the company's seal to the mortgage was evidence that the mortgage itself had been properly approved by the company.[38]

[5.016] In advising on an appropriate practice to be adopted, despite the rule in *Turquand's case* as applied by Carroll J,[39] the current practice of calling for a certified copy of a board resolution should continue[40] – to do otherwise might run the risk of not being seen to be acting in accordance with best practice.[41]

The ability to rely on the minutes is supported by Finlay J's decision in *Allied Irish Banks Ltd v Ardmore Studios International (1972) Ltd.*[42] Finlay J held that it was sufficient to rely on a copy of a board resolution, certified by a director and by the company secretary, showing the date of the board resolution and that the borrowing was approved at the meeting. The absence of notice to a third

---

[36] As explained by Jervis CJ (1856) 6 El & Bl 327 at 332: "We may now take for granted that the dealings with these companies are not like dealings with other partnerships, and that the parties dealing with them are bound to read the statute and the deed of settlement. But they are not bound to do more. And the party here on reading the deed of settlement would find, not a prohibition from borrowing, but a permission to do so on certain conditions. Finding that the authority might be made complete by a resolution, he would have a right to infer the fact of a resolution authorising that which on the face of the document appeared to be legitimately done."

[37] *Ulster Investment Bank Ltd v Euro Estates Ltd and Drumkill Ltd* [1982] ILRM 57.

[38] See also *County of Gloucester Bank v Rudry Merthyr Steam and House Coal Colliery Company* [1895] 1 Ch 629.

[39] In *Ulster Investment Bank Ltd v Euro Estates Ltd and Drumkill Ltd* [1982] ILRM 57 at 65.

[40] See also *Lingard's Bank Security Documents* (5th edn) at paras 2.13 to 2.20.

[41] See *Roche and Roche v Peilow and Peilow* [1986] ILRM 189.

[42] *Allied Irish Banks Ltd v Ardmore Studios International (1972) Ltd* (30 May 1973, unreported) HC.

director or any actual minutes of the board meeting[43] were considered by Finlay J to be "classical examples of an irregularity in the internal management of the company".[44]

[5.017] Under common law any action carried out by a director or directors without authorisation from the board can be ratified by the board retrospectively[45] provided the director whose action is sought to be ratified must have purported to act for the company, and at the time of the ratification the company must have been capable of entering into the transaction.

Matters concerning security

(a) Corporate certificate

[5.018] Typically, at the time of entering into any security documentation, a company will be required to provide a certificate, usually known as a corporate certificate or a directors' certificate, whereby directors of the company certify certain factual matters relating to the company such as solvency, absence of litigation and other events/information concerning the company which should be best known by the directors. It is not anticipated that this would change even where there is only one director. In such event the single director will be signing the certificate.

(b) Sealing of security

[5.019] It is not anticipated that the security itself will in any way change as a result of the Companies Act 2014 including the execution of an agreement under seal. However, the attesting requirements have been made more flexible than the previous requirements of Regulation 115 of Part I of Table A to the Companies Act 1963. Unless a company's constitution provides otherwise, the following provisions will apply: A director need no longer attest to the sealing, but there must still be two signatories. As before, a company's seal can be used only by the authority of its directors or of a committee of directors.[46] The agreement to which the seal is affixed is to be signed by a director or by some other person appointed for that purpose by the directors (or a committee of

---

[43] See also *Re Burke Clancy & Company Ltd* (23 May 1974, unreported) HC, Kenny J, where the absence of any minute in the minute book did not affect the validity of the borrowing.

[44] Finlay J followed the decision in *Duck v Tower Galvanising Company Ltd* [1901] 2 KB 314 which held that a company's debenture was validly created notwithstanding that no directors of the company had been appointed and no resolution to issue the debentures had been passed.

[45] See *Firth v Staines* [1897] 2 QB 70; approved and applied in the Supreme Court by Kenny J in *Bank of Ireland Finance Ltd v Rockfield Ltd* [1979] IR 21 at 35.

[46] Section 43(2)(a) of the Act.

directors), and countersigned by the company's secretary, or a director or by such person appointed for the purpose by the directors (or a committee of directors).[47]

The provisions are varied slightly to accommodate the use of the seal by a registered person.[48]

(c) Enforcement of share charges

[5.020] In taking security over shares, typically a lender will seek to have the directors' veto arising under Regulation 3 of Part II of Table A overridden where a share transfer is presented for registration by a chargee or its receiver. Nothing will change here and this will still be a requirement as the equivalent of Regulation 3 is now incorporated in the Companies Act 2014[49] and there will have to be a specific change to a company's constitution by special resolution to override the veto.

(d) Guarantees and security given by company for the benefit of directors and connected parties

[5.021] The restrictions on companies giving guarantees and security for obligations of directors and connected parties as set out in s 31 of the Companies Act 1990 are re-enacted in s 239 of the Act with certain modifications as outlined in Ch 4, *Changes in the Law of Directors' Duties*. The principal change to the law on this area arises in the form of the validation procedure whereby an accountant's certificate is no longer required. The validation procedure, now known as the summary approval procedure, is the same procedure as for validating financial assistance and is outlined below in paras **[5.039]** to **[5.046]**.[50]

While large financings in practice involve parent/subsidiary guarantees which will come within the exemption provided by s 243 of the Act, the change brought about by dropping the requirement for an accountant's certificate should ease the ability of the many family connected corporate businesses to raise finance more readily.

Financial assistance given by way of security

[5.022] At any time where security is to be taken, whether it be a guarantee, mortgage, charge or pledge, the statutory requirements for the giving of

---

47 Section 43(2)(b) of the Act.
48 Section 43(3) of the Act where the agreement will be countersigned in the manner provided in s 43(2).
49 Section 95(1)(a).
50 As recommended in para 5.2.14 of the First Report (in 2001) of the Company Law Review Group.

financial assistance must be considered.[51] Section 82(2) and (4) of the Act provides that, subject to certain specified exceptions (set out in sub-ss (5) and (6)), it shall not be lawful for a company[52] to give, directly or indirectly, or by means of a loan or guarantee, the provision of security[53] or otherwise, any financial assistance for the purpose[54] of an acquisition[55] made or to be made by any person of any shares in the company, or, where the company is a subsidiary company, in its holding company. Accordingly, the financial assistance section should still appear on every practitioner's check-list in advising on financing transactions.

(a) Directly or indirectly

[5.023] The reference to "directly or indirectly" has been retained from s 60 of the Companies Act 1963. The word "indirectly" has caught a transaction where a company lent money to a person who deposited the funds with a bank who lent the same amount to a purchaser who used that loan to purchase shares in the company.[56] However, the scope for financial assistance applying is now more limited by the deletion of the words "*in connection with*" (which were in s 60 of the Companies Act 1963). These words were regarded by the High Court as

---

51 For a brief historical background see Ussher, *Company Law in Ireland* (Sweet & Maxwell, 1986) p 319; for consideration of similar English provisions see Roberts, *Financial Assistance for the Acquisition of Shares* (Oxford University Press, 2005); see also Smith, "The Parameters of Financial Assistance Explored: Current Limitations and Proposed Amendments" (Royal Irish Academy Dublin, 9 November 2011); Ambrose, "Financial Assistance: Do we really need prevention and the cure" (2012) 19 CLP 47.

52 "Company" is defined in s 2(1) of the Act as meaning that subject to s 10, "a company formed and registered under this Act, or an existing company"; "existing company" is defined under the same section as "a company formed and registered in a register kept in the State under the Joint Stock Companies Acts, the Companies Act, 1862, the Companies (Consolidation) Act 1908" or the Companies Act 1963; s 10 provides that "unless expressly provided otherwise, a reference ... to a company is a reference to a private company limited by shares".

53 "A usual way, and maybe the only way, in which a company could give financial assistance by means of the provision of a security in circumstances which would not amount to the giving of financial assistance by means of a loan or guarantee would be by entering into a debenture" [which incorporated a charge]: Fisher J in *Heald v O'Connor* [1971] 2 All ER 1105 at 1109.

54 In *Chaston v SWP Group Plc* [2003] 1 BCLC 675, the English Court of Appeal held that to constitute a breach of this prohibition it was sufficient if even only one of the purposes was to assist in the acquisition.

55 "Acquisition" in relation to shares, means acquisition by subscription, purchase, exchange or otherwise: see s 82(1) of the Act.

56 *Selanger United Rubber Estates Ltd v Cradock (No 3)* [1968] 2 All ER 1073.

having "wide import",[57] thereby leading to a cautious approach by practitioners who required any doubtful transactions to be validated.

(b) Purpose

[5.024] What has happened here is that under the Companies Act 1963, s 60, the prohibition applied to "any financial assistance for the purpose of or in connection with a purchase or subscription", whereas the Companies Act 2014, s 82 states "any financial assistance for the purpose of an acquisition". Because of the previous reference to *"in connection with"*, there was in practice no analysis of "for the purpose" because a prospective financial assistance transaction was always caught by the words "in connection with".

[5.025] In analysing the phrase "for the purpose of" it is difficult to improve upon the analysis of Catherine Roberts in her published work *Financial Assistance for the Acquisition of Shares*,[58] where in considering similar provisions under the English Companies Act 1985 she stated:[59]

> "A company providing the financial assistance must have the object of assisting the acquisition of shares. It is not sufficient if the provision of the financial assistance is in connection with or associated with the acquisition of shares or if the provision of the financial assistance results in assisting in an acquisition of shares. The question that has to be asked is what was the object of a company in providing financial assistance.
>
> A careful analysis of the particular facts of a transaction must take place in order to ascertain whether direct or indirect financial assistance has been given for the purpose of the acquisition or for the purpose of reducing or discharging the liability so incurred.
>
> Even if there is financial assistance in a transaction it will not breach the prohibition unless it is for the purpose of an acquisition of shares."

[5.026] The Act does not prohibit a financial assistance transaction where the company's "principal purpose" in giving the financial assistance is not to give it for the purpose of any such acquisition of shares or if the financial assistance is only an "incidental part of some larger purpose of the company". This exception applies only where the assistance is given in good faith and in the interests of the company.[60]

---

57 Murphy J in *Eccles Hall Ltd v Bank of Nova Scotia, Paramount Enterprises Ltd and O'Keeffe* (3 February 1995, unreported) HC.

58 Roberts, *Financial Assistance for the Acquisition of Shares* (Oxford University Press, 2005).

59 Roberts, *Financial Assistance for the Acquisition of Shares* (Oxford University Press, 2005) at para 6.09

60 Section 82(5) of the Act.

In analysing the House of Lords' decision in *Brady v Brady*[61] of the equivalent carve-out in the English legislation, Catherine Roberts wrote:[62]

"The phrase 'in good faith in the interests of the company' had to be construed as a single composite expression. That phrase imposed a subjective test, that is to say whether those who procured the giving of the financial assistance were acting in the genuine belief and perception that what was being done was for the advancement of the corporate and commercial interests of T Brady & Sons Limited. In order to rely on that single composite phrase, it required those who were responsible for the acts in question to act in the genuine belief that what was being done was in the company's interests."

[5.027] In *Plaut v Steiner*[63] it was held that the financial assistance could not have been given in good faith and in the interests of the company as to do so would have rendered the company insolvent.

(c) Statutory non-application of prohibition

[5.028] The prohibition on the giving of financial assistance does not apply to several types of transactions which are set out in s 82(6) of the Act. These broadly replicate s 60(12) of the Companies Act 1963 as amended by s 56(1) of the Investment Funds, Companies and Miscellaneous Provisions Act 2005,[64] and include:

"(a) the giving of financial assistance in accordance with the Summary Approval Procedure;

(e) where the lending of money is part of the ordinary business of the company, the lending of money by a company in the ordinary course of its business;

(h) the giving of financial assistance –

(i) by means of a loan of guarantee, the provision of security or otherwise to discharge the liability under, or effect that which is commonly known as a refinancing of, any arrangement or transaction that gave rise to the provision of financial assistance, being financial assistance referred to in subsection (2) that has already been given by the company in accordance with the Summary Approval Procedure or section 60(2) of the Act of 1963; or

(ii) by means of any subsequent loan or guarantee, provision of security or otherwise to effect a refinancing of –

(I) refinancing referred to subparagraph (i); or

---

61 *Brady v Brady* [1989] AC 755.
62 *Brady v Brady* [1989] AC 755 at para 8.10.
63 *Plaut v Steiner* (1989) 5 BCC 352.
64 Recommended in 2001 by the Company Law Review Group, see First Report at para 5.4.

> (II) refinancing referred to in this subparagraph that has been
> previously effected (and this subparagraph shall be read
> as permitting the giving of financial assistance to effect
> such subsequent refinancing any number of times)."

[5.029] The first of these exceptions, and likely to be the most significant in practice, is the new summary approval procedure outlined below in paras **[5.039]** to **[5.046]**. It should be noted though that, following on from the European Communities (Public Limited Companies Subsidiaries) Regulations 1997,[65] s 82(7) of the Act provides that:[66]

> "... a private limited subsidiary shall not provide financial assistance in
> accordance with the Summary Approval Procedure for the purpose of the
> acquisition of shares in its parent public company."

However, s 82(8) of the Act provides that the Minister for Jobs, Enterprise and Innovation may by regulations "specify circumstances in which a private limited subsidiary ... may avail of the Summary Approval Procedure".

Public companies are prohibited from giving financial assistance.[67] If the company is a DAC, it should of course have the power under its memorandum and articles of association to enter into the transaction.[68]

[5.030] The fifth exception (set out in para (e)), the lending of money by a company in the ordinary course of business where the lending of money by that company is part of its ordinary business, was the subject of a criminal trial in the matter of the *DPP v Fitzpatrick McAteer and Whelan*.[69]

[5.031] The refinancing exception (set out in para (h)), was broadly brought into effect in 2005 following a recommendation from the Company Law Review Group.[70] This exception has been extended to cover a subsequent refinancing of any arrangement or transaction which gives rise to financial assistance which was validated. This was the intention of the Investment Funds, Companies and Miscellaneous Provisions Act 2005[71] but the language of that legislation in omitting reference to guarantees did not follow correctly the CLRG recommendation. Thus the 2005 refinancing exemption has been of little use in practice. Accordingly, the Act should obviate the unnecessary requirement to

---

[65] SI 67/1997.
[66] This is subject to s 82(8) of the Act, which enables the Minister to make regulations specifying circumstances in which a private limited subsidiary (of a PLC) may avail of the summary approval procedure.
[67] While s 82 of the Act applies to PLCs, the summary approval procedure does not apply to PLCs for this purpose: s 1002(3) of the Act.
[68] See para **[5.004]**.
[69] *DPP v Fitzpatrick McAteer and Whelan* (Circuit Criminal Court, 2014).
[70] See paras 5.4.3 and 5.4.4 of the First Report of the Company Law Review Group in 2001.
[71] Section 56, implemented on 30 June 2005 (SI 323/2005).

validate a refinancing, and in this regard the language of the exemption was further refined at the Committee Stage of the Bill.

(d) Notice of breach

[5.032] Although the opening words of s 82(2) of the Act provide that "it shall not be lawful for a company" to carry out certain transactions,[72] the unlawfulness is in practice overridden by subs (9) which states:

> "Any transaction in breach of this section shall be voidable at the instance of the company against any person (whether a party to the transaction or not) who had notice of the facts which constitute such contravention."

There is no change here from s 60(14) of the Companies Act 1963. The courts have held that if the transaction is to be avoided by the company, the company must prove that the person seeking to uphold the transaction had actual notice and not simply constructive notice of the breach. In *Lombard and Ulster Banking Ltd v The Governor and Company of the Bank of Ireland and Brookhouse School*[73] Costello J held that subs (14) means:[74]

> "(a) that although a transaction in breach of the section is illegal it is only "voidable", not void, and (b) it is only voidable against a person who had notice of the facts which constituted the breach."

In practice, the person who will seek to avoid a transaction (which contravenes s 82) will be a liquidator of the company, so that the company's unsecured creditors may benefit at the expense of the secured creditor. Hence, the need for every lender and its advisers to be ever mindful of s 82.

[5.033] The judiciary have utilised this subsection to prevent a company receiving a windfall, or its unsecured creditors obtaining payment of debts due to them, as a result of obtaining financial assistance in breach of the statutory requirements.

In *Bank of Ireland Finance Ltd v Rockfield Ltd*,[75] the bank granted a loan to persons who wished to purchase a hotel. Security for the loan was to be an equitable mortgage by way of deposit of the title deeds to the hotel. The borrowers used the loan to purchase shares in the defendant, the owner of the hotel. McWilliam J in the High Court held that the bank should have had notice of the purpose for which the borrowers intended to use the moneys advanced and therefore the mortgage could be avoided by the defendant. In reply to the

---

[72] Giving rise to a category of offence for the company and every officer of the company who is in default (Companies Act 2014, s 82(11)).

[73] *Lombard and Ulster Banking Ltd v The Governor and Company of the Bank of Ireland and Brookhouse School* (2 June 1987, unreported) HC, Costello J.

[74] *Lombard and Ulster Banking Ltd v The Governor and Company of the Bank of Ireland and Brookhouse School* (2 June 1987, unreported) HC, Costello J at p 10.

[75] *Bank of Ireland Finance Ltd v Rockfield Ltd* [1979] IR 21.

bank's contention that, on the authority of Lindley LJ,[76] the doctrine of constructive notice did not apply to commercial transactions, McWilliam J concluded:[77]

> "I fully accept the view expressed by Lindley LJ but it seems to me that there must be some limit to the extent to which a person may fail to accept information available to him or fail to make the inquiries normal in his line of business so as to leave himself in the position that he has no notice of something anyone else in the same line of business would have appreciated."

However, the Supreme Court found "considerable difficulty in understanding what the judge meant by this passage",[78] and unanimously allowed the appeal. The Supreme Court held that the transaction between the bank and the borrowers was the loan of money and that it was not the loan of money for the purpose of buying shares in the defendant company; the defendant could not invoke the subsection as the defendant had failed to establish that prior to the transaction the bank had actual notice of the facts alleged to constitute a breach of that section.

[5.034] Although there is no legal obligation on a bank (or other lender) to enquire as to how its funds lent to a company will be utilised,[79] the Supreme Court's decision gives judicial approval for a bank to lend money without knowing or even enquiring precisely how the funds are to be utilised. The bank was thus able to avoid the illegality under s 82 by not having actual knowledge of the basic details of the project being financed by them. Although this was a decision of five judges[80] of the Supreme Court it would be unwise to rely upon it in the context that any prudent lender will almost invariably be aware, and should be aware, of how its finance is to be utilised. Nonetheless, it is a useful decision to support the validity of security given in contravention of s 82 if the person relying on the security can show that he did not have notice of the facts of the transaction.

[5.035] The decision in fact was applied by Costello J in *Lombard and Ulster Banking Ltd v The Governor and Company of the Bank of Ireland and Brookhouse School*.[81] Although the parties to the transaction understood at the time that the procedure envisaged by s 82's predecessor s 60 of the Companies Act 1963 needed to be complied with, Costello J found that there was non-

---

[76] In *Manchester Trust v Furness* [1895] 2 QB 539 at 545.

[77] *Bank of Ireland Finance Ltd v Rockfield Ltd* [1979] IR 21 at 28.

[78] *Bank of Ireland Finance Ltd v Rockfield Ltd* [1979] IR 21 at 35 per Kenny J (the other four members of the court agreeing with him).

[79] See Harman LJ in *Re Introductions Ltd* [1969] 1 All ER 887 at 890.

[80] O'Higgins CJ, Henchy J, Griffin J and Parke J each of whom agreed with the judgment of Kenny J.

[81] *Lombard and Ulster Banking Ltd v The Governor and Company of the Bank of Ireland and Brookhouse School* (2 June 1987, unreported) HC.

compliance in at least two respects, namely, the statutory declaration was not made at the appropriate time and the resolution passed was not a special resolution.[82] Costello J held that although it was not shown that s 60 had been complied with, as the evidence showed that the plaintiff had no knowledge of the failure to comply with s 60, the charge was held to be valid.[83] It thus came down to a question of notice, Costello J stating:[84]

> "if a lender knows that an attempt to validate a prohibited transaction and avoid breaching the section by adopting the procedures set out in subsection (2), (3) and (4) is to be made I do not think he has notice of any breach within the meaning of the subsection unless it can be shown (a) that there was in fact non-compliance with the subsections and (b) that he knew of the facts which resulted in non-compliance.

> ... as to the nature of the 'notice', it is not sufficient for the liquidator to show that if Lombard and Ulster had made proper inquiries that they would have ascertained that the company had failed to comply with the subsections. It must be shown that Lombard and Ulster had 'actual notice' of the facts which constituted the breach, that is (a) that they or their officials actually knew that the required procedures were not adopted or that they knew facts from which they must have inferred that the company had failed to adopt the required procedures, or (b) that an agent of theirs actually knew of the failure or knew facts from which he must have inferred that a failure had occurred (see *Bank of Ireland v Rockfield*). 'Constructive notice' of the failure is not sufficient for subsection (14)."

[5.036] The Supreme Court's decision in *Bank of Ireland Finance Ltd v Rockfield Ltd*[85] and in particular its interpretation as to "notice" under subs (14) was applied also by Murphy J in *Eccles Hall Ltd v Bank of Nova Scotia, Paramount Enterprises Ltd and O'Keeffe*.[86] Murphy J said[87] it was clear from the Supreme Court's judgment that:

> "the word 'notice' as used in that subsection (and indeed in all legislation relating to commercial as distinct from conveyancing matters) is 'actual notice' as opposed to and distinct from 'constructive' notice."

82 *Lombard and Ulster Banking Ltd v The Governor and Company of the Bank of Ireland and Brookhouse School* (2 June 1987, unreported) HC at p 9.
83 For a criticism of this decision and the earlier Supreme Court decision see Lynch (1988) 10 DULJ 146.
84 *Lombard and Ulster Banking Ltd v The Governor and Company of the Bank of Ireland and Brookhouse School* (2 June 1987, unreported) HC at p 10.
85 *Bank of Ireland Finance Ltd v Rockfield Ltd* [1979] IR 21.
86 *Eccles Hall Ltd v Bank of Nova Scotia, Paramount Enterprises Ltd and O'Keeffe* (3 February 1995, unreported) HC.
87 *Eccles Hall Ltd v Bank of Nova Scotia, Paramount Enterprises Ltd and O'Keeffe* (3 February 1995, unreported) HC at p 16.

[5.037] The interpretation of notice being actual notice, and the more onerous requirement (for a company or its liquidator) to show actual rather than constructive notice, should not give a false sense of security to banks (or other lenders). The High Court's decision in *Re Northside Motor Company Ltd, Eddison v Allied Irish Banks Ltd*[88] should jolt any bank and its lawyer out of any complacency enjoyed from other court decisions. Essentially in that case moneys were advanced to a shareholder to acquire further shares in a company; the company undertook to guarantee repayment of the advance – a classic and straightforward s 60 transaction. Costello J considered the bank to be aware of the non-compliance with the section and accordingly the company was entitled to avoid the guarantee.

(e) Transaction voidable

[5.038] Where compliance with the requirements of s 82 of the Act has not been fully carried out it would be wrong for any bank and its lawyer to draw comfort from the fact that, as such a transaction is voidable[89] at the instance of the company only, the shareholders and directors are known to the bank and are unlikely to seek to avoid the transaction or might be estopped from avoiding it having been a party to it or sanctioned it albeit improperly. In the event of the company having a receiver or liquidator appointed to it, the liquidator if not the receiver will see it as his duty (to the company's creditors) to challenge the transaction or at least seek the directions of the court.[90]

Summary approval procedure

[5.039] The Act introduces a new procedure which is to apply, inter alia, to transactions for financial assistance and for guarantees and security given by companies for directors and connected persons, either activity being referred to as "a restricted activity".[91] The law has been simplified by providing that the same procedure be carried out for both types of transaction.[92] This validation procedure, previously commonly referred to and misnamed as a "whitewash",[93]

---

88 *Re Northside Motor Company Ltd, Eddison v Allied Irish Banks Ltd* (24 July 1985, unreported) HC, Costello J.
89 Section 82(9) of the Act.
90 See the remarks of Harman J in *Re NL Electrical Ltd, Ghosh v 3i plc* [1994] 1 BCLC 22 at 25 (the Irish decisions have invariably resulted from applications for directions by liquidators).
91 Section 200 of the Act. These are two of seven transactions which can be approved utilising the SAP: see para **[2.063]**.
92 As recommended by the Company Law Review Group's First Report in 2001 at para 5.2.14; the same procedure applies also for a members' voluntary winding up.
93 Whitewash means to plaster over with a white composition: to cover or coat with whitewash. (contd.../)

is now called the summary approval procedure. The summary approval procedure entails compliance with the following conditions:[94]

(1)   a special resolution of the company must be passed approving the restricted activity, the resolution being passed not more than 12 months prior to the commencement of the activity; and

(2)   a copy of the directors' declaration (referred to below) is forwarded to each member of the company with the notice of the special resolution or where the special resolution is to be by way of written resolution a copy of the directors' declaration is appended to the proposed text of the resolution.

There is no change in law here to the current financial assistance validation.

[5.040] The Summary Approval Procedure may be availed of by private companies limited by shares, designated activity companies, companies limited by guarantee.[95] However, a private company which is a subsidiary of a public limited company cannot avail of the procedure.[96]

(a) Declaration of directors

[5.041] The declaration should be signed by a majority of the directors (where there is an even number of directors more than one-half of the number of directors must make the declaration).[97] The declaration should be made at a meeting of the directors held not earlier than 30 days before the passing of the special resolution.[98]

[5.042] The matters to be addressed in the directors' declaration are to be expanded in the case of a financial assistance validation (but currently in the procedure in respect of directors and connected persons validation) so as to include, the circumstances in which the transaction or arrangement is to be entered into[99] and the nature of the benefit which will accrue to the company directly or indirectly from entering into the transaction or arrangement.[100]

---

[93]   (\....contd) To give a fair appearance to; to cover up, conceal, or gloss over the faults or blemishes. To clear (a bankrupt or insolvent) by judicial process from liability for his debts. To beat (the opponents) so that they fail to score: *The Shorter Oxford English Dictionary.*

[94]   Section 202(1) of the Act.

[95]   Sections 964(1) and 1173(1) of the Act.

[96]   Section 82(7) of the Act.

[97]   Majority means, "the greater number or part; more than half": *The Shorter Oxford English Dictionary*; or, "a number that is more than half of a total": *Black's Law Dictionary* (7th edn, West Group, 1999).

[98]   Section 202(6) of the Act.

[99]   Section 203(1)(a) of the Act.

[100] Section 203(1)(e) of the Act.

[5.043] In determining whether the company will be able to pay or discharge its debts and other liabilities in full, the directors will not be required to assume (where relevant) either that the company will be called upon to pay moneys on foot of a guarantee given or, as the case may be, that security given will be realised.[101]

[5.044] Currently, unless all of the company's members vote in favour of the requisite special resolution, the transaction whereby the financial assistance is to be given cannot be carried out before the expiry of 30 days after the date of that resolution. The 30-day waiting period no longer applies where members holding more than 90 per cent in nominal value of each class of issued voting shares have voted in favour of the special resolution (but continues to apply where a special resolution is passed but without 90 per cent of its votes cast in favour of the resolution).[102] This can be helpful if there is a shareholder or shareholders (holding less than 10 per cent of the share capital) who is not or are not readily contactable, and thus in such circumstances a financing transaction can be facilitated.

[5.045] Unlike the new arrangement for validating a transaction, formerly otherwise prohibited by s 31 of the Companies Act 1990 (or indeed under the former financial assistance provisions in the UK), there is no requirement for an accountant's report for the summary approval procedure.

[5.046] An appropriate procedure for availing of the new summary approval procedure is to hold a meeting of the board of directors of the company giving the guarantee or security. Assuming both a quorum and a majority of the directors are present (and none of the directors is conflicted from voting on the issues), the board considers the relevant issues, and if comfortable with these issues, resolves that the guarantee or security be given. The directors will make a declaration and then resolve that a meeting of the members be called to consider and, if thought fit by them, to pass a special resolution authorising the giving of the guarantee or the security.

(b) Benefit to the company

[5.047] The directors' declaration must state "the nature of the benefit which will accrue to the company directly or indirectly from entering into the transaction or arrangement".[103] Thus, in the first instance it is for the directors, acting in the course of their duty as directors, in managing the business of the company to decide whether the guarantee or security is for the benefit of the company.[104] Although there is some, albeit limited, case law on the need for

---

[101] Section 203(2) of the Act.
[102] Section 211(2) of the Act.
[103] Section 203(1)(e) of the Act.
[104] Under the Companies Act 2014.

corporate benefit in giving a guarantee or security, the leading UK publications are remarkably sparse in dealing with the issue.[105] In considering other common law jurisdictions for guidance, one needs to be aware that in some jurisdictions guarantees given at an undervalue are prohibited by statute.[106]

[5.048] Nowadays, in lending transactions, even without a statutory requirement to consider the benefit accruing to the company, it is invariably the practice that a guarantee will be given by a company only where the company's board of directors has concluded that the company obtains a benefit in giving the guarantee.[107] The question arises as to how the directors are to assess whether or not the giving of a guarantee is for the company's benefit. In *Charterbridge Corporation, Ltd v Lloyds Bank, Ltd*[108] Pennycuick J stated:[109]

> "The proper test ... must be whether an intelligent and honest man in the position of a director of the company concerned, could, in the whole of the existing circumstances, have reasonably believed that the transaction was for the benefit of the company."

[5.049] If the guarantee and/or security is being given to support indebtedness being provided to another company which is part of the group of companies of which the guarantor is a member, the directors may well take the view that the finance being made available to a fellow group member benefits all companies in the group including the guarantor.[110] Support for this line of interpretation can be found in *Re PMPA Garage (Longmile) Ltd*[111] (referred to in the next paragraph), and also by the New Zealand Court of Appeal[112] which indicated

---

[105] With the exception of *Lingard's Bank Security Documents* (5th edn, Butterworths) Ch 4; see also the Australian publication edited by Burton, *Directions in Finance Law* (1990, Butterworths) ch 7.

[106] In the UK, Insolvency Act 1986, s 238.

[107] In the absence of a benefit to the corporate guarantor, the beneficiary's lawyer is likely to advise that the guarantee may be unenforceable, despite the decision of McWilliam J in *Re Metro Investment Trust Ltd* (26 May 1977, unreported) HC; for further reading see Parkinson, "Non-Commercial Transactions and the Interest of Creditors" (1984) 5 Co Law 55; Dawson, "Commercial Benefit" (1991) [107] LQR 202; Price, "Intra-Group Guarantees" (1997) PLC (May p 15).

[108] *Charterbridge Corporation, Ltd v Lloyds Bank, Ltd* [1969] 2 All ER 1185.

[109] *Charterbridge Corporation, Ltd v Lloyds Bank, Ltd* [1969] 2 All ER 1185 at 1194 where Pennycuick J elaborates further on the incorrect approaches of considering only the company's interest, or only the group's interest.

[110] Although the directors should be mindful of the position as indicated at para 1925 of the Cork Committee's "Report on Insolvency Law and Practice" (Cmnd 8558): "... each company in a group is a separate legal entity, and the directors of one company are not entitled to sacrifice the interests of that company to the interests of the group as a whole ... the existence of separate groups of creditors of each company requires the directors of each company to have separate regard to its particular interests."

[111] *Re PMPA Garage (Longmile) Ltd* [1992] 1 IR 315.

[112] *Nicholson v Permakraft (NZ) Ltd* [1985] 1 NZLR 242.

that a cloistered approach to a view of the law which requires directors to focus on the interests of the company and ignore the interests of the group as a whole "should be put aside as out of touch with reasonable commercial practice".[113]

[5.050] In *Re PMPA Garage (Longmile) Ltd*[114] a number of companies in the PMPA group guaranteed each other's indebtedness for advances made to them by PMPS, another group member. Murphy J acknowledged that a director of a subsidiary is often placed in a dilemma and held that, in discharging his duties to a company, a director is entitled to consider the interests of the group as a whole. He said:[115]

> "In the nature of things companies associated with each other as parent and subsidiary or through common shareholders or who share common management and common titles or logos cannot safely ignore the problems of each other. Even the most independently minded director of any such related company would necessarily recognise that he should and perhaps must protect the interests of the group as a whole or else take steps to secure that the particular company disassociates itself from the group."

Murphy J held that the execution of the guarantees, insofar as it allowed each company to borrow money or enjoy the prospect of borrowing money, had benefited each guarantor in the group.[116]

[5.051] Subsequent to that decision, Finlay Geoghegan J held that considering the group position must be balanced by the fact that the directors are required to fully inform themselves about the company's affairs and must show evidence of a real consideration of whether significant transactions or operations to be undertaken were desirable in the interest of the company or could be said to be for the benefit of the company. In *Re 360 Atlantic (Ireland) Ltd: O'Ferral v Coughlan*,[117] Finlay Geoghegan J held that (1) where a group corporate structure existed, a director of the wholly-owned Irish subsidiary must be able to establish at a minimum that he informed himself about the affairs of the Irish subsidiary company as distinct from any other company within the group. There must be evidence of a real consideration by the directors of whether significant transactions or operations to be undertaken were desirable in the interest of the Irish subsidiary company; (2) there was no evidence that the directors, either

---

113 *Nicholson v Permakraft (NZ) Ltd* [1985] 1 NZLR 242 at 251 per Cooke J.
114 *Re PMPA Garage (Longmile) Ltd* [1992] 1 IR 315.
115 *Re PMPA Garage (Longmile) Ltd* [1992] 1 IR 315 at 324.
116 *Re PMPA Garage (Longmile) Ltd* [1992] 1 IR 315 at 327: "it was in the interest and for the benefit of each individual company to ensure and promote the success of the other companies in the group and that in addition to the benefits secured indirectly in that way the individual companies also enjoyed at least the opportunity, and perhaps the reality, of advances ... which could only have been obtained on the security of the fellow members of the group as a whole."
117 *Re 360 Atlantic (Ireland) Ltd: O'Ferral v Coughlan* [2004] 4 IR 266.

collectively with their fellow directors or individually, addressed in a substantive way or determined whether significant transactions entered into by the company were in the interests of the company; and (3) notwithstanding the almost total dependence of the company on other companies within the group, it was not permissible for the directors of the company to effectively abdicate all decision-making in relation to the affairs of the company.

[5.052] More recently, the Supreme Court held in *Re Mitek Holdings Ltd: Grace v Kachkarand*,[118] that (1) although the inter-relationships of companies in a group might affect the extent of a director's responsibilities and it might be normal and permissible to take account of group policy, the separate corporate existence of an Irish subsidiary company could not be ignored and its rights and property interests had to be independently considered; (2) in permitting corporate group contributions at a time when the companies were unable to meet their obligations to creditors, the directors did not act responsibly in relation to the affairs of the companies; and (3) in allowing security to be created over the assets of the companies at a time when it was apparent the companies were insolvent, the directors did not act responsibly in relation to the affairs of the companies.

In practice, in recent years greater emphasis is placed on the recording of the commercial benefit in the minutes to at least dissuade liquidators from taking an action for lack of commercial benefit. This is an important point for the company and its directors. Directors who cause the company to give a guarantee without benefit to the company could leave themselves open to a court compelling them to make a contribution in respect of misfeasance.[119]

(c) Directors' liability

[5.053] A lawyer advising directors making the declaration should point out to them the provisions of s 210(1) of the Act which provide that any director making the declaration:

> "without having reasonable grounds for the opinion that the company having entered into the transaction or arrangement will be able to pay or discharge its debts and other liabilities in full as they fall due during the period of 12 months after the date of the relevant act may be subject to a declaration by the court that the directors making the declaration shall be personally responsible, without any limitation of liability, for all or any of the debts or other liabilities of the company."[120]

[5.054] Furthermore, if the company is wound up within 12 months after the date of the making of the declaration and its debts are not paid or provided for in

---

[118] *Re Mitek Holdings Ltd: Grace v Kachkarand* [2010] 3 IR 374.
[119] Section 612 of the Act.
[120] Section 210(1) of the Act.

full within 12 months after the commencement of the winding up, "it shall be presumed, until the contrary is shown, that each director of the company who made the declaration did not have reasonable grounds for his or her opinion".[121]

The first part of this section is new and should focus the minds of the directors and in certain circumstances may be a cause of concern and even result in the transaction not proceeding. The directors, of course, could be liable for reckless trading,[122] or where the company is insolvent at the time the guarantee is given the directors will be liable to the company's creditors for failing to preserve the company's assets for its creditors.[123]

(d) Filing the directors' declaration

[5.055] A copy of the declaration must be delivered to the Registrar of Companies not later than 21 days after the date on which the financial assistance is commenced namely the security provided.[124] Late delivery, even by one day, invalidates the transaction the subject of the summary approval procedure;[125] in such cases the procedure must be re-started.

[5.056] The importance of strict compliance (as to the filing under the section's predecessor s 60 of the Companies Act 1963) was emphasised by the High Court in *Lombard and Ulster Banking Ltd v The Governor and Company of the Bank of Ireland and Brookhouse School*,[126] where Costello J stated:[127]

> "The section makes illegal the granting of financial assistance (as defined) and if exemption for a transaction ... is claimed because of the adoption of the procedures laid down ... then strict compliance is necessary. It is not sufficient to show that all the shareholders had authorised their solicitors to take the necessary steps and that they subsequently ratified what in fact was done. If the procedural requirements were not adopted the transaction is an illegal one, if in fact it involved the granting of financial assistance ..."

[5.057] All may not be lost as an amendment was made at Committee Stage of the Bill whereby the court, on the application of any interested party, may declare that, notwithstanding a failure to comply with the filing deadline, the restricted activity shall be valid. To make such a declaration the court must be satisfied that it would be just and equitable to do so.[128]

---

[121] Section 210(2) of the Act.
[122] Section 610 of the Act.
[123] See the Supreme Court's decision in *Re Frederick Inns Ltd (in Liquidation)* [1994] 1 ILRM 387.
[124] Section 203(3) of the Act.
[125] Section 201(3) of the Act.
[126] *Lombard and Ulster Banking Ltd v The Governor and Company of the Bank of Ireland and Brookhouse School* (2 June 1987, unreported) HC, Costello J.
[127] *Lombard and Ulster Banking Ltd v The Governor and Company of the Bank of Ireland and Brookhouse School* (2 June 1987, unreported) HC, Costello J at p 9.
[128] Section 203(4) of the Act.

(e) Form of declaration

[5.058] Section 202(6) of the Act provides that the declaration shall be made by a majority of the directors at a meeting held not earlier than 30 days prior to the meeting at which the special resolution is to be passed. The contents of the declaration are regulated by s 203(1), which reads:

"The declaration shall state –

(a)   the circumstances in which the transaction or arrangement is to be entered into;

(b)   the nature of the transaction or arrangement;[129]

(c)   the person or persons to or for whom the transaction or arrangement is to be made;

(d)   the purpose for which the company is entering into the transaction or arrangement;

(e)   the nature of the benefit which will accrue to the company directly or indirectly from entering into the transaction or arrangement; and

(f)   that the declarants have made a full inquiry into the affairs of the company and that, having done so, they have formed the opinion that the company, having entered into the transaction or arrangement (the "relevant act"), will be able to pay or discharge its debts and other liabilities in full as they fall due during the period of 12 months after the date of the relevant act."

In England it has been held that in interpreting the requirements of the equivalent English section the severe consequences of non-compliance had to be kept in mind; thus a borderline case was likely to be decided in favour of compliance.[130]

(f) Cancellation of the special resolution

[5.059] If the special resolution of the members of the company validating the transaction is passed, by the holders of less than 90 per cent in nominal value of the voting shares, then the guarantee or security cannot be given before the expiry of 30 days after the special resolution has been passed.[131] The holders of not less than 10 per cent in nominal value of the company's issued share capital or any class thereof may apply to the court to have the resolution varied provided such application is made within 30 days after the date on which the special

---

[129]   Language such as "the granting of a guarantee supported by a fixed and floating charge over the company's assets in favour of [name of financier]" should be sufficient: see *Re SH & Company (Realisations) 1990 Ltd* [1993] BCLC 1309.

[130]   See *Re SH & Company (Realisations) 1990 Ltd* [1993] BCLC 1309 where Mummery J stated at 1318: "In future solicitors responsible for completing such a statutory declaration should err on the side of caution."

[131]   Section 211(2) of the Act.

resolution is passed.[132] In that event the resolution will take effect only to the extent sanctioned by the court.[133] A person who has consented to, signed or voted in favour of the special resolution cannot join in the application to cancel the resolution.[134]

Registration of charges

(a) Development of the requirement for registration of charges

[5.060] The system for public registration of charges created by companies was established in 1900[135] following the implementation of the 1895 Davey Report.[136] The categories of charges subject to registration were expanded from four to six by the Companies Act 1907[137] and retained by the Companies (Consolidation) Act 1908.[138] Following Ireland's independence from the United Kingdom, the first time consideration was given to any company law reform was in the 1950s by the Company Law Reform Committee chaired by Arthur Cox.[139] The Report of that Committee gave rise to the Companies Act 1963 which in most respects mirrored the English Companies Act 1948 as well as incorporating some recommendations of the Jenkins Committee which reported in 1962 in the United Kingdom.[140] Section 99 of the Companies Act 1963 and s 112 of the Companies Act 1990 extended the category of charges requiring registration.[141] In the year 2013, 7,207 mortgages or charges were registered in the Companies Registration Office.[142]

[5.061] The first serious consideration to reforming the law applicable to registration of corporate security was undertaken by the Company Law Review Group.[143] In its First Report[144] the Company Law Review Group stated:[145]

"The Group believes it is illogical to have a requirement to register some categories of charges but not others, as the secured creditor in each case has

---

[132] Section 211(4), (6) of the Act.
[133] Section 211(7) of the Act.
[134] Section 211(5) of the Act.
[135] Companies Act 1900, s 14.
[136] C7779.
[137] Section 10.
[138] Section 93.
[139] Reported in 1958.
[140] (Cmnd 1749); for a critical analysis of the English system, a system adopted with modification by Ireland, see Gretton, "Registration of Company Charges" (2002) Edin LR 146.
[141] Further additional amendments proposed by the Companies (No 2) Bill 1987 were not enacted.
[142] See *Annual Report of the Companies Registration Office* at p 6.
[143] Established by the Company Law Enforcement Act 2001, s 67.
[144] Issued on 31 December 2001.
[145] Para 5.12.1.

priority. However, EU developments on the registration or otherwise of charges need to be considered. Company law reform on the registration and priority of charges is to be considered in the Review Group's second programme."

The Company Law Review Group's detailed recommendations in its Second Report[146] form the basis of the law of registration brought into effect by ss 408–421 of the Act.

[5.062] Simultaneously in the early part of the 21st century, the United Kingdom considered the reform of the law of registration of corporate security.[147] Many of the new provisions in both jurisdictions have similar themes,[148] although unlike on previous occasions, the provisions in Ireland were considered without regard to the concurrent and mainly later deliberations in the United Kingdom.

(b) Registration of all but excluded security

[5.063] Every "charge" (as defined) created by a company is void against the company's liquidator or any creditor of the company where particulars of the charge are not filed for registration with the Companies Registration Office in accordance with either the one-stage procedure or the two-stage procedure outlined in s 409 of the Companies Act 2014.[149] The courts' application of this statutory provision, or its predecessor s 99 of the Companies Act 1963, is a stark reminder to every solicitor not to overlook filing the necessary particulars.[150] As before, when a charge becomes void from the absence of filing, the money secured by it shall immediately become payable.[151]

---

[146] Issued in March 2004.

[147] *Registration of Company Charges*, October 2000, URN 00/31213; *Modern Company law for a Competitive Economy: Final Report* (June 2001); *Registration of Security Interests: Company Charges and Property other than Land*, Law Commission Consultation Paper No 164 (2002); *Company Security Interests*, Law Commission Consultation Paper No 176 (2004); Company Security Interests, Law Commission No 296 (2005) Cm 6654; Department of Trade and Industry, *The Registration of Companies' Security Interests (Company Charges)*, July 2005; for a very informative article on the development in the UK see Graham, "Registration of Company Charges" [2014] JBL175.

[148] Charges requiring registration are not listed: now all charges require registration save for certain designated exceptions

[149] Section 409(1) of the Act; this provision is "without prejudice to any contract or obligation for repayment of the money secured by the charge": s 409(6).

[150] See *Carroll Group Distributors Ltd v G&F Bourke Ltd and Bourke Sales Ltd* [1990] ILRM 285 and in *Re Shannonside Holdings (in Liquidation)* (20 May 1993, unreported) HC, Costello J.

[151] Section 409(6) of the Act.

[5.064] A new provision is that where particulars of a charging document are filed, but the particulars omit one or more properties to which the charge relates, the charge will be void (as against the company's liquidator, and any creditor) in respect of the omitted properties.[152]

[5.065] The first point to consider is whether any particular document is a "charge" within the meaning of the Act. Section 408(1) of the Act provides:

"... 'charge', in relation to a company, means a mortgage or a charge, in an agreement (written or oral), that is created over an interest in any property[153] of the company (and in section 409(8) and sections 414 to 421 includes a judgment mortgage) but does not include a mortgage or a charge in an agreement (written or oral), that is created over an interest in –

(a)   cash;

(b)   money credited to an account of a financial institution, or any other deposits;

(c)   shares, bonds or debt instruments;

(d)   units in collective investment undertakings or money market instruments; or

(e)   claims and rights (such as dividends or interest) in respect of any thing referred to in any of the foregoing paragraphs (b) to (d)."[154]

The categories of these exclusions are taken from much, but not all, of the European Communities (Financial Collateral Arrangements) Regulations 2010.[155] Furthermore the Minister for Jobs, Enterprise and Innovation is empowered to add to the list of exclusions by ministerial order where "the Minister considers it is necessary or expedient to do so in consequence of any Community act ... relating to financial collateral arrangements."[156] Accordingly, a significant change here is that charges over all, but certain excluded, assets are registrable rather than a charge over certain assets specifically falling within a list of assets (as most recently set out in s 99(2) of the Companies Act 1963 (as amended)).

---

[152]   Section 409(2) of the Act.

[153]   Property includes "assets or undertaking": see s 408(1) of the Act.

[154]   See also s 408(3) of the Act.

[155]   SI 626/2010 (as amended by SI 318/2011); these regulations repealed the initial regulations brought into effect in 2004, SI 1/2004 and SI 89/2004 which give effect to Directive 2002/47/EC; it appears these Regulations would not have exempted registration of a floating charge over these assets, unlike the Companies Act 2014, as a result of this definition: see *Re FZG Realisations Ltd (in Liquidation)* [2014] 1 BCLC 313.

[156]   Section 408(2) of the Act.

[5.066] The application of s 409 to "a company" applies to an LTD, a DAC, a PLC, a CLG and a UC as well as an existing company.[157] Particulars of a charge created by a company over property outside the State must be filed in accordance with the Companies Act 2014.[158] The registration provisions of the Act apply also to an external company that establishes a branch in the State.[159]

(c) Security for financial contracts

[5.067] The requirement to register particulars of charges over assets (other than excluded assets)[160] applies notwithstanding the provisions of the Netting of Financial Contracts Act 1995.[161] This again is new, as recommended by the Company Law Review Group's Second Report.[162]

At first this may seen confusing because it is not contemplated that security over assets typically subject to netting, such as cash or securities, would be subject to registration arising out of the European Communities (Financial Collateral Arrangements) Regulations 2010,[163] or under the Companies Act 2014 because of the definition of "charge".

However, where it is relevant is where non-financial collateral assets, such as land or machinery, are charged to secure the obligations of a debtor under a financial contract. This is a practice which prevailed in the late 1990s, but seems to have gone out of fashion on the grounds of cost. The way it worked was that if a creditor granted the debtor a number of facilities such as invoice discounting, a term loan, a revolving credit facility, a guarantee facility and required the debtor to enter into a hedging agreement to counteract an interest rate rise or a currency exposure, the security for the repayment of the facility granted by the debtor to the creditor would be subject to a stay on enforcement if an examiner was appointed to the debtor.

Where the facility was significant, the creditor in addition to taking the all sums security would take a second set of security to cover only the obligations due to it under the financial contract. This became particularly cumbersome if there were a number of lenders in a lending syndicate. While one set of security in favour of one of the lenders as security agent might be taken to secure all sums, it is necessary by virtue of the definition of financial contract in the Netting of Financial Contracts Act 1995, to take separate security for each creditor to secure the debtor's obligations under the financial contract to that

---

[157] Namely, "a company formed and registered in a register kept in the State under the Joint Stock Companies Acts, the Companies Act 1862, the Companies (Consolidation) Act 1908 or the [Companies Act] 1963": see s 2(1) of the Act.
[158] Section 409(7) of the Act.
[159] Section 1301(2) of the Act; "external company" is defined in s 1300(1).
[160] Under s 408(1), see para [5.063].
[161] Section 421 of the Act.
[162] See para 8.18.2.
[163] SI 626/2010 (as amended by SI 318/2011).

creditor, if such security is to achieve its primary purpose. The primary purpose of such security is that if an examiner were appointed to the company, thereby putting a stay on the all sums security, the separate hedging security could be enforced under the Netting of Financial Contracts Act 1995. This could effectively circumvent the operation of the examinership, as the charged assets to secure the hedging would be taken to make whole the secured swap counterparties leaving the examiner with a diminished or even worthless asset pool to save the company.

[5.068] A literal reading of s 4 of the Netting of Financial Contracts Act 1995 would mean that such hedging security would not require registration under s 409 of the Act. In practice, such security was usually registered. Section 421 of the Act is designed to ensure such security is registered for transparency purposes (although it will not apply to assets falling outside the definition of charge, which more usually apply as collateral to financial contracts).

(d) New registration procedure

[5.069] There are now two methods or procedures whereby particulars of charges may be filed correctly with the Companies Registration Office. The first, known as the one-stage procedure, involves filing with the Companies Registration Office the prescribed particulars of the charge in the prescribed form.[164] The filing must be done "not later than 21 days after the date of the charge's creation".[165]

[5.070] The second method is known as the two-stage procedure. This procedure entails:[166]

(a) delivering a notice (in the prescribed form containing the prescribed particulars) to the Companies Registration Office that the company *intends to create* a charge; and

(b) not later than 21 days after the delivery of the notice, delivering a further notice (to the Companies Registration Office) stating that the charge referred to in the first notice *has been created*.

In the event that the second notice is not delivered within the 21-day time period, the first notice "shall be removed" by the Companies Registration Office.[167]

[5.071] While the first method is simpler, and represents the pre-Companies Act 2014 approach, the second method is preferable as regards protecting the priority of the charge being created. It is therefore a safer practice for a lender or security holder to require compliance with the two-stage procedure when a

---

[164] The form of particulars is likely to be set out in a statutory instrument.
[165] Section 409(3) of the Act.
[166] Section 409(4) of the Act.
[167] Section 409(5) of the Act.

company is creating a charge. The weakness of the first approach has been highlighted in the Second Report of the Company Law Review Group where it is stated:[168]

> "8.3.2 However, the present system can create anomalies because, aside from priority under any specialist registries dealing with particular assets, charges acquire their priority from the date they are created not the date they are registered, provided they are subsequently registered within the 21-day period. An example to illustrate the defect in the present system is as follows: A lender may arrange to make available finance to a corporate borrower on day 10 subject to receiving a charge over the borrower's assets, at the time it advances the loan, and obtaining also at that time a search from the CRO (carried out in day 10), showing that the borrower has no outstanding charges registered against it. If the lender files the form C1 in the CRO (containing the prescribed particulars of the charge created on day 10) and such filing is made on day 12, the lender might reasonably assume that it has priority over any other charge created by the borrower. However, aside from priority under any specialist registries dealing with particular assets,[169] if the corporate borrower had created a charge on the same assets on day 2 (8 days prior to day 10) but had not registered particulars of the charge until day 20, this latter charge would in fact rank in priority to the charge given on day 10, as it had been created although not filed, prior to the date of creation of the day 10 charge.
>
> 8.3.3 Thus, for example, charge 'A', created on day 2 over specific assets, takes priority over charge 'B' on the same assets, created on day 10, even if its particulars are not filed with the CRO, and thus publicly known, until day 20 and charge 'B' is disclosed on day 12. The lender in respect of charge 'B' has no notice of the existence of charge 'A' at the time of the creation of his charge.
>
> 8.3.4 This system is clearly open to abuse; in the example given the lender although taking all appropriate precautions will not have attained a first ranking charge. Although to date there has been no evidence of abuse, and whilst irrelevant in cases of charges over real property which are the subject of the vast majority of charges created, the Review Group believe it should not be left open for abuse to the detriment of potential providers of finance."

---

[168] Issued in March 2004; see also McGrath, "a charge may have priority for up to 21 days prior to its becoming discoverable by a search of the register" in "Chopping down Dante's wood? – Article 9 of the Uniform Commercial Code and Personal Property Security Law in Ireland" (2006) 13(7) CLP 179.

[169] Registry of Deeds, Land Registry, Shipping Register, International (Cape Town) Registry, Patents Register, Trade Marks Register and Agricultural Chattel Mortgage Registers.

Following the acceptance of the CLRG's recommendation and enactment of the two-stage procedure, the State now has a notice filing system for registration of company charges.

(e) Registration form

[5.072] The prescribed particulars of a charge by a company, which are required to be filed with the Registrar of Companies, must be completed and filed online.[170] Where the one-stage filing procedure is used, the relevant form is Form C1. This form will require insertion of the incorporation number of the company, the name of the company, the description of the charging document,[171] the date of the charge followed by short particulars of the property charged, the name and address of the chargeholder as well as presenter details and signatures on behalf of the company and the chargeholder.

Although the Form C1 specifically states the manner in which the particulars should be verified, perhaps historically the greatest number of rejections of filed Forms C1 result from the inaccurate completion of the verification.[172] The usual procedure is that although it is the statutory duty of the company creating the charge to submit the prescribed particulars,[173] the security holder will arrange for the filing of the particulars (as such filing is essentially for the benefit of the security holder). The chargee's solicitor should ideally prepare the Form C1 simultaneously with the engrossment of the charge. At the time the charge is executed, a person duly authorised on behalf of the company, usually a director, the secretary or a solicitor, will sign the form and indicate his or her position in relation to the company. The chargeholder's solicitor will then verify the particulars by signing where indicated for verification and shall state the nature of his or her interest, for example, solicitor for the chargeholder.

[5.073] Where the two-stage procedure is being used, a Form C1A should be completed for the first filing. This form is identical to the Form C1 except the date of charge will not be entered (it being unknown at the time of filing). The second filing of the two-stage procedure will require the completion and filing of a Form C1B. This will be a simple form which will state the incorporation number of the company, the name of the company, the date Form C1A was submitted to the Registrar of Companies, the submission number of the first filing and the date of the creation of the charge; this will be followed by the signature blocks of both parties and the presenter's details.

---

[170] See www.cro.ie.

[171] The options for description are set out in the Notes to the form although it is not clear why a description is required.

[172] See Power, *Practice and Procedure in the Companies Registration Office* (The Irish Centre for Commercial Law Studies) 11 December 1997.

[173] Section 410 of the Act.

[5.074] The filing of particulars of a charge on property in the State created by an external company in accordance with the Companies Act 214, s 1301(4), is to be completed on a Form F8 where the one-stage procedure is used, and F8A and F8B where the two-stage procedure is used. Details to be competed on these forms are the same as for the C1, C1A and C1B forms save that in the case of F8 and F8A the company's country of origin is to be specified as well as its principal place of business in the State.[174]

[5.075] There is specifically no requirement to deliver the charge or a copy of it to the Companies Registration Office and, if there is such a delivery, the Registrar of Companies is under no duty and indeed has no power to examine it.[175]

[5.076] Where one or more persons entitled to a charge, transfers its interest to another person the particulars of the other person "may be delivered" in the prescribed form to the Companies Registration Office.[176] This provision appears to be optional, but it would be in the interest of the transferee to require that such particulars be delivered to ensure it receives notices issued to the security holder by the Companies Registration Office in respect of the charge. Having a prescribed form for notifying the Registrar of the change of chargee is new – the form is C17.

(f)   21-day time period

[5.077] The particulars of the charge are to be delivered to the Companies Registration Office in the case of the one-stage procedure, "not later than 21 days after" the creation of the charge[177] and in the case of the two-stage procedure, "not later than 21 days after" the delivery of the first notice (of intention to create a charge) to the Companies Registration Office.[178]

[5.078] Where an instrument is dated, the date on the instrument is *prima facie* evidence that that was the date of its execution or creation.[179] The safest procedure for any solicitor to follow is to regard the date of creation of a charge as being the date of its execution[180] or where this cannot be ascertained, the date

[174] See www.cro.ie.
[175] Section 409(9) of the Act.
[176] Section 409(8) of the Act.
[177] Section 409(3) of the Act.
[178] Section 409(4) of the Act.
[179] See Bosanquet J in *Anderson v Weston and Badcock* (1840) CP 6, Bing NC 292 at 300.
[180] See *Re Columbian Fireproofing Company Ltd* [1910] 2 Ch 120 and *Esberger & Sons Ltd v Capital and Countess Bank* [1913] 2 Ch 366; see also Buckley J in *Re The Harrogate Estates Ltd* [1903] 1 Ch 498 at 502: "The twenty-one days ... run from the date, not of the resolution which authorised the charge, but from the date at which the charge was created in favour of a person entitled to the benefit of the charge."

the chargor's board resolved to execute the security.[181] In this context, the wording of the resolution is important. For example, where a board approves the terms of a charge and resolves that it be created and that a director or directors be authorised to execute the charge or a sealing committee be authorised to seal the charge, the date of execution, even if subsequent, may be regarded as the date of creation.[182] The concept of execution and holding in escrow, which traditionally have been followed by some lending institutions, and which is a practice the author believes is likely to give rise to muddle and inadvertence if not strictly adhered to, was given judicial recognition in *Re CL Nye Ltd.*[183] In that case a charge was sealed and handed undated to the bank's solicitor. The following month the solicitor reported to the bank that the title was valid and the security good whereupon the bank advanced money to the company. Although the case was decided on other issues,[184] Harman LJ found that the date of creation of the security was the date the charge became effective, namely, the date when the solicitor reported that the security was good.[185]

Where a deed of charge is not dated and there are no escrow arrangements, the date of creation of the charge has been held to be the date the deed of charge is executed.[186] It is submitted that though the date of creation of the charge is the date the executed charge is delivered to the chargee or its agent; such date is usually the date of execution.

(g) *Conclusiveness of certificate of charge*

[5.079] The Registrar of Companies is required to give "a certificate of the registration of any charge";[187] subject to a few exceptions,[188] the certificate of registration issued by the Registrar is "conclusive evidence" that the requirements as to the registration of the charge have been complied with.[189]

---

181 See *Re Olderfleet Shipbuilding and Engineering Company Ltd* [1922] 1 IR 26.

182 In *Re Olderfleet Shipbuilding and Engineering Company Ltd* [1922] 1 IR 26 the shareholders passed a resolution authorising the issue of debentures and subsequently the directors passed a resolution to issue the debentures – it was held that the debentures were created on the date of the directors' resolution rather than the date of the shareholders' resolution.

183 *Re CL Nye Ltd* [1970] 3 All ER 1061, [1970] 2 WLR 158.

184 See para **[5.081]**.

185 See, however, *Alan Estates Ltd v WG Stores Ltd* [1981] 2 WLR 892 where the English Court of Appeal held by a majority that when all conditions of an escrow were satisfied, the title which passed under the deed related back so as to operate as between grantor and grantee from the time of the conditional delivery of the instrument.

186 See *Esberger v Capital and Counties Bank* [1913] 2 Ch 366.

187 Section 415(1) of the Act.

188 See para **[5.083]** and in the case of fraud see para **[5.084]**; see also *Re Advantage Healthcare (T10) Ltd* [2000] BCC 985 where the certificate was held to be "meaningless and worthless".

189 Section 415(2) of the Act.

However, it should be noted that under the new Act the certificate will not be conclusive evidence in respect of any property charged particulars of which have not been delivered to the Companies Registration Office.[190]

[5.080] The statutory conclusiveness of the certificate of registration has given rise to litigation challenging such conclusiveness.[191] However, the judiciary have consistently complied with the wording of the legislation, even where to do so has resulted in condoning or at least permitting sloppiness on the part of those filing the particulars. In *Lombard and Ulster Banking (Ireland) Ltd v Amurec Ltd (in liq)*[192] the company acquired ballroom premises in November 1972. At the closing of the sale, the bank's solicitor took the conveyance (which was undated) and the mortgage (also undated). The mortgage was a mortgage of the ballroom premises to secure moneys advanced to the company to enable it to purchase the premises. The company was unable to pay the stamp duty on the conveyance and it was not until March 1974 that the bank decided to pay the duty, at which stage current dates were inserted in the conveyance and mortgage.[193] Particulars of the mortgage were delivered to the Registrar of Companies who subsequently issued a certificate of registration. Following the company's liquidation, the liquidator claimed that the mortgage was void for non-registration within 21 days of its creation. In giving judgment Hamilton J said:[194]

> "... I have considerable sympathy with the submissions made by [counsel for the liquidator], I am, however, bound by the terms of Section 104 of the Companies Act, 1963 ... the wording of Section 104 is clear and unambiguous ... I have ... no alternative but to hold that the charge is a valid charge and is not void against the liquidator."

[5.081] In complying strictly with the provisions of s 104 (equivalent to Companies Act 2014, s 415), Hamilton J followed the English decisions[195] of *Re Eric Holmes (Property) Ltd (in liq)*[196] and *Re CL Nye Ltd*.[197] In the former case, particulars of two equitable mortgages by deposit of title deeds were delivered to the Registrar of Companies on 11 July with a date of creation given as 23 June,

---

[190] Section 415(3) of the Act.

[191] For further reading see an excellent article by O'Riordan and Pearce, "The Conclusiveness of Certificates of Registration of Company Charges" (1986) Gazette 281; see also Pye, "The s 104 Certificate of Registration" (1985) 3 ILT 213 and McCormick, "Conclusiveness in the Registration of Company Charge Procedure" (1989) 10 Co Law 175.

[192] *Lombard and Ulster Banking (Ireland) Ltd v Amurec Ltd (in liq)* (1978) 112 ILTR 1.

[193] This procedure resulted in the evasion/avoidance of penalty stamp duty.

[194] *Lombard and Ulster Banking (Ireland) Ltd v Amurec Ltd (in liq)* (1978) 112 ILTR 1 at 5.

[195] Where s 98(2) of the English Companies Act 1948 is equivalent to s 415 of the Companies Act 2014.

[196] *Re Eric Holmes (Property) Ltd (in liq)* [1965] 2 All ER 333.

[197] *Re CL Nye Ltd* [1970] 3 All ER 1061.

although in fact they were created on 5 June. The company's liquidator contended that the mortgages were void for want of registration within 21 days of their creation. Pennycuick J held that although the particulars delivered to the Registrar were incorrect, once the certificate of registration had issued it was impossible to take the case out of that section. Pennycuick J observed:[198]

> "It is, I think, possible that there is some lacuna in the Act here, inasmuch as the Act gives, apparently, protection where the certificate is made upon the basis of particulars which are incorrect and might even be fraudulent."

In the latter case, on facts not dissimilar to the facts Hamilton J had to contend with, on the purchase of premises by the company, the bank's solicitor took the executed but undated transfer and charge on 28 February. On 9 March the solicitor reported to the bank that the title was valid and the security was good, whereupon the bank advanced funds to the company. On 3 July the solicitor applied for registration of the charge which he dated 18 June. The Registrar duly issued a certificate of registration. The Court of Appeal reversed the High Court's decision[199] and held that although it considered the charge to have been delivered in escrow on 28 February and to have become effective on 9 March, as the certificate of registration was "conclusive" the charge was valid and binding on the company's liquidator.

[5.082] More recently, Laffoy J set out the position clearly and emphatically:[200]

> "The conclusiveness of the certificate of registration relates to compliance with the statutory registration requirements. There is a wealth of authority for the proposition that, because of the conclusiveness of the certificate, the registration of the charge cannot be challenged even when the registration requirements have not in fact been observed."

(h) Certificate open to judicial review

[5.083] The line of decisions on the Registrar's certificate indicate that the judiciary are not prepared to review the basis on which the certificate has been given even where the certificate has been issued on a false assumption, for example, particulars being submitted within 21 days of the charge's creation. However, in 1984 Mervyn Davies J held in England that the Registrar's decision to register a charge was open to judicial review.[201] The Court of Appeal however would have none of this and, on appeal by the Registrar, held[202] that the

---

[198] *Re Eric Holmes (Property) Ltd (in liq)* [1965] 2 All ER 333 at 344.

[199] The High Court had found against the bank on the grounds that the bank's solicitor had misstated the date of the charge and that no man can take advantage of his own wrong.

[200] In *re Investment Options and Solutions Ltd* [2010] IEHC 107.

[201] In *R v Registrar of Companies, ex p Esal (Commodities) Ltd (in liq)* [1985] BCLC 84; see also *Insolvency Law & Practice* (1985) Vol 1, p 20.

[202] In *R v Registrar of Companies, ex p Central Bank of India* [1985] BCLC 465; see also *Insolvency Law & Practice* (1986) Vol 2, p 118.

Registrar's decision was not open to judicial review.[203] In that case, the Registrar in finding the particulars to be incorrect returned them to the chargee for correction and, following their correct re-submission by the chargee, he issued a certificate of registration on the basis that they had been correctly submitted in the first instance so as to come within the statutory 21-day period required for registration. The Court of Appeal held that the English equivalent of s 415 precluded evidence being adduced to challenge the correctness of the Registrar's decision to register a charge; and that the Registrar had jurisdiction finally and conclusively to determine any question as to whether or not the requirements as to registration had been complied with.

In Ireland the judiciary have shown a greater willingness to consider a judicial review and it is possible that the Irish courts may not take the same line as the English Court of Appeal if an applicant can demonstrate that the Registrar has clearly acted outside the scope of his authority.[204] It has been suggested that the conclusiveness of the Registrar's certificate is constitutionally dubious.[205]

(i) *Practical consequences of conclusiveness of certificate*[206]

[5.084] The judicial decisions upholding the conclusive nature of the Registrar's certificate issued pursuant to the former equivalent of s 415 mean that, once a certificate referring to a mortgage or charge has been issued, that mortgage or charge cannot be challenged for want of registration within 21 days of creation.[207] However, in certain instances the conclusiveness of the certificate could be challenged on the grounds of fraud.[208]

[5.085] It may be possible for a person to obtain damages against the Registrar of Companies for negligence, either in the issue of a certificate or in failing to

---

[203] Other than by the Attorney General as the section does not bind the Crown.

[204] For further discussion on the prospect of a judicial review see O'Riordan and Pearce, "The Conclusiveness of Certificates of Registration of Company Charges" (1986) ILSI Gazette 281.

[205] See McGrath, "Missing an opportunity? A response to Part A7 of the draft Companies Bill 2007" (2007) 14(7) CLP 135.

[206] See also Gough, *Company Charges* (2nd edn, 1996) Ch 29.

[207] See *Lombard and Ulster Banking (Ireland) Ltd v Amurec Ltd (in liq)* (1978) 112 ILTR 1 and Laffoy J in *re Investment Options and Solutions Ltd* [2010] IEHC 107; see also *Re Eric Holmes (Property) Ltd (in liq)* [1965] 2 All ER 333, *Re CL Nye Ltd* [1970] 3 All ER 1061 and *First City Corporation Ltd v Downsview Nominees Ltd* [1990] 3 NZLR 265.

[208] See the remarks of Slade LJ in *R v Registrar of Companies, ex p Central Bank of India* [1985] BCLC 465 at 491 and those of Lord Templeman in *Sun Tai Cheung Credits Ltd v Attorney General of Hong Kong* [1987] 1 WLR 948 at 953; see also McCormick, "Conclusiveness in the Registration of Company Charge Procedure" (1989) 10 Co Law 175.

transcribe correctly the details of the Form C1 onto the relevant company file.[209] In an English Court of Appeal decision[210] concerning the Land Registry, Lord Denning MR stated:[211]

> "Suppose, now, that a clerk in the registry makes a mistake. He omits to enter a charge: or wrongly gives a clear certificate: with the result that the encumbrancer loses the benefit of it. Who is to suffer for the mistake? Is the incumbrancer to bear the loss without any recourse against anyone? Surely not. The very object of the registration system is to secure him against loss. The system breaks down utterly if he is left to bear the loss himself.
>
> Who, then, is to bear the loss? The negligent clerk can, of course, be made to bear it, if he can be found and is worth the money – which is unlikely. Apart from the clerk himself, there is only one person in law who can be made responsible. It is the Registrar. He must answer for the mistakes of the clerk and make compensation for the loss. He is a public officer and comes within the settled principle of English law that, when an official duty is laid on a public officer, by statute or by common law, then he is personally responsible for seeing that the duty is carried out."[212]

[5.086] Although the Registrar of Companies has an obligation on receiving particulars of a charge to enter in the appropriate company register the date of the charge, short particulars of the property charged, and the persons entitled to the charge,[213] a person inspecting the company file[214] should not rely on the accuracy of the particulars filed. He should endeavour to obtain a copy of the mortgage/charge from the company to ascertain the extent of the property charged and the amount secured thereby. The following words of Bankes LJ stated over 90 years ago still apply today:[215]

> "... when once the Registrar has given his certificate that the registration was complete, and that the mortgage or charge was created by an instrument, identifying it, in my opinion you have to go to the instrument to see what was actually charged, there being nothing in the statute which says that when once

---

209 See *First City Corporation Ltd v Downsview Nominees Ltd* [1990] 3 NZLR 265 where the Registrar issued a certificate of registration of charge but failed to enter the particulars of the charge in the company's file; see also Lightman J in *re Advantage Healthcare (T10) Ltd* [2000] BCC 985; although see the Privy Council's decision in *Yuen Kum Yeu v Attorney General for Hong Kong* [1988] AC 175.

210 *Ministry of Housing and Local Government v Sharp* [1970] 2 QB 223.

211 *Ministry of Housing and Local Government v Sharp* [1970] 2 QB 223 at 265.

212 Lord Denning MR went on to say: "It is not open to the public officer to say: 'I get low fees and small pay. It is very hard to make me *personally* responsible.' By law he is responsible. He will, of course, if he is wise insure himself against his liability; or get the Government to stand behind him."

213 Section 414(1) of the Act.

214 Any person on payment of a fee may inspect a company's file: s 414(2) of the Act.

215 *National Provincial and Union Bank of Ireland v Clarnby* [1924] 1KB 431 at 444.

registration has taken place the register shall be the evidence of the extent of the charge."[216]

[5.087] It should be noted however that if the mortgage/charge is invalid for any reason (other than for non-registration) the issue of a certificate of registration of charge by the Registrar of Companies does not remedy such invalidity.[217] The certificate just confirms that the mortgage/charge cannot be challenged for want of registration within the required time period.[218]

[5.088] The conclusiveness of the certificate does not apply to property the prescribed particulars of which have not been included in the C1 filed with the Companies Registration Office.[219] This new provision avoids the injustice highlighted by the facts in *National Provincial and Union Bank of England v Charnley*,[220] where the company mortgaged leasehold premises together with moveable plant. The particulars filed with the Registrar of Companies referred to the leasehold premises but not to the moveable plant. The certificate of registration was duly issued. The English Court of Appeal held that as the certificate identified the instrument of charge and certified that the mortgage or charge thereby created had been duly registered, the certificate in effect certified the due registration of all the charges created by the instrument (including that over the moveable plant).

(j) Priority of registered charges

[5.089] Prior to the enactment of the Companies Act 2014, in the absence of priority rules applicable in other registers,[221] the priority of charges over the same property, in the absence of agreement between the security holders, ranked in the order in which the charge was created (provided particulars of such charge were filed in the Companies Registration Office within 21 days of its creation).[222]

---

[216] Bankes LJ in *National Provincial and Union Bank of England v Charnley* [1924] 1 KB 431 at 444.

[217] See the remarks of Slade LJ in *R v Registrar of Companies, ex p Central Bank of India* [1985] BCLC 465 at 490; eg a charge could be invalid for being an unfair preference under s 604 of the Act.

[218] See Laffoy J in *re Investment Options and Solutions Ltd* [2010] IEHC 107.

[219] Section 415(3) of the Act.

[220] *National Provincial and Union Bank of England v Charnley* [1924] 1 KB 431; see also *Re Mechanisations (Eaglescliffe) Ltd* [1964] 3 All ER 840 which involved the misstatement of the amount secured by the charge (not required now under the Companies Act 2014).

[221] Eg the Registry of Deeds, the Land Registry, the registers applicable to agricultural stock, the Trade Marks Register, the Patents Register, the Shipping Register and the International Registry (under the Cape Town Convention).

[222] Thus giving rise to the potential difficulty highlighted by the Company Law Review Group, see para **[5.071]**.

[5.090] Where the two-stage registration filing is carried out,[223] the date of receipt by the Companies Registration Office of the notice of intention to create a charge is deemed to be the date of receipt of the charge.[224] This is a further encouragement for security holders to require that the two-stage procedure be adopted. It gives rise to what may be considered an odd situation in that the priority of such a charge runs from a date before it was actually created. However, as the notice filing will be entered on the company's register in the Companies Registration Office, other potential creditors should not be prejudiced as they will or ought to have carried out a search of the register.

[5.091] Section 412(3) of the Act specifically regulates the priority of competing charges which, in the absence of priority governed by other registers or agreement between the security holders, will no longer be governed by the time of creation but by the order by which the particulars of the charge were received by the Companies Registration Office.[225] This order though is subject to any rule of law as to priority by virtue of notice which remains unaffected by the provisions of the Act.[226]

[5.092] Apart from notice though, and that in itself has uncertainty surrounding it,[227] any relevant rule of law is modified by the priority set out by s 412(3) of the Act.[228] This raises the question whether an earlier floating charge will now have priority over a later fixed charge. If the floating charge had priority the subsequent fixed charge would rank behind not only this floating charge but the preferential creditors which are required to be paid before the holder of a floating charge.[229] In practice the holder of the subsequent fixed charge should enter into an intercreditor or interlender agreement with the floating charge holder to regulate their respective priorities; this will depend upon the company giving the security being able to negotiate a satisfactory outcome with both chargees. However, such a contention, that the earlier floating charge retains priority over the later fixed, ignores s 619 of the Act which imports the bankruptcy rules within company law as to the rights of secured and unsecured creditors. Under these rules,[230] a fixed chargeholder takes the assets held under a fixed charge outside the bankruptcy or liquidation of the chargor. In respect of assets subject only to a floating charge, preferential creditors have priority.[231]

---

[223] Under s 409(4) of the Act; see para **[5.070]**.

[224] Section 412(4)(b) of the Act.

[225] Section 412(3) of the Act, another common law jurisdiction which changed to this order is Zambia: see Zambian Companies Act 1994, s 101.

[226] Section 412(2) of the Act.

[227] See paras **[5.094]** to **[5.101]**.

[228] Section 412(2) of the Act.

[229] Section 621 of the Act; for an example of the application of this see *Re Portbase Clothing Ltd* [1990] Ch 388.

[230] Bankruptcy Act 1988, s 76 First Sch, para 24.

[231] Section 621 of the Act.

[5.093] The priority rule can be overridden by an agreement between the competing security holders,[232] and in practice this is usually but not always done typically through a priority agreement, an interlender agreement or an intercreditor agreement prepared usually by the solicitor acting for the first or principal security holder.[233]

(k) Notice

[5.094] The issue as to priority raises the question of notice.[234] There is a practice that debentures incorporating a floating charge contain a restriction on the chargor creating further charges in priority to or *pari passu* with the floating charge. Such a restriction was designed to avoid the floating charge holder losing priority over the charged assets to a subsequent fixed charge created by the chargor over the same assets. Although such a restriction, known as a negative pledge, was invariably contained in a deed incorporating a floating charge, a practice had developed of inserting details of the negative pledge in the charge's prescribed particulars being filed in the Companies Registration Office on the basis that such filing would put subsequent intended chargeholders on notice of the negative pledge.

[5.095] There was some uncertainty as to whether a person who takes a fixed charge from a company is fixed with notice that a prior floating charge exists which prohibits the creation of a charge, to rank *pari passu* with or in priority to the floating charge.[235] Irish publications on company law have given scant reference to it[236] and the English publications do not have a common approach.[237] What emerged as something of a consensus is that the practice of inserting in the form containing the prescribed particulars, notice of the restriction (contained in the debenture) on the creation of further charges did not

---

[232] Section 412(5) of the Act.

[233] Such an agreement will usually set out the agreed procedure for enforcement of the security and the distribution of proceeds. It may also incorporate an agreement between the creditors as to when a demand may be made against the chargor for payment or discharge of the secured obligations or liabilities.

[234] For an outstanding treatment of this difficult area of law, as applicable to England, see Calnan, *Taking Security* (3rd edn, Jordans, 2013) ch 7.

[235] "It is an important and unresolved question as to what aspects of charges registration gives notice": Penn & Shea, *The Law Relating to Domestic Banking* (2nd edn, Sweet & Maxwell, 2000) at para 19-051.

[236] Although see Ussher, *Company Law in Ireland* (Sweet & Maxwell, 1986) at pp 424–429 and see Courtney, *The Law of Companies* (3rd edn, Bloomsbury Professional, 2012) at paras 18.080–18.084 and 18.089.

[237] See *Gore-Browne on Companies*: "the issue of constructive notice remains open to argument" at para 18.14 (44th edn).

give rise to constructive notice, as notice of such restriction is not a matter which falls within the prescribed particulars which required to be filed.[238]

[5.096] In 1979, the Supreme Court regarded it as settled law that there is no duty on a bank to examine the terms of a prior debenture created by a company to ascertain whether there is a prohibition on the creation of further charges.[239] The Supreme Court regarded it as "common"[240] in debentures to have such a restriction, yet somehow considered the bank would not be fixed with notice of such prohibition.[241] It is submitted that a bank cannot be said "to have acted in good faith" when, in preparing to take security, it, or its solicitor, fails to carry out a search in the Companies Registration Office and ignores a prior floating charge notwithstanding the almost universal practice of such charge incorporating a restriction on the creation of further security ranking *pari passu* with or in priority to it.[242]

[5.097] There seems no reason why a person intending to take security and making a search in the Companies Registration Office on discovering a prior debenture should not ask the prospective chargor for sight of such debenture. It should be difficult to maintain that the security was taken in good faith without having made such preliminary enquiries.[243] In reality this is what happens in practice where the amount to be secured is not insignificant. The test for a purchaser in good faith indicated by the Supreme Court[244] in 1979 (the same year in which it ruled on in *Welch v Browmaker (Ireland) Ltd and the Governor*

---

[238] See *Palmer's Company Law* (25th edn) at para 13.043, *Goode on Legal Problems of Credit and Security* (5th edn) at para 2.28, and Gough, *Company Charges* (2nd edn, 1996) at p 814; see also Gower in *Principles of Modern Company Law*, who acknowledges this difficulty at p 475 (4th edn) having erased what he stated at p 422 (3rd edn) namely: "It is submitted that if this is done [filing notice of the restriction], notice is given to all the world so that neither a legal nor an equitable mortgagee can take priority."

[239] Henchy J in *Welch v Bowmaker (Ireland) Ltd and The Governor and Company of the Bank of Ireland* [1980] IR 251 at 256.

[240] *Welch v Bowmaker (Ireland) Ltd and The Governor and Company of the Bank of Ireland* [1980] IR 251 at 256.

[241] It seems in Scotland that actual notice of a prohibition may be presumed where a subsequent chargee has failed to make inquiries the result of which he knew might prejudice his position of being unaware of such a restriction: see Palmer (25th edn) at para 13.137.

[242] See also the Supreme Court's test of good faith in *Somers v Weir* [1979] IR 94, 113 ILTR 81.

[243] See also *Lingard's Bank Security Documents* (5th edn) at para 1.9: "It is odd that notice of the existence of a debenture was held in the old cases not to impose any duty to call for a copy of the document or to involve notice of the contents."

[244] *Somers v Weir* [1979] IR 94; 113 ILTR 81.

and Company of the Bank of Ireland) could be applied equally to a chargee, namely:[245]

> "The question whether a purchaser has acted in good faith necessarily depends on the extent of his knowledge of the relevant circumstances. In earlier times the tendency was to judge a purchaser solely by the facts that had actually come to his knowledge. In the course of time it came to be held in the Court of Chancery that it would be unconscionable for the purchaser to take his stand on the facts that had come to his notice to the exclusion of those which ordinary prudence or circumspection or skill should have called to his attention. When the facts at his command beckoned him to look and inquire further, and he refrained from doing so, equity fixed him with constructive notice of what he would have ascertained if he had pursued the further investigation which a person of reasonable care and skill would have felt proper to make in the circumstances."

[5.098] Thus, in *Cox v Dublin City Distillery Company*[246] a bank which took a pledge of whisky was unable to rely on the pledge as it was shown that the bank was familiar with the prior debentures of the pledgor which prohibited the creation of further security in priority to the floating charge under the debentures.

[5.099] Following the recommendation of the Company Law Review Group,[247] the Companies Act 2014 has simplified the task of the practitioner in the preparation of the filing form by providing that the Registrar shall not be under a duty to enter on the chargor's file in the Companies Registration Office what the Act describes as "extraneous material" and receipt by the Registrar of particulars of such extraneous material shall have no effect.[248] Extraneous material includes details of a negative pledge or other covenants applicable to the charged assets, such as a requirement to pay proceeds of book debts into a specified account or specifying events which give rise to a crystallisation of the floating charge.[249] Thus a prospective chargee will not have notice of any negative pledge but should be expected to request a copy of the previous charges filed against the company.

[5.100] One exception to the rule excluding extraneous material is made for prescribed particulars of floating charges granted to the Central Bank which

---

[245] *Somers v Weir* [1979] IR 94; 113 ILTR 81 *per* Henchy J at 108 and 88 respectively.

[246] *Cox v Dublin City Distillery Company* [1906] 1 IR 446.

[247] Second Report issued March 2004 at paras 8.5.1 to 8.5.4.

[248] Section 412(6) of the Act; the Bill provided that the Registrar shall not enter any extraneous material on the register but a late change introduced and passed at the Second Report stage on 30 September 2014 provided that the Registrar shall not be under a duty to register such material, therein giving the Registrar some flexibility but opening the Registrar to submissions, which is undesirable.

[249] Section 412(6) and (8) of the Act; this includes restrictions in a charge on the company borrowing moneys or obtaining credit.

may include such extraneous material.[250] The background to this anomaly is that the initial requirement for charges granted to the Central Bank was introduced by the Central Bank and Financial Services Authority of Ireland Act 2004 under the auspices of the Department of Finance, whereas the legislation governing companies is the remit of the Department of Jobs, Enterprise and Innovation.[251]

[5.101] While the provisions of s 412(6) of the Act making the Registrar under no duty to file "extraneous material" leaves the unsatisfactory majority Supreme Court decision (in *Welch v Bowmaker (Ireland) Ltd and the Governor and Company of the Bank of Ireland*) intact, in view of the practice of subsequent chargees to seek the terms of prior charges, the effect of the Supreme Court decision is more likely to apply where a company in difficulty obtains emergency financing from a willing lender who may wish to take security anyway and give notice of that security, once taken, to the prior chargee, thereby forcing that chargee to rule its account to avoid losing priority for subsequent advances made by it.[252] However, as a result of the Supreme Court's inconsistent decisions in 1979,[253] uncertainty does remain until a further decision of the Supreme Court on appropriate facts.[254]

(l)   *Satisfaction and release of charged property*

[5.102] Particulars of a charge created by a company will remain on the company's file in the Companies Registration Office indefinitely. The Registrar of Companies will file a note on the company's file that a charge has been satisfied where the Registrar receives satisfactory evidence of the release. The Registrar may accept as evidence of a charge's release a statement in the prescribed forms being a C6 in the case of a full discharge and a C7 in the case of a partial discharge.[255]

Where a charge is released or discharged, the company should file a statement in a prescribed form with the Companies Registration Office to ensure that the charge on the company's file is shown as having been satisfied and discharged. The statement must be signed by two directors of the company

---

[250] Section 412(7) of the Act.

[251] For more background see the Second Report of the Company Law Review Group at paras 8.5.5 to 8.5.8.

[252] See the Rule in *Clayton's Case* [1816] 1 Mer 572.

[253] 14 February 1979: *Somers v Weir* [1979] IR 94; and 9 July 1979: *Welch v Bowmaker (Ireland) Ltd and the Governor and Company of the Bank of Ireland* [1980] IR 251.

[254] For a further discussion on the uncertainty, see McGrath, "The Company Charge Registration in Ireland; Some Reflections on the Reform Proposals in the Companies Consolidation and Reform Bill 2012" [2013] JBL 303.

[255] See www.cro.ie.

or by one director and the company's secretary.[256] There is now no requirement to swear the statement.

[5.103] Where a statement is signed in the knowledge that it is false the signatory is guilty of a category 2 offence.[257] Furthermore, where the signatory in making such false statement "did not honestly believe on reasonable grounds that the statement was true", a court may, on the application of the liquidator or examiner or receiver or any creditor or contributor of the company, declare that the signatory shall be personally liable, without limitation of liability, for all or such part as the court may specify of the debts and other liabilities of the company.[258] This is new and is the logical penalty for enabling a form to be filed without being sworn which, in practice, often proves cumbersome particularly where officers are located in different jurisdictions.

For a court to declare a signatory personally liable for a company's debt on foot of the misstatement, the court is required to come to the view that the making of the statement:

    "(a)   contributed to the company being unable to pay its debts;

    (b)   prevented or impeded the orderly winding-up of the company; or

    (c)   facilitated the defrauding of the creditors of the company."[259]

(m) Abolition of Slavenburg filing

[5.104] As is currently the position, an external company which sets up a branch in the State is required to file particulars of charges over property in the State.[260] A significant change is that where an external company establishes a branch, but does not register as an external company under ss 1302(1) and (2) or 1304 (as appropriate) any charge which it creates will be incapable of being registered (whether by the company or a person interested in the charge).[261] Accordingly, all charges created by an external company which should have, but has not, registered as a branch will be void as against its liquidator and creditors as the consequences of not registering a registrable charge, as set out in Part 7 of the Act, will apply to them.[262]

---

[256] Section 416(4) of the Act.
[257] Section 416(5) of the Act.
[258] Section 416(6) and (7) of the Act.
[259] Section 416(6) of the Act.
[260] Section 1301(1), (2) and (4) of the Act.
[261] Section 1301(5) of the Act.
[262] Section 1301(4) of the Act.

Chapter 6

Corporate Restructuring: Schemes, Mergers and Divisions

by
Lyndon MacCann SC

Introduction

[6.001] The purpose of this chapter is to review and analyse the changes made by the Companies Act to the area of company law relating to the restructuring of companies, other than the restructuring of an insolvent company in the context of an examinership, which is dealt with separately in Ch 7.[1] The relevant provisions are to be found in Part 9. These provisions deal with the following:

1. Schemes of arrangement and compromises between a company and some or all of its members and/or creditors, including schemes involving the reconstruction or amalgamation of companies;
2. The compulsory acquisition of dissenting shareholders in a take-over;
3. Mergers of two or more Irish companies;
4. The division of an existing Irish company into two or more companies.

[6.002] Previously, such activities were governed primarily by ss 210 to 204 of the Companies Act 1963 and by the European Communities (Mergers and Division of Companies) Regulations 1987, 2008 and 2011.

[6.003] In the case of cross-border mergers of companies, these continue to be governed by the provisions of the European Communities (Cross-Border Mergers) Regulations 2008 which in turn implement Council Directive No 2005/56/EC.

Schemes of arrangement

[6.004] Chapter 1 of Part 9 deals with schemes of arrangement and is, broadly speaking, the successor to ss 201 to 203 of the Companies Act 1963.

---

[1] It is beyond the scope of this chapter to do more than consider the way in which the existing law on these areas has been changed. For a discussion of the pre-existing law relating to the restructuring of companies, see Courtney, *The Law of Companies* (3rd edn, Bloomsbury Professional, 2012) at Ch 9, paras 9.091 to 9.108, Ch 21.

(a) The calling of scheme meetings

[6.005] The first main change to be noted is that whereas scheme meetings of members and/or creditors could previously only be summoned by order of the High Court, now under s 450 they may be convened by the directors.[2] However, if the directors do not exercise that power, then they may still be summoned by order of the High Court on foot of an application made by:

(a)   the company itself; or

(b)   any creditor or member of the company; or

(c)   in the case of a company being wound up, by the liquidator.[3]

[6.006] Presumably this change in the law to allow for scheme meetings to be convened merely by resolution of the directors was intended to reduce costs by potentially eliminating one of the court applications from the whole scheme process. Furthermore, it would appear to have been intended for use in circumstances where there was little difficulty in determining how the relevant class meetings should be composed.

[6.007] The relevance of getting class composition right is that the courts have long held that if the company segregates members or creditors into the wrong classes, that mistake may prove to be fatal to the whole scheme.[4] Previously, the court would not rule in advance regarding the proper class to which a particular member or creditor belonged. However, a practice has been emerging in recent years whereby the Irish courts, following the example of their UK counterparts, will be prepared to give preliminary directions as to class composition when ordering the summoning of meetings.[5] That practice has now been put on a legislative footing by s 450(5) of the Act which provides that:

> "Without prejudice to the court's jurisdiction under section 453(2)(c) to determine whether the scheme meetings that have been held comply with the general law referred to in subsection (2), the court, in exercising its jurisdiction to summon meetings under subsection (3), may, in its discretion, where it considers it just and convenient to do so, give directions as to what are the appropriate scheme meetings that must be held in the circumstances concerned."

There are several points to be noted about this power of the court. First, it arises only in circumstances where the court is being asked to summon the scheme meetings; it is not capable of being invoked in circumstances where the meetings are being convened by the directors themselves. Second, although the

---

2   Section 450(1) of the Act.
3   Section 450(3) and (4) of the Act.
4   *Re Pye (Ireland) Ltd* (11 March 1985, unreported) HC (Costello J). See also *Re Hellenic Trust Ltd* [1975] 3 All ER 382; *Re T & N Ltd (No 3)* [2007] 1 BCLC 563.
5   *Re Millstream Recycling Ltd* [2010] 4 IR 463; *Re Hawk Insurance Company Ltd* [2001] 2 BCLC 480.

subsection does not expressly so provide, nevertheless it is to be presumed that the court's existing practice will continue to apply whereby it will only give directions as to class composition if those members and creditors who stand to be affected by the court's directions have been put on notice of the application (whether by advertisement or by service of the court papers) and have had an opportunity to be heard on the issue.

[6.008] The facility to obtain preliminary directions as to class composition may, of itself, mean that applying to court to summon scheme meetings will continue to be a more attractive option than having the meetings convened by the directors, at least in circumstances where there is any degree of complication in relation to class composition. However, there is another practical reason why applying to court to have the meetings summoned may still be the more common course of action. This is because s 450 says nothing about the manner in which scheme meetings are to be convened and conducted.

[6.009] Scheme meetings are not general meetings and thus the ordinary provisions of the Companies Acts, including the provisions of Table A of the 1963 Act, did not automatically apply to them. Thus, the practice when applying to have the scheme meetings summoned was to ask the court to give directions as to practical matters such as the length of notice to be given, the form of proxies to be used, the time limits for submitting proxies, the procedure for demanding and taking polls, the quorum, etc.

[6.010] Insofar as the scheme meetings involve classes of members, it is possible that s 197(1) of the Act might be invoked. It states that:

> "The provisions of this Part, and the provisions of the constitution of a company relating to general meetings, shall, as far as applicable, apply in relation to *any meeting* of any class of member of the company." (Emphasis added.)

Arguably this wording is wide enough to apply a scheme meeting involving a class of members of the company. However, it does not purport to apply nor could it apply to meetings of classes of creditors.

That being so, if the proposed scheme is going to involve a compromise or arrangement with the company's creditors or any class or classes of creditors (and holders of share options are, technically, creditors of the company) then the company may have little option but to have the scheme meetings summoned by order of the court rather than having them convened by resolution of the board of directors.

(b) Staying proceedings against the company

[6.011] Irrespective of whether the scheme meetings have been convened by the directors or summoned by the court, s 451 provides that application may be made to the court to stay all proceedings or to restrain further proceedings against the company for such period as the court sees fit. The application may be made by the following persons:

(a) the company;

(b) the directors;

(c) any creditor or member of the company; or

(d) in the case of a winding up, the liquidator.

So, for example, even though the scheme meetings might have been convened by the directors, the application for a stay on proceedings could be made by any one of the potential applicants identified above.

[6.012] This power to grant a stay on proceedings broadly mirrors s 201(2) of the Companies Act 1963. Unfortunately, the legislature has not taken the opportunity to expand the scope of the potential stay that may be granted by the court. Only existing and potential "proceedings" (ie legal proceedings) may be stayed or restrained under s 451. Other acts on enforcement by creditors, such as the appointment of a receiver, the taking of possession of mortgaged property and the repossession of goods subject to retention of title, hire-purchase or leasing arrangements, continue to be permitted.

Thus, schemes of arrangement by way of examinership rather than pursuant to Part 9 will probably continue to be the more viable option for insolvent companies.

(c) Continued availability of schemes to foreign companies

[6.013] Under the former legislation, the scheme of arrangement procedure could be invoked by "any company liable to be wound up" under the Companies Acts 1963 to 2013.[6] This was held to confer jurisdiction on the court, *inter alia*, to summon scheme meetings and to sanction a scheme involving a foreign company provided that the company had some connection with the State which might render it liable to be wound up here as an unregistered company, as where a contract sought to be effected by the scheme was stated to be governed by Irish law.[7] It is to be noted, that while no equivalent legislative provision is to be found in Part 9 of the Companies Act because the Act is structured so that Part 9 applies only to LTDs, the substantive position is preserved by s 1430 which provides that Chapter 1 (other than s 455) of Part 9 *"shall apply to any company liable to be wound up under this Act"*.

---

6 Section 201(7) of the Companies Act 1963.

7 See *Re Drax Holdings Ltd* [2004] 1 BCLC 10; *Re Primacom Holdings GmbH* [2011] EWHC 3746 (Ch); *Re Vietnam Shipbuilding Industry Group* [2014] 1 BCLC 400.

(d) The requisite majority

[6.014] One area where the legislature did not take the opportunity to make what would have been a welcome amendment, is in relation to the prescribed majority to be obtained at each scheme meeting. Under s 453 it continues to be a "special majority", which is defined in s 449(1) as being:

> "a majority in number representing at least 75 per cent in value of the creditors or class of creditors or members of class of members, as the case may be, present and voting either in person or by proxy at the scheme meeting."

By continuing to require a majority in number of the members of the class, irrespective of the value of their respective claims, the legislature affords to objectors who may well have a relatively small economic stake in the company, a potentially disproportionate right of veto in respect of a scheme of arrangement that has the overwhelming support in value of the affected members and/or creditors.

(e) Power of State creditors to vote for a compromise

[6.015] A new provision enacted by s 453(4) of the Act states that:

> "Where a State Authority[8] is a creditor of the company, such authority shall be entitled to accept proposals under this section notwithstanding –
>
> (a)   that any claim of such authority as a creditor would be impaired under the proposals; or
>
> (b)   any other enactment."

This subsection, which is new to schemes of arrangement, but already existed for examinerships,[9] has as its purpose the removal of any doubt as to whether public bodies, in particular, the Revenue Commissioners, would be acting *ultra vires* in voting to approve a scheme of arrangement which resulted in payment to them of less than 100 cent in the euro.

(f) Conditions for the scheme to become binding

[6.016] Under s 454(1), which reflects the pre-existing legal position, the order of the court approving the scheme of arrangement becomes effective upon delivery of a copy of the order to the Registrar of Companies. This must occur within 21 days of the making of the order.

Before the court can sanction the scheme, s 453(1)(a) stipulates that it must have been approved by a special majority at each scheme meeting. There is

---

[8]   A "State Authority" is defined in s 453(5) as meaning the State, a Minister of the Government, a local authority or the Revenue Commissioners.

[9]   See s 23(5) of the Companies (Amendment) Act 1990.

nothing new here. What is new, however, at least in legislative terms, is the requirement under s 453(2)(b) that:

> "notice –
>
> i.   of the passing of such resolution or resolutions at the scheme meeting or scheme meetings; and
>
> ii. that an application will be made under paragraph (c) to the court in relation to the compromise or arrangement, is advertised once in at least 2 daily newspapers circulating in the district where the registered office or principal place of business of the company is situated."

[6.017] Heretofore the question of advertising has been a matter for the discretion of the court when giving directions as to the hearing of the petition to sanction the scheme. In practice, the court has tended to direct that the petition be advertised at least once in *Iris Oifigiúil* and in two national daily newspapers, with advertisements also being placed in foreign newspapers in circumstances where the company does business abroad. It is to be anticipated that the court will continue to give such directions as to foreign advertising in appropriate cases.

[6.018] It is also notable that s 453(2) does not state the period of time in advance of the hearing of the petition, by which the notice must appear in the relevant publications. Undoubtedly the court will be anxious to ensure that affected members and creditors will continue to receive *meaningful* notice of the application and will thus continue to direct that such notice is advertised two to three weeks before the petition is actually heard.

Compulsory acquisition of shares in a take-over

[6.019] Chapter 2 of Part 9 broadly reflects what was s 204 of the Companies Act 1963 and provides a right for an offeror to buy out shareholders dissenting from a take-over scheme, contract or offer which has received the requisite level of approval, as well as conferring on such dissenting shareholders a right to insist on being bought out.

[6.020] The offeror must have received acceptances in respect of at least 80 per cent in value of the shares affected before these rights are triggered. However, under s 458(1) and (2) the offeror's right to compulsorily acquire the rights of dissentients is further limited in a case where at the date of the publication of the offer "shares in the offeree company are … already in the beneficial ownership of the offeror to a value greater than 20 per cent of the aggregate value of those shares and the shares affected." In such circumstances, the offeror's right of compulsory acquisition is not triggered unless he has obtained acceptances which not only comprise at least 80 per cent in value of the shares affected *but also represent not less than 50 per cent in number of the holders of those shares.*

[6.021] In some respects this change in the law is more onerous than had been the case previously. This is because one must look not only at the extent of the offeror's pre-existing holding in the class of shares affected, but also at the extent of his holdings in all classes of shares in the company, whereas under s 204, one only had to look at the extent of his pre-existing holding of shares affected.

[6.022] In other respects, however, it is less onerous, in that he now only has to have acceptances in respect of at least 80 per cent in value and more than 50 per cent in number of the shares affected, whereas previously he had to have received acceptances in respect of not less than 80 per cent in value and not less than 75 per cent in number of the shares affected.

[6.023] It is to be noted, however, that this additional requirement under s 458 only applies in respect of the right of the offeror to compulsorily buy out the dissentients. It does not apply in relation to the dissentients' right to call on the offeror to buy them out.

[6.024] With regard to the foregoing, it is to be noted that s 460(2) of the Act spells out certain instances where shares are to be deemed to be in the beneficial ownership of the offeror at the date of the publication of the offer. They are as follows:

> "For the purposes of this Chapter –
>
> (a)   shares in the offeree company in the beneficial ownership of a subsidiary of the offeror shall be deemed to be in the beneficial ownership of the offeror; and
>
> (b)   the acquisition of the beneficial ownership of shares in the offeree company by a subsidiary of the offeror shall be deemed to be the acquisition of such beneficial ownership by the offeror."

It is significant, however, that the legislature has not seen fit to stipulate that account be taken of shares in the offeree company which are held by the offeror's holding company, notwithstanding the fact that the acceptance in respect of those shares may be no more independent than acceptance by the offeror's subsidiaries.

[6.025] Section 459 of the Act contains useful new provisions in relation to the mechanics for the service of notices on dissenting shareholders, including provision for the service of notices by electronic means in certain circumstances. Provision is also made for the mode of service in the case of joint holders of a share, as well as in the case of dead or bankrupt shareholders and certain classes of foreign shareholders.

Mergers and divisions of companies

[6.026] Perhaps the most significant changes to the law which have been effected by Part 9 of the Act are those concerning the merger and division of domestic companies. They are to be found in Chapters 3 and 4 respectively of Part 9. Previously, mergers and divisions of domestic companies could only be effected in the case of PLCs pursuant to the European Communities (Mergers and Divisions of Companies) Regulations 1987 and the European Communities (Mergers and Divisions of Companies) (Amendment) Regulations 2008. Because of the limited range of companies to which they applied, they were rarely used. The relevant statutory provisions relating to the merger and division of domestic PLCs are now to be found in Chapters 16 and 17 respectively of Part 17 of the Act.

Mergers of companies

[6.027] The provisions of Chapter 3 of Part 9 of the Act are based upon the European Communities (Cross-Border Mergers) Regulations 2008 which, as their title suggests, relate to mergers between Irish companies and companies from different states within the European Economic Area (the EEA). In this regard, it should be noted that the 2008 Regulations have not been repealed and continue to govern cross-border mergers.

(a) Types of merger

[6.028] Insofar as domestic mergers are concerned, there are three types of merger process, namely "merger by acquisition", "merger by absorption" and "merger by formation of a new company".[10]

[6.029] A "merger by acquisition" is a process pursuant to which an existing company acquires all the assets and liabilities of one or more transferor companies in exchange for the allotment by it of shares to the members of those transferor companies, with or without an accompanying cash payment, and pursuant to which those transferor companies are dissolved without going into liquidation.[11]

[6.030] A "merger by absorption" is a process whereby, on being dissolved and without going into liquidation, a wholly-owned subsidiary transfers all of its assets and liabilities to its holding company.[12]

[6.031] A "merger by formation of a new company" is a process whereby one or more transferor companies, on being dissolved without going into liquidation, transfer all of their respective assets and liabilities to a newly formed company

---

[10] Section 461(1) of the Act.
[11] Section 463(1) of the Act.
[12] Section 463(1) of the Act.

in exchange for the allotment by it of shares to the members of those transferor companies.[13]

(b) The documents to be prepared

[6.032] The first step in the merger process is for the directors of the merging companies to draw up and approve written common draft terms of merger which must, at a minimum, set out the matters prescribed by s 466(2).

[6.033] Except in the case of a merger by absorption, an explanatory report must also be prepared and approved in respect of each merging company, by its board of directors, explaining, at a minimum, the common draft terms of merger and the legal and economic grounds for and implications of the proposed merger, with particular reference to the proposed share exchange ratio, organisation and management structures, recent and future commercial activities and the financial interests of the holders of the shares and other securities in the company.[14] The requirement for an explanatory report may be dispensed with, *inter alia*, if all of the holders of voting shares in each of the merging companies so agree.[15]

[6.034] Subject to some exceptions set out in s 468(2) there must also be drawn up for the members of each merging company an expert's report which must:

(a)   state the method or methods used to arrive at the proposed share exchange ratio;

(b)   give the opinion of the expert as to whether the proposed share exchange ratio is fair and reasonable;

(c)   give the opinion of the expert as to the adequacy of the method or methods used in the case in question;

(d)   indicate the values arrived at using each such method;

(e)   give the opinion of the expert as to the relative importance attributed to such methods in arriving at the values decided on; and

(f)   specify any valuation difficulties which have arisen.[16]

[6.035] The board of each merging company may appoint its own expert (or two or more boards may appoint the same person or persons). Alternatively, all of the merging companies may apply to the court to appoint a common expert.[17] The expert must be a statutory auditor and not only must not have been an officer or employee of any of the merging companies in the 12 months before the date of the common draft terms of merger but also, subject to certain

---

[13]   Section 463(1) of the Act.
[14]   Section 467(1), (2) and (3) of the Act.
[15]   Section 467(4) of the Act.
[16]   Section 467(7) of the Act.
[17]   Section 468(3) of the Act.

exceptions, must not be connected with any of the officers of any of the merging companies.[18]

[6.036] Where the latest statutory financial statements of any of the merging companies relate to a financial year ended more than six months before the date of the common draft terms of merger and the summary approval procedure is not being employed to effect the merger, then, subject to certain exceptions, if that company is availing itself of the exemption from the requirement to hold a general meeting, it must prepare a merger financial statement (with accompanying statutory auditor's report) in the format of its last annual balance sheet and must be made up to a date not earlier than the first day of the month preceding the date of the common draft terms of merger.[19]

(c) Registration, publication and inspection of documents

[6.037] Unless the summary approval procedure is being employed to effect the merger, at least 30 days before the date of passing of their respective resolutions approving the common draft terms of merger, each of the merging companies must deliver to the Registrar of Companies a copy of the draft terms of merger and a notice in the prescribed form specifying its name and registered office, its legal form and its registered number.[20] Notice of the delivery of the common draft terms of merger to the Registrar of Companies must then be published by the Registrar in the *CRO Gazette* and by each merging company in one national daily newspaper. The notice published by each of the merging companies must likewise appear in the relevant newspapers at least 30 days before the passing of the resolutions approving the merger.[21] The notice as so published must include:

(a) a statement that copies of the common draft terms of merger, the directors' explanatory report, the statutory financial statements of each of the merging companies for the preceding three financial years and (where relevant) the expert's report are available for inspection by the respective members of each merging company at each company's registered office; and

(b) a statement that the common draft terms of merger may be obtained from the Registrar.[22]

[6.038] The publication requirements of s 470 may be avoided by a merging company if it published free of charge on its website for a continuous period of

---

[18] Section 468(6) of the Act.
[19] Section 469 of the Act.
[20] Section 470(1), (2) and (4) of the Act. There is provision in s 470(6) for these periods to be extended if the company's website has been disrupted for a continuous period of at least 24 hours or for separate periods totalling not less than 72 hours.
[21] Section 470(1), (2) and (4) of the Act.
[22] Section 470(3) of the Act.

at least two months, commencing at least 30 days[23] before the date of the general meeting at which the merger is to be voted on and ending at least 30 days after that date, a copy of the common draft terms of merger and published in the *CRO Gazette* and once at least in one daily newspaper notice of the publication on its website of the common draft terms of merger.

[6.039] Section 471 in turn confers on the members of each merging company an express right of inspection, free of charge, of those documents referred to in the notices published by the merging companies.

(d) Approval of the merger

[6.040] The next step in the process is for the merger to be approved by each of the merging companies. In this regard, s 472 provides the merging companies with two options.

Use of summary approval procedure

[6.041] First, they may elect to employ the summary approval procedure in which case, as provided for in Chapter 7 of Part 4 of the Act, on the passing of the resolution referred to in s 202(1)(a)(ii) by each of the merging companies, the merger shall, in accordance with the common draft terms of merger and any supplemental document, take effect on the date specified in the common draft terms of merger or in that supplemental document, as the case may be.[24] According to s 472(2) and (3), the approval of the merger using the summary approval procedure has the same consequential effects as if the merger had been confirmed by court order, with the same preservation of rights of holders of securities and with the same civil and criminal liability arising for untrue statements in the merger documents.

[6.042] The Summary Approval Procedure ("SAP") has been considered elsewhere in this guide.[25] In the case of merger, Chapter 7 of Part 4 sets out the way in which each of the merging companies can authorise the merger to be put into effect by unanimous resolution of its members and by its directors making a certain declaration.[26] Unlike other restricted activities, which can be carried out using the SAP in respect of which a special resolution suffices, in the case of merger the authority from the members must be by way of a unanimous resolution.[27] The unanimous resolution must be passed not more than 12 months

---

[23] Section 470(5) of the Act.
[24] Section 472(2) of the Act.
[25] See, Ch 2, *Changes in the Basics: Constitutions, Share Capital and Governance*, at para **[2.063]** *et seq* and Ch 5 *Taking Security, the Summary Approval Procedure and the Registration of Charges*, at para **[5.039]** *et seq*.
[26] Section 201(2) of the Act.
[27] Section 202(1)(a)(ii).

prior to the commencement of the carrying on of the merger by each of the merging companies. The terms of the resolution must be that the common draft terms of merger are approved.[28]

In addition, the merging companies must forward with each notice of the meeting at which the unanimous resolution is to be passed (or if the written means for passing the resolution is used, the merging companies must append to the proposed text of the unanimous resolution) a copy of a declaration of the directors.

[6.043] The directors' declaration must be in writing and made at a meeting of the directors held not earlier than 30 days before the date of the meeting (or if passed by written means, not earlier than 30 days before the date of the last member to sign it): s 202(6). In the case of merger, each declaration by the directors (or by a majority of them) must state:

(a)   the total amount of the assets and liabilities of the merging company in question as at the latest practicable date before the date of making of the declaration and in any event at a date not more than 3 months before the date of that making; and

(b)   that the declarants have made a full inquiry into the affairs of the company and the other merging companies and that, having done so, they have formed the opinion that the successor company (within the meaning of Chapter 3 of Part 9) will be able to pay or discharge the debts and other liabilities of it and the transferor company or companies in full as they fall due during the period of 12 months after the date on which the merger takes effect.

A copy of each declaration must be delivered to the Registrar not later than 21 days after the date on which the carrying on of the merger is commenced: s 206(2).

It should be noted, however, that by reason of s 209(1), this declaration will have no effect unless it is accompanied by a document, prepared by the directors, either –

"(a)   confirming that the common draft terms of merger provide for such particulars of each relevant matter as will enable each of the prescribed effects provisions to operate without difficulty in relation to the merger; or

(b)   specifying such particulars of each relevant matter as will enable each of those effects provisions to operate without difficulty in relation to the merger."

"Prescribed effects provisions" is defined to mean s 480(3)(a) to (i) as that provision has effected by virtue of s 472(2).

---

[28]   Section 202(7) of the Act.

Section 202(5) provides that on the delivery, in accordance with s 206, to the Registrar of the declarations of both companies' directors, the Registrar shall register the dissolution of the transferor company (or companies where more than one is merging into a successor).

Use of alternative approval and confirmation procedure

[6.044] If the merging companies do not elect to employ the summary approval procedure, then they must instead comply with the approval procedure laid down in ss 473 to 482 of the Act.

In the first instance, the common draft terms of merger must be approved by a special resolution passed at a general meeting of each of the merging companies.[29] Each such meeting must be held not earlier than 30 days after the publication of the notices referred to above.[30] If the merger will involve a variation of class rights, then separate class approval will also be required in accordance with the provisions of Chapter 4 of Part 3 of the Act.[31]

The notice convening each meeting must contain a statement of every shareholder's entitlement to obtain on request, free of charge, copies of the merger documents referred to in the aforementioned notices.[32]

[6.045] In the case of each transferor company, the directors must inform the general meeting of that company of any material change in the assets and liabilities of that company that has occurred between the date of the common draft terms of merger and the date of the general meeting.[33] They must similarly inform the directors of the successor company of any such changes "as soon as practicable"[34] and the directors of the successor company must likewise inform the general meeting of that company of any such changes in the assets and liabilities of any transferor company that have been so communicated to them.[35]

[6.046] Approval of the common draft terms of merger by special resolution will not be required of any transferor company, in the case of a merger by absorption; nor will it be required of the successor company in the case of a merger by acquisition if the following conditions have been satisfied:[36]

---

29   Section 473(2) of the Act.
30   Section 473(2) of the Act.
31   Section 475 of the Act.
32   Section 473(3) of the Act. Under s 474, if a shareholder has so consented, he may be given notice electronically and rather than being sent hard copies of the documentation, it will suffice that he can download them from the website.
33   Section 473(4) of the Act.
34   Section 473(4) of the Act.
35   Section 473(5) of the Act.
36   Section 473(6) and (7) of the Act.

(a) at least 30 days before the passing by it of the special resolution approving the merger, the transferor company duly published in at least one national daily newspaper, the notice required of it under s 470;[37]

(b) during the notice period the members of the successor company were entitled to inspect the merger documents and financial statements in accordance with s 471 and to obtain copies of those documents on request; and

(c) during the notice period a general meeting to vote on the merger has not been requisitioned by one or more members holding not less than 5 per cent of the paid up voting share capital.

(e) Purchase of minority shares

[6.047] Where the merger has been duly approved by each of the merging companies, s 476 affords the right for minority shareholders in any of the transferor companies to demand that they be bought out for cash by the successor company at a price determined in accordance with the share exchange ratio set out in the common draft terms of merger. In this regard a "minority shareholder" is defined as meaning the following:

(a) Any shareholder other than the successor company, in a case where the successor company (not being one formed for the purpose of the merger) holds 90 per cent or more of the voting shares in the transferor company;

(b) In any other case, a shareholder who voted against the resolution.

The demand to be bought out must be made not later than 15 days after the "relevant date". In the second of the scenarios in which the person is a "minority shareholder" the "relevant date" is simply stated as being the date on which the relevant transferor company passed the special resolution. However, in the first scenario, the "relevant date" is the date of the publication of the notice required under s 470. Since that notice must be published at least 30 days before the special resolution is passed, the period of 15 days from the relevant date will have expired before the special resolution has been passed. Thus, on a literal reading of the legislation, a minority shareholder in a transferor company in which the successor company holds at least 90 per cent of the voting shares, could lose his right to be bought out before that right had even accrued!

---

[37] If there is more than one transferor company, and they pass their respective special resolutions on different dates, the notices in question must have been duly published not earlier than 30 days before the first of the special resolutions was passed.

(f) Confirmation by the court

[6.048] Once the merger has been duly approved by each of the merging companies they must then make a joint application to the court for an order confirming the merger.[38] The application must give details of any minority shareholder who has sought to be bought out under s 476 and must give details of the steps which the successor company proposes to take to comply with that demand.

Creditor protection

[6.049] In order to ensure that creditors of the merging companies are protected, s 478 expressly stipulates that they have a right to be heard by the court in relation to the confirmation of the merger. Presumably, therefore, the court will have to give directions as to the advertising and/or service of the application on creditors in advance of the hearing taking place.

[6.050] In the case of the holders of securities, other than shares, in any of the transferor companies, to which special rights are attached, s 479 affords additional protection. They must be given rights in the successor company at least equivalent to those possessed in the transferor company unless:

(a) the alteration of rights in the successor company has been approved by a majority of the holders of those securities at a meeting held for that purpose; or

(b) the alteration of rights has been individually approved by all of the holders of those securities; or

(c) the holders of those securities are entitled under the terms of those securities to be bought out by the successor company.

The confirmation order

[6.051] If the court is satisfied that:

(a) the requirements of Chapter 3 have been complied with;

(b) proper provision has been made for any minority shareholder who has requested to be bought out under s 476;

(c) proper provision has been made for any objecting creditor; and

(d) the rights of holders of securities under s 479 have been complied with,

it may make an order under s 480 confirming the merger from such date as it appoints.

---

[38] Section 477 of the Act.

[6.052] Certain consequences are stated to flow automatically from the making of the confirmation order. These include the following:

   (a) the transfer of all assets and liabilities of the transferor companies to the successor company;

   (b) in the case of a merger by acquisition or a merger by formation of a new company, the members of the transferor company or companies except the successor company becoming members of the successor company;

   (c) the continuation by or against the successor company of pending legal proceedings to which any of the transferor companies were parties;

   (d) the automatic dissolution of the transferor companies and the substitution of the successor company for the transferor companies in relation to every contract, agreement or instrument to which any of the transferor companies were parties. In this regard, all such contracts, agreements and other instruments automatically vest in the successor company even if they were expressly stated to be unassignable and thus personal to the relevant transferor company.[39]

[6.053] It should also be noted that s 481 expressly provides that, if the court sees fit to do so for the purpose of enabling the merger to have effect, it may include in the confirmation order a provision for the giving of financial assistance in relation to the acquisition of shares that would otherwise be unlawful under s 82 and may also permit a reduction in company capital that might otherwise be prohibited under s 84.

[6.054] Once the court has made the confirmation order, it must send a certified copy to the Registrar who must register both the order and the fact of the dissolution of the transferor companies and must also within 14 days publish notice of the delivery of the order to him in the *CRO Gazette*.[40]

(g) Civil and criminal liability

[6.055] In order to protect persons who might be adversely affected by the merger, ss 483 and 484 provide for the imposition of civil and/or criminal liability for certain classes of misconduct connected with the merger process.

In particular, s 483(1) provides that:

"Any shareholder of any of the merging companies who has suffered loss or damage by reason of misconduct in the preparation or implementation of the merger by a director of any such company or by the expert, if any, who has made a report under section 468 shall be entitled to have such loss or damage made good to him or her by –

---

[39] See s 480(4) of the Act.
[40] Section 482 of the Act.

(a)   in the case of misconduct by a person who was a director of that company at the date of the common draft terms of merger – that person;

(b)   in the case of misconduct by any expert who made a report under section 468 in respect of any of the merging companies – that person."

Section 483(2) goes on to provide that without prejudice to the generality of the civil liability imposed by subs (1) any shareholder of any of the merging companies who has suffered loss or damage arising from the inclusion of any untrue statement in the common draft terms of merger and/or any explanatory report and/or any expert's report and/or any merger financial statement will be entitled to have that loss or damage made good. In the case of untrue statements in the common draft terms of merger and/or any explanatory report and/or any merger financial statement, the persons with liability to compensate are the persons who were directors of that company at the date of the common draft terms of merger. In the case of an untrue statement in an expert's report, it is the expert himself who has liability.

[6.056] A director will not be liable under subs (2) if:

(a)   he or she can prove that the document in question was issued without his or her knowledge or consent and that, on becoming aware of its issue, he or she immediately informed the shareholders of that company that the document was so issued without his or her consent; or

(b)   that as regards any untrue statement he or she had reasonable grounds, having exercised all reasonable care and skill, for believing and did believe, up to the time when the merger took effect, that the statement was true.[41]

Likewise the expert may avoid liability for an untrue statement in his or her report if he or she proves:

(a)   that, on becoming aware of the statement, he or she immediately informed the company and its shareholders of the untruth; or

(b)   that he or she was competent to make the statement and had reasonable grounds for believing and did believe up to the time when the merger took effect, that the statement was true.[42]

[6.057] In relation to the question of criminal liability, s 484 provides that where any untrue statement has been included in the common draft terms of merger and/or any explanatory report and/or any merger financial statement, the following persons will be guilty of a category 2 offence:

(a)   each of the persons who was a director of any of the merging companies at the date of the common draft terms of merger or, in the case of an

---

[41]   Section 484(3) of the Act.
[42]   Section 483(4) of the Act.

explanatory report or merger financial statement, at the date of that document's preparation; and

(b)   any person who authorised the issue of the document.

The expert and any person who authorised the issue of the expert's report will also be guilty of a category 2 offence.

In any such criminal proceedings it is a defence for the accused to prove that, having exercised all reasonable care and skill, he or she had reasonable grounds for believing and did believe, up to the time of the issue of the document, that the statement in question was true.

Divisions of companies

[6.058] Turning now to the division of companies, Chapter 4 of Part 9 of the Act provides a procedure which is broadly equivalent to that which previously applied to PLCs under Part III of the European Communities (Mergers and Divisions of Companies) Regulations 1987, as amended by the European Communities (Mergers and Divisions of Companies) (Amendment) Regulations 2008.

[6.059] According to s 486, the provisions of Chapter 4 apply only if none of the companies involved is a PLC[43] and provided also that at least one of the companies involved in the division is a private company limited by shares.

[6.060] Two types of division are provided for, namely a "division by acquisition" and a "division by formation of new companies".[44]

[6.061] A "division by acquisition" is a process whereby two or more successor companies (of which one or more but not all may be a new company) acquire between them all the assets and liabilities of a transferor company in exchange for the allotment by them of shares to the members of the transferor company, with or without an accompanying cash payment, and pursuant to which the transferor company is dissolved without going into liquidation.[45]

[6.062] A "division by formation of new companies" is a process consisting of the same elements as a division by acquisition, save that the successor companies have all been formed for the purpose of the acquisition of the assets and liabilities of the transferor company.[46]

[6.063] The procedure for effecting a division is similar but not identical to that laid down by Chapter 3 for mergers.

---

[43]   As already explained above, mergers and divisions of PLCs are now governed by Chapters 16 and 17 of Part 17 of the Act.

[44]   Section 485(1) of the Act.

[45]   Section 487(1) of the Act.

[46]   Section 487(2) of the Act.

(a)   The documents to be prepared

[6.064] The first step in the division process is for the directors of the participating companies to draw up and approve written common draft terms of division which must, at a minimum, set out the matters prescribed by s 490.

[6.065] An explanatory report must also be prepared and approved in respect of each participating company, by its board of directors, explaining, at a minimum, the common draft terms of division and the legal and economic grounds for and implications of the proposed division, with particular reference to the proposed share exchange ratio, organisation and management structures, recent and future commercial activities and the financial interests of the holders of the shares and other securities in the company.[47] The requirement for an explanatory report may be dispensed with, *inter alia*, if all of the holders of voting shares in each of the participating companies so agree.[48] In addition, there will be no requirement for an explanatory report in relation to a company involved in a division by formation of new companies where the shares in each of the successor companies are allocated to the shareholders of the transferor company in proportion to their rights in the capital of that company.[49]

[6.066] Subject to some exceptions set out in s 492(2) there must also be drawn up for the members of each participating company an expert's report which must:

(a)   state the method or methods used to arrive at the proposed share exchange ratio;

(b)   give the opinion of the expert as to whether the proposed share exchange ratio is fair and reasonable;

(c)   give the opinion of the expert as to the adequacy of the method or methods used in the case in question;

(d)   indicate the values arrived at using each such method;

(e)   give the opinion of the expert as to the relative importance attributed to such methods in arriving at the values decided on; and

(f)   specify any valuation difficulties which have arisen.[50]

[6.067] The board of each participating company may appoint its own expert (or two or more boards may appoint the same person or persons). Alternatively, all of the participating companies may apply to the court to appoint a common expert.[51] The expert must be a statutory auditor and not only must not have been an officer or employee of any of the participating companies in the 12 months

---

[47]   Section 491(1), (2) and (3) of the Act.
[48]   Section 491(4) of the Act.
[49]   Section 491(5) of the Act.
[50]   Section 491(7) of the Act.
[51]   Section 491(3) of the Act.

before the date of the common draft terms of division but also, subject to certain exceptions, must not be connected with any of the officers of any of the participating companies.[52]

[6.068] Where the latest statutory financial statements of any of the participating companies relate to a financial year ended more than six months before the date of the common draft terms of division, then, subject to certain exceptions, if that company is availing itself of the exemption from the requirement to hold a general meeting, it must prepare a division financial statement (with accompanying statutory auditor's report) in the format of its last annual balance sheet that must be made up to a date not earlier than the first day of the month preceding the date of the common draft terms of division.[53]

(b) Registration, publication and inspection of documents

[6.069] At least 30 days before the date of passing of their respective resolutions approving the common draft terms of division, each of the participating companies must deliver to the Registrar of Companies a copy of the draft terms of division and a notice in the prescribed form specifying its name and registered office, its legal form and its registered number.[54] Notice of the delivery of the common draft terms of division to the Registrar of Companies must then be published by the Registrar in the *CRO Gazette* and by each participating company in one national daily newspaper. The notice published by each of the participating companies must likewise appear in the relevant newspapers at least 30 days before the passing of the resolutions approving the division.[55] The notice as so published must include:

(a) a statement that copies of the common draft terms of division, the directors' explanatory report, the statutory financial statements of each of the participating companies for the preceding three financial years and (where relevant) the expert's report are available for inspection by the respective members of each participating company at each company's registered office; and

(b) a statement that the common draft terms of division may be obtained from the Registrar.[56]

[6.070] The publication requirements of s 494 may be avoided by a participating company if it published free of charge on its website for a continuous period of

---

[52] Section 491(6) of the Act.
[53] Section 492 of the Act.
[54] Section 494(1), (2) and (4) of the Act. There is provision in s 494(6) for these periods to be extended if the company's website has been disrupted for a continuous period of at least 24 hours or for separate periods totalling not less than 72 hours.
[55] Section 494(1), (2) and (4) of the Act.
[56] Section 494(3) of the Act.

at least two months, commencing at least 30 days[57] before the date of the general meeting at which the division is to be voted on and ending at least 30 days after that date, a copy of the common draft terms of division and published in the *CRO Gazette* and once at least in one daily newspaper notice of the publication on its website of the common draft terms of division.

[6.071] Section 495 in turn confers on the members of each participating company an express right of inspection, free of charge, of those documents referred to in the notices published by the participating companies.

(c) Approval of the division

[6.072] The next step in the process is for the division to be approved by each of the participating companies. In this regard, it should be noted that in contrast to the procedure for the approval of mergers pursuant to Chapter 3 of Part 9, there is no provision for the use of the summary approval procedure for the purpose of giving effect to a division of companies pursuant to Chapter 4. Rather, there is one unified approval and confirmation procedure, laid down by ss 496 to 504.

[6.073] In the first instance, the common draft terms of division must be approved by a special resolution passed at a general meeting of each of the participating companies.[58] Each such meeting must be held not earlier than 30 days after the publication of the notices referred to above.[59] If the division will involve a variation of class rights, then separate class approval will also be required in accordance with the provisions of Chapter 4 of Part 3 of the Act.[60]

[6.074] The notice convening each meeting must contain a statement of every shareholder's entitlement to obtain on request, free of charge, copies of the merger documents referred to in the aforementioned notices.[61]

[6.075] In the case of the transferor company, the directors must inform the general meeting of that company of any material change in the assets and liabilities of that company that has occurred between the date of the common draft terms of division and the date of the general meeting.[62] They must similarly inform the directors of the successor companies of any such changes "as soon as practicable"[63] and the directors of the successor companies must likewise inform the general meeting of those companies of any such changes in

---

[57] Section 494(5) of the Act.
[58] Section 496(2) of the Act.
[59] Section 496(2) of the Act.
[60] Section 498 of the Act.
[61] Section 498(3) of the Act. Under s 497, if a shareholder has so consented, he may be given notice electronically and rather than being sent hard copies of the documentation, it will suffice that he can download them from the website.
[62] Section 496(4) of the Act.
[63] Section 496(4) of the Act.

the assets and liabilities of the transferor company that have been so communicated to them.[64]

[6.076] Approval of the common draft terms of division by special resolution will not be required of any particular successor company, in the case of a division by acquisition, if the following conditions have been satisfied:[65]

(a) at least 30 days before the passing by the transferor company of the special resolution approving the division, the particular successor company duly published in at least one national daily newspaper, the notice required of it under s 494;

(b) during the notice period the members of the particular successor company were entitled to inspect the division documents and financial statements in accordance with s 495 and to obtain copies of those documents on request; and

(c) during the notice period a general meeting to vote on the division has not been requisitioned by one or more members holding not less than 5 per cent of the paid up voting share capital.

(d) Purchase of minority shares

[6.077] Where the division has been duly approved by each of the participating companies, s 499 affords the right for minority shareholders in the transferor company to demand that they be bought out for cash by the successor companies at a price determined in accordance with the share exchange ratio set out in the common draft terms of division. In this regard a "minority shareholder" is defined as meaning the following:

(a) any shareholder other than a successor company, in a case where a successor company (not being one formed for the purpose of the division) holds 90 per cent or more of the voting shares in the transferor company;

(b) in any other case, a shareholder who voted against the resolution.

The demand to be bought out must be made not later than 15 days after the "relevant date". In the second of the scenarios in which the person is a "minority shareholder" the "relevant date" is simply stated as being the date on which the transferor company passed the special resolution. However, in the first scenario, the "relevant date" is the date of the publication of the notice required under s 494. This gives rise to the same anomaly as has been described above in relation to the merger of companies. In particular, it is to be noted that since that notice must be published at least 30 days before the special resolution is passed, the period of 15 days from the relevant date will have expired before the special

---

64 Section 496(5) of the Act.
65 Section 496(6) and (7) of the Act.

resolution has been passed. Thus, on a literal reading of the legislation, a minority shareholder in a transferor company in which the successor company holds at least 90 per cent of the voting shares, could lose his right to be bought out before that right had even accrued!

(e) Confirmation by the court

[6.078] Once the division has been duly approved by each of the participating companies they must then make a joint application to the court for an order confirming the division.[66] The application must give details of any minority shareholder who has sought to be bought out under s 499 and must give details of the steps which the successor companies propose to take to comply with that demand.

Creditor protection

[6.079] In order to ensure that creditors of the merging companies are protected, s 501 expressly stipulates that they have a right to be heard by the court in relation to the confirmation of the division. Presumably, therefore, the court will have to give directions as to the advertising and/or service of the application on creditors in advance of the hearing taking place.

[6.080] Furthermore, s 501(2) specifies that where a liability of the transferor company has not been allocated by the common draft terms of division and it is not possible, by reference to an interpretation of the draft terms of division, to determine the manner in which it is to be allocated, the liability is to become, jointly and severally, the liability of all of the successor companies. Similarly, subs (3) stipulates that if provision is not made by the common draft terms of division for the allocation of a liability incurred by, or which otherwise becomes attached to, the transferor company on or after the date of those draft terms then, subject to any other provision that the court may make in the order confirming the division, the liability becomes, jointly and severally, the liability of all of the successor companies.

[6.081] In the case of the holders of securities, other than shares, in the transferor company, to which special rights are attached, s 502 affords additional protection. They must be given rights in one or more of the successor companies at least equivalent to those possessed in the transferor company unless:

(a)   the alteration of rights in a successor company has been approved by a majority of the holders of those securities at a meeting held for that purpose; or

(b)   the alteration of rights has been individually approved by all of the holders of those securities; or

---

[66]   Section 500 of the Act.

(c)   the holders of those securities are entitled under the terms of those securities to be bought out by a successor company.

The confirmation order

[6.082] If the court is satisfied that:

(a)   the requirements of Chapter 4 have been complied with;

(b)   proper provision has been made for any minority shareholder who has requested to be bought out under s 499;

(c)   proper provision has been made for any objecting creditor; and

(d)   the rights of holders of securities under s 502 have been complied with,

it may make an order under s 503 confirming the merger from such date as it appoints.

[6.083] Certain consequences are stated to flow automatically from the making of the confirmation order. These include the following:

(a)   the members of the transferor company becoming members of one or more of the successor companies as provided by the common draft terms of division;

(b)   the transfer of all assets and liabilities of the transferor company to the relevant successor company or companies;

(c)   the continuation by or against the successor companies (or such of them as the court may specify) of pending legal proceedings to which the transferor company was a party;

(d)   the automatic dissolution of the transferor company and the substitution of the relevant successor company or companies for the transferor company in relation to every contract, agreement or instrument to which the transferor company was a party. In this regard, all such contracts, agreements and other instruments automatically vest in the relevant successor company or companies even if they were expressly stated to be unassignable and thus personal to the transferor company.[67]

[6.084] It should also be noted that s 504 expressly provides that if the court sees fit to do so for the purpose of enabling the division to have effect, it may include in the confirmation order a provision for the giving of financial assistance in relation to the acquisition of shares that would otherwise be unlawful under s 82 and may also permit a reduction in company capital that might otherwise be prohibited under s 84.

[6.085] Once the court has made the confirmation order, it must send a certified copy to the Registrar of Companies who must register both the order and the fact

---

[67]   See s 503(4) of the Act.

of the dissolution of the transferor company and must also within 14 days publish notice of the delivery of the order to him in the *CRO Gazette*.[68]

(f) *Civil and criminal liability*

[6.086] In order to protect persons who might be adversely affected by the division, ss 506 and 507 provide for the imposition of civil and/or criminal liability for certain classes of misconduct connected with the division process.

In particular, s 506(1) provides that:

"Any shareholder of any of the companies involved in the division who has suffered loss or damage by reason of misconduct in the preparation or implementation of the division by a director of any such company or by the expert, if any, who has made a report under section 492 shall be entitled to have such loss or damage made good to him or her by –

    (a)   in the case of misconduct by a person who was a director of that company at the date of the common draft terms of division – that person;

    (b)   in the case of misconduct by any expert who made a report under section 492 in respect of the companies involved in the division – that person."

Section 506(2) goes on to provide that without prejudice to the generality of the civil liability imposed by subs (1) any shareholder of any of the participating companies who has suffered loss or damage arising from the inclusion of any untrue statement in the common draft terms of division and/or any explanatory report and/or any expert's report and/or any division financial statement will be entitled to have that loss or damage made good. In the case of untrue statements in the common draft terms of division and/or any explanatory report and/or any division financial statement, the persons with liability to compensate are the persons who were directors of that company at the date of the common draft terms of division. In the case of an untrue statement in an expert's report, it is the expert himself who has liability.

[6.087] A director will not be liable under subs (2) if:

    (a)   he or she can prove that the document in question was issued without his or her knowledge or consent and that, on becoming aware of its issue, he or she immediately informed the shareholders of that company that the document was so issued without his or her consent; or

    (b)   that as regards any untrue statement he or she had reasonable grounds, having exercised all reasonable care and skill, for believing and did believe, up to the time when the division took effect, that the statement was true.[69]

---

[68]   Section 505 of the Act.
[69]   Section 506(3) of the Act.

Likewise the expert may avoid liability for an untrue statement in his or her report if he or she proves:

(a) that, on becoming aware of the statement, he or she immediately informed the company and its shareholders of the untruth; or

(b) that he or she was competent to make the statement and had reasonable grounds for believing and did believe up to the time when the division took effect, that the statement was true.[70]

[6.088] In relation to the question of criminal liability, s 507 provides that where any untrue statement has been included in the common draft terms of division and/or any explanatory report and/or any division financial statement, the following persons will be guilty of a category 2 offence:

(a) each of the persons who was a director of any of the merging companies at the date of the common draft terms of division or, in the case of an explanatory report or division financial statement, at the date of that document's preparation; and

(b) any person who authorised the issue of the document.

The expert and any person who authorised the issue of the expert's report will also be guilty of a category 2 offence.

In any such criminal proceedings it is a defence for the accused to prove that, having exercised all reasonable care and skill, he or she had reasonable grounds for believing and did believe, up to the time of the issue of the document, that the statement in question was true.

---

[70] Section 506(4) of the Act.

Chapter 7

Insolvency and Rescue

by
Professor Irene Lynch Fannon

Introduction

[7.001] This chapter will describe changes to previously existing legislation enacted in the new Companies Act in relation to insolvency and rescue processes and insolvency rules generally. It is not therefore intended to provide a full description of all of the laws regarding these matters but to focus on changes. Readers are referred to Lynch Fannon and Murphy, *Corporate Insolvency and Rescue*[1] for a more complete treatment of the laws in this area. Accordingly, there will be a discussion of the provisions relating to receivers, schemes of arrangement,[2] examinerships, and windings up. The latter will include a discussion on compulsory or court windings up (liquidations) and voluntary windings up (liquidations), both creditors' and members'. Although the actual processes will be the focus of this chapter, where relevant particular issues, for example the position of preferential creditors in insolvency, matters concerning transactional avoidance and other issues, will also be dealt with as these provisions appear in the relevant parts under discussion.

Structure

[7.002] This chapter considers the following matters:

1. An overview of major changes;
2. Receivers;
3. Reorganisations;[3]

---

[1] Lynch Fannon and Murphy, *Corporate Insolvency and Rescue* (2nd edn, Bloomsbury Professional, 2012). See also Lynch, Marshall and O'Farrell, *Corporate Insolvency and Rescue* (Butterworths, 1996).

[2] Schemes of arrangement are used in relation to corporate rescues and restructurings in insolvency situations. Note that here there is some interface with the discussion in Ch 6, *Corporate Restructuring: Schemes, Mergers and Divisions*.

[3] See generally, Lynch, Marshall and O'Farrell, *Corporate Insolvency and Rescue* (Butterworths, 1996) Ch 12 on Other Forms of Rescue; Lynch Fannon and Murphy, *Corporate Insolvency and Rescue* (2nd edn, Bloomsbury Professional, 2012) Ch 14 on Other Forms of Rescue.

4. Exminership; and

5. Winding up.

An overview of major changes

[7.003] This section highlights the principal changes which will take place in the area of insolvency and rescue law, broadly speaking, under the new Companies Act 2014. They are as follows:

1. Powers of receivers are enumerated in this legislation for the first time.[4]

2. The scheme of arrangement process included in the provisions on mergers and acquisitions has been simplified with a significant reduction in the requirement of court hearings to, in theory at least, a sole court hearing rather than three.[5]

3. The jurisdiction of the Circuit Court will extend to the appointment of examiners in relation to small companies (as defined in s 350) of the Act to assist with the rescue of small and medium enterprises (SMEs). This change had been in the original drafts of the Bill but was extracted from the legislation and enacted in advance in December 2013 when the Companies (Miscellaneous Provisions) Act 2013 was passed. These provisions were enacted before the main body of the Act because of the perception that steps needed to be taken urgently to address corporate rescue in the SME sector. However, this legislation, insofar as it affects examinerships, is now replaced again by provisions in the consolidated legislation.[6]

4. There will be some use of the Summary Approval Procedure which is a feature of the new legislation. The summary approval procedure is outlined in Part 4, Chapter 7, of the legislation.[7] It is applicable to a number of areas of the legislation where hitherto particular actions of a company had to be approved through special resolution accompanied by a statutory declaration of solvency. Examples include reduction in share capital and transactions regarding the provision of financial assistance in the purchase of shares. In the liquidation area this will apply to voluntary liquidations. This is required by s 579 regarding the commencement of members' voluntary windings up.

5. The legislation has been designed so that there is greater uniformity between the three types of windings up (liquidation); namely, court windings up (sometimes referred to as official or compulsory); and voluntary windings up, both members' and creditors' voluntary windings up. This has implications for the role of the court in official

---

4   Section 437 of the Act.
5   Sections 449–455 of the Act.
6   Section 509 of the Act.
7   Section 202 of the Act.

liquidations, the role of liquidators generally, and also involves some changes to the role of the creditors' committees of inspection which will be described below.[8]

6. The regulation of insolvency practitioners, in particular, the requirement that those acting as liquidators hold particular qualifications, heralds a long overdue professionalisation of the role of liquidators in Ireland. There are also provisions regarding the role of the Supervisory Authority in relation to the appointment of non-qualified individuals as liquidators in limited circumstances and in relation to the requirement for professional indemnity.[9] The requirements regarding qualifications of liquidators are also applied to examiners by virtue of s 519.

7. There are some changes made in relation to the avoidance of transactions and the distribution of assets on liquidation.[10]

8. The terms of the EU Insolvency Regulation are enacted and referred to as required, although there will be changes in this area emanating from the EU Commission in the medium to short term.[11]

9. There are some changes in relation to foreign subsidiaries.

[7.004] This chapter will focus on changes to pre-existing legislation on insolvency and rescue law which have now been enacted in the Companies Act 2014. Some areas of divergence between English and Irish insolvency and rescue law will be considered, as there is a significant level of divergence at this point in time.

Receivers[12]

[7.005] Part 8 of the Companies Act 2014, which deals with receivers, is divided into a number of Chapters, namely:

- Chapter 1: Interpretation;
- Chapter 2: Appointment of receivers;

---

8   Sections 666–668 of the Act.
9   Sections 633–635 of the Act.
10 Sections 603–608 of the Act.
11 The EU Insolvency Regulation 1346/2000 was enacted as part of Irish law in the European Communities (Corporate Insolvency) Regulations 2002 (SI 333/2002). Lynch Fannon and Murphy, *Corporate Insolvency and Rescue* (2nd edn, Bloomsbury Professional, 2012) Ch 1; Moss, Fletcher and Isaacs, *The EC Regulation on Insolvency Proceedings – A Commentary and Annotated Guide* (2nd edn, Oxford University Press, 2009). Currently there are proposals emanating from the European Commission to amend the Regulation. See COM (2012) 744 'Proposal for a Regulation of the European Parliament and Council amending Council Regulation (EC) No 1346/2000'. In this context see Commission Recommendation of 12.3.2014 C (2014) 1500/final 'A new approach to Business Failure and Insolvency'.
12 See generally Lynch Fannon and Murphy, *Corporate Insolvency and Rescue* (2nd edn, Bloomsbury Professional, 2012) Chs 6 and 7.

- Chapter 3: Powers and duties of receivers;
- Chapter 4: Regulation of receivers and enforcement of their duties.

As stated, this chapter will focus on significant changes to existing law.

(a) Powers and duties of receivers[13]

[7.006] Section 437 represents a significant change in that this provision enumerates the powers of a receiver. To begin with the section states in s 437(1) that a receiver has the power to do "in the State and elsewhere all things necessary or convenient to be done for, or in connection with, or incidental to the attainment of the objectives for which the receiver was appointed." The purpose of enumerating the receiver's powers is to address problems arising from "poorly drafted debentures" which have led to cases where the receiver have been left in doubt as to powers available. Section 437 is modelled on s 420 of the Australian Corporations Act 2001.

[7.007] There are two questions of interest, the first concerning principles of statutory interpretation and the second regarding the jurisdictional reach of this provision. Despite the broad terminology of s 437(1), is it the case that once the powers have been explicitly enumerated as the section goes on to do, the broad introductory statement is confined by the subsequent enumeration of powers? To address the potential for litigation on this point, s 437(2) explicitly states that the enumeration of the powers in this section is "without prejudice to the generality of subsection (1)" and so this matter seems to be clear. Nevertheless s 437(4) recognises that it is possible that the receiver's powers may be limited by the court or "the instrument under which the receiver was appointed" and states that s 437(1) and (2) are subject to such provisions. Accordingly the final determinant of a receiver's powers will be the court order or instrument appointing him or her.

[7.008] The second question, which is more pertinent in current contexts, concerns the jurisdictional reach of the provision which specifically refers to "the State and elsewhere". Whether the powers of a receiver are recognised or enforceable in other jurisdictions depends entirely on reciprocity of arrangements between Ireland and other jurisdictions. The EU Insolvency Regulation[14] does not apply to receiverships (as receivership is not a formal insolvency process) and so the likelihood that the appointment of a receiver over assets located in another jurisdiction and the consequent recognition of the

---

13 Lynch Fannon and Murphy, *Corporate Insolvency and Rescue* (2nd edn, Bloomsbury Professional, 2012) Ch 6, pp 231–238; Ch 7, pp 247–261.

14 Article 1(1) of the EU Insolvency Regulation 3486/2000 enacted in Ireland under the European Communities (Corporate Insolvency) Regulations 2002 (SI 333/2002). Lynch Fannon and Murphy, *Corporate Insolvency and Rescue* (2nd edn, Bloomsbury Professional, 2012) Ch 1, pp 19–33.

exercise by a receiver of his powers is diminished. There will of course be situations where creditors of an Irish company who are located in other jurisdictions may wish to pursue their own remedies including initiating insolvency procedures in their home jurisdiction. This is a definite possibility as the appointment of a receiver is not a process recognised, and therefore procedurally protected, under the provisions of the EU Insolvency Regulation.[15]

[7.009] Leaving these questions to be resolved in another forum, s 437(2) states that the powers enumerated in s 437 are in addition to powers conferred by order, instrument or any other law. Section 437(3) goes on to enumerate the powers which specifically include the power to borrow money (s 437(d)) and the power to carry on the business of the company (s 437(h)). The receiver may also bring or defend proceedings or do any other act in the name of the company (s 437(j)). Finally, amongst other powers the receiver is specifically empowered to "engage or discharge employees on behalf of the company" (s 437(m)). All of these enumerated powers are reflective of existing practice and law. There are other powers specifically mentioned but a number of questions arise:[16]

(a) the status of borrowings of the receiver in priority in a subsequent liquidation if that were to arise;

(b) whether the power of the receiver to sue in the company's name survives the appointment of a liquidator, a matter which has arisen in case law;[17]

(c) the potential application of the European Communities (Protection of Employees on Transfer of Undertakings) Regulations 2003 in relation to the discharge of employees;[18]

(d) rights of third parties are protected under the provisions of s 437(5) which states that "the conferral on a receiver, by this section, of powers in relation to property of a company does not affect any rights in relation to that property of any other person other than the company".

[7.010] Section 438 allows the receiver and other parties affected to apply to the court for directions. This may include guidance as to the exercise of additional powers.

[7.011] Finally, in relation to powers and duties of a receiver, s 439 repeats the existing obligation imposed on a receiver by s 316A of the 1963 Act as inserted

---

[15] See n 11. Article 3 and Recitals 12, 13 and 17 of the EU Insolvency Regulation 1346/2000 allow for the initiating of territorial proceedings where the creditor has particular interests relating to the assets of the debtor and there is a jurisdictional connection between the claim and the assets/debtor.

[16] See Lynch Fannon and Murphy, *Corporate Insolvency and Rescue* (2nd edn, Bloomsbury Professional, 2012) Ch 7, pp 261–270.

[17] Romer LJ in *Gough's Garages Ltd v Pugsley* [1930] 1 KB 615 at 626.

[18] Lynch Fannon and Murphy, *Corporate Insolvency and Rescue* (2nd edn, Bloomsbury Professional, 2012) Ch 7.

by s 172 of the 1990 Act to "exercise all reasonable care to obtain the best price reasonably obtainable as at the time of sale". There is no further clarification of the extent and nature of this obligation provided in this legislation so therefore existing case law and commentary is relevant. So for example there is still a hanging question, which is particularly relevant in a volatile property market, as to the relevant time period in which the receiver operates to get the best price "reasonably obtainable" and whether there is any obligation on the receiver to make some judgment regarding the time at which he or she is to get the best price reasonably obtainable. Most importantly, when exercising this judgment is there a possibility of a broader more expansive obligation based on a general duty of care in negligence?[19] On balance, and given the re-enactment of the legislative provision in its original format, and despite some litigation surrounding this question in the intervening years, the answer is most likely no.

(b) Regulation of receivers and enforcement of their duties

[7.012] The Director of Corporate Enforcement may request the books of a receiver under s 446 re-enacting s 53 of the Company Law Enforcement Act.

[7.013] Section 448 provides for the possibility that a professional body of which a receiver is a member may report its findings regarding particular types of misconduct on the part of a receiver to the Director of Corporate Enforcement. Types of misconduct include not maintaining appropriate records (s 448(1)(a)) or the commission of certain offences (s 448(1)(b)).

[7.014] There is no explicit requirement regarding the professional standardisation of those appointed to receiverships in this legislation. As described below, the Act introduces very explicit requirements regarding liquidators[20] which are applied to examiners by virtue of s 519 although not very explicitly so,[21] but there does not seem to be any explicit statement regarding the professional qualifications of those acting as receivers.

Reorganisations, acquisitions, mergers and divisions

[7.015] Part 9 of the Companies Act 2014 deals with the above matters and is considered in detail in Ch 6 of this text. However, the use of schemes of arrangement under this Part as a corporate rescue device will be considered below.

---

[19] Lynch Fannon and Murphy, *Corporate Insolvency and Rescue* (2nd edn, Bloomsbury Professional, 2012) Ch 7 where this matter and the case law thereon is discussed at length.

[20] See paras **[7.089]–[7.094]**.

[21] See paras **[7.032]–[7.033]**.

(a) Schemes of arrangement

[7.016] Part 9 of the Act deals generally with reorganisations, acquisitions, mergers and divisions. There is, however, an insolvency and rescue dimension to these provisions. Accordingly, this chapter will consider the application of the revised version of the original s 201 of the Companies Act 1963 which is re-enacted in the new legislation.[22]

[7.017] The provisions of Part 9, Chapter 3, ss 449–455 of the new Companies Act are relevant to corporate rescue. An interesting development in the current, post-crisis era of insolvency and rescue practice has been the use of the older scheme of arrangement legislation in England, which has enjoyed "something of a renaissance".[23] These provisions originally in the Irish legislation in ss 201–204 are mirrored in the Companies Act (UK) 2006 in ss 895–899.

[7.018] Schemes of arrangement have proved particularly attractive in England to a particular type of corporate rescue, especially for companies with cross-border trade and where parts of the corporate group span a number of European jurisdictions. Successful rescues have been facilitated in English courts for a number of European companies in cases such as *Re Seat Pagine Gialle SpA*,[24] *Re NEF TelecomCo BV*,[25] *Re Cortefiel SA*,[26] *Re Primacom Holdings GmbH*[27] and *Re Rodenstock GmbH*[28] where these companies have successfully availed of English schemes.[29] Interestingly, in Ireland these provisions are also present but have not been utilised with such great effect as they have been in England. (In passing it should be mentioned that schemes of arrangement provided for in ss 201–204 ought not to be conflated with the use of the term schemes of arrangement under the examinership process.)

[7.019] The great advantage to the modern usage of schemes of arrangement as a rescue device under English law is that these are not covered by the EU

---

[22] See generally Lynch, Marshall and O'Farrell, *Corporate Insolvency and Rescue* (Butterworths, 1996) Ch 12 and Lynch Fannon and Murphy, *Corporate Insolvency and Rescue* (2nd edn, Bloomsbury Professional, 2012) Ch 14.

[23] Payne, "Cross Border Schemes of Arrangement and Forum Shopping" (2014) 14 European Business Organisation Law Review 563–589, 567.

[24] *Re Seat Pagine Gialle SpA* [2012] EWHC 3686.

[25] *Re NEF TelecomCo BV* [2012] EWHC 2944.

[26] *Re Cortefiel SA* [2012] EWHC 2998.

[27] *Re Primacom Holdings GmbH* [2012] EWHC 164.

[28] *Re Rodenstock GmbH* [2011] EWHC 1104. See also *Re APCOA Parking (UK) Ltd & Ors* [2014] EWHC 997.

[29] For a consideration of how successful the scheme of arrangement has been in facilitating corporate rescue under English law see the following discussion in Payne, "Cross Border Schemes of Arrangement and Forum Shopping" (2014) 14 European Business Organisation Law Review 563–589. See further Payne, *Schemes of Arrangement, Theory and Structure* (Cambridge University Press, 2014).

Insolvency Regulation[30] and so foreign companies can quite happily avail of the English (or Irish) provisions without running the danger that "home country creditors" can initiate secondary or territorial proceedings in accordance with the procedures outlined in that Regulation. This is an advantage which the Irish provisions also have, as Chapter 1 of Part 9 is expressed to apply to any company liable to be wound up under the Act and not just "companies" as defined by s 2(1).[31] No issues as to COMI ("centre of main interests") as provided for in the EU Regulation arise. Nor will there be a difficulty if additional proceedings arise elsewhere as the scheme of arrangement, rescue and compromise with main creditors can proceed with the approval of the court. The English courts have accordingly utilised their discretion provided under the legislative framework with great effect and have facilitated a voluntary and very flexible corporate rescue regime.[32] The assertiveness of judicial discretion in approving schemes, despite objections of some creditors, has been extremely effective particularly in relation to approving schemes supported by significant creditors even where other creditors are disadvantaged. Such creditors, when deemed to be "out of the money" have been held to have no *locus standi* to object effectively. In effect, a form of "cram-down" on particular creditors has been fashioned through use of pre-pack negotiations before the court approval stage.[33] A further advantage is that the company avoids the stigma of insolvency if it can utilise this process without recourse to more formal processes, such as examinership.[34]

[7.020] In that context it is worth noting that the Act has streamlined existing provisions. Section 450(1) has removed the requirement that court approval is required to convene scheme meetings of members and more importantly, in this context, creditors, where the directors convene the meetings. It is therefore open to the directors to convene meetings of creditors "or the class concerned of them" or meetings of members "or the class concerned of them". Conversely, where directors have not convened the initial meetings, s 450(3) requires court approval or involvement at this early stage. (This might be where a major creditor initiates a scheme.) Section 450(4) goes on to provide that a creditor may request that a meeting is held. Section 451 also provides that once the

---

30 See n 11.

31 See s 1430 of the Act.

32 See above n 25–29 for case law on how the English courts have addressed questions of jurisdiction in this context.

33 The combined use of schemes of arrangement with pre-packaged administrations has facilitated cram-down on classes of creditors under this legislation. See eg *Re Bluebrook Ltd* [2009] EWHC 2114 for treatment of creditors who were "out of the money" and *Sea Assets v PT Garuda Indonesia* [2001] EWCA 1696.

34 See *Re Pye (Ireland) Ltd* (17 November 1984, unreported) HC and (11 March 1985, unreported) SC; *Re Millstream Recycling Ltd* [2009] IEHC 571 is an example of a modern scheme of arrangement under Irish law.

scheme process is initiated the court can grant a stay on proceedings which can be of indefinite duration, thus re-enacting s 201(2) of the 1963 Act.[35] Section 453(2)(b) eliminates the need for the second court hearing advertising the passing of the scheme. Sections 453 and 455 govern the sanctioning of the scheme by the court. Effectively, the required number of court hearings in the scheme of arrangement process has been reduced from three to one.

[7.021] The simple point to make is that this process, hitherto underutilised in Irish law, has now been further streamlined and is governed by a simply structured legal framework. It is possible that for some companies or groups this may present a better way to rescue a business than that available under examinerships. There are a number of advantages to schemes of arrangement under these provisions as compared even with examinerships, which are considered to be very effective:

   (i)   there is a lot less court involvement and therefore the process can be simple, speedy and cheaper;

   (ii)   there is no threshold requirement to initiate the rescue process *viz* there is no requirement for a "reasonable prospect" of the company surviving;

   (iii)   there is no necessity for an independent report;

   (iv)   there are no additional legal requirements regarding what must be rescued;[36]

   (v)   there is no stigma of insolvency for the company and its operations;

   (vi)   nor is there a triggering of other provisions regarding directors' liability and the liability of other officers under reckless or fraudulent trading provisions. Nor are the provisions regarding disqualification and restriction of directors and other officers triggered;

   (vii)   finally, there is a broad ranging discretion given to the court in the final approval process with a lot less precedential authority in terms of case law in relation to approval, providing a great deal of flexibility to the court.

[7.022] These factors, considered with the decoupling from the EU Insolvency Regulation, surely provide opportunities for Irish companies, European companies wishing to avail of more rescue friendly processes than those available in home jurisdictions, and their advisors.

---

[35] See Lynch Fannon and Murphy, *Corporate Insolvency and Rescue* (2nd edn, Bloomsbury Professional, 2012) Ch 14 at p 623 for a discussion of the relationship between this process and the appointment of a receiver.

[36] *Re Clare Textiles Ltd*. [1993] 2 IR 213. Lynch Fannon and Murphy, *Corporate Insolvency and Rescue* (2nd edn, Bloomsbury Professional, 2012) p 492.

Examinership[37]

[7.023] Part 10 of the Companies Act dealing with examiners is divided into a number of Chapters including:

- Chapter 1: Interpretation;
- Chapter 2: Appointment of an examiner;
- Chapter 3: Powers of an examiner;
- Chapter 4: Liability of third parties for debts of a company in examination;
- Chapter 5: Conclusion of examinership.

As stated, this chapter will focus on significant changes to existing law.

(a) Interpretation

[7.024] Section 508(2) specifically states that this Part is subject to the EU Insolvency Regulation.[38]

[7.025] Section 508 adds the concept of "shadow director" to the definition of directors in the section on interpretation.

(b) Appointment of an examiner

[7.026] The main change in relation to examinerships which was envisaged by this legislation has already become part of Irish law. The original Bill envisaged that the Circuit Court could take jurisdiction in relation to the appointment of examiners to smaller companies, thus making the process cheaper and more accessible to the SME sector. The compelling attraction of this initiative led this part of the Bill to be extracted and enacted as the Companies (Miscellaneous Provisions) Act 2013 in December 2013. Some cases have been heard already under the legislation, the first concerning the appointment of an examiner to Celbridge Playzone in Naas in April 2014 leading to the rescue of the company which employed 27 employees.[39] The Act reconsolidates this legislation into the main legislation. Accordingly, Chapter 2 addresses this jurisdictional question.

[7.027] Section 509 (7)(b) provides that for companies which fall to be treated as "a small company by virtue of s 350" based on information from the latest financial year of the company, references to the court in the section will be construed as referring to the Circuit Court. Accordingly, the Circuit Court now has jurisdiction to hear applications to appoint an examiner for those companies.

---

[37] Lynch Fannon and Murphy, *Corporate Insolvency and Rescue* (2nd edn, Bloomsbury Professional, 2012) Chs 12 and 13.

[38] See n 11.

[39] (2014) *Irish Independent* 3 April.

[7.028] Similarly, the Circuit Court has jurisdiction under s 517(8) to appoint an examiner to a related company where that related company can be treated as a small company by virtue of s 350.

[7.029] The examinership legislation has received a lot of attention since its original enactment in the Companies (Amendment) Act 1990. It was substantially amended in 1999 and has enjoyed close scrutiny and attention from practitioners and the courts alike. A number of additional changes are worth noting.

[7.030] Section 510(5) and (6) cross refer to the National Asset Management Agency Act 2009 (NAMA Act 2009) and provide that a court cannot appoint an examiner to a company where that company has obligations in relation to an asset that has been transferred to NAMA, unless a copy of the petition to appoint an examiner has been served on NAMA and the court has heard NAMA in relation to the order to appoint. (This is provided for in s 234 of the NAMA Act 2009.)

[7.031] Similarly, under s 517(6) the court cannot appoint an examiner to a related company where the related company has similar obligations in relation to assets belonging to the related company unless NAMA has been served with notice and the court has heard any submissions from NAMA.

[7.032] Section 519 provides, as did the previous legislation, that a person shall not be qualified to be appointed or to act as an examiner of a company unless he or she would be qualified to act as its liquidator. The new provisions on professional standardisation of liquidators are discussed below. Although not explicitly described in relation to examiners it must be the case that these standards now apply by virtue of this s 519.[40]

[7.033] Section 522 includes an amendment of s 6 of the Companies (Amendment) Act 1990. A provisional liquidator already appointed may be appointed as examiner of the company or be required to cease to act. This is reflective of the more limited effect the appointment of a provisional liquidator will have in the future which is described below.

(c) Powers of an examiner

[7.034] Section 524(9) is new and provides that no liability shall attach to an examiner nor will the examiner be regarded as being in breach of any professional or legal duty by reason of the examiner's compliance with the section in its entirety. Section 524 is equivalent to s 7 of the Companies (Amendment) Act 1990 and details the powers of the examiner.

---

[40] See paras **[7.091]**–**[7.094]**. Section 519(2) provides that it is a category 2 offence for a person to act as an examiner of a company where he or she is not qualified to do so.

[7.035] Specific provisions which have been inserted to address particular eventualities include the insertion of s 542(6)(b), which allows for a scheme to specifically provide for a reduction of capital following the decision of Finlay Geogheghan J in *Re McEnaney Construction Ltd*,[41] where it was held that a scheme under the examinership legislation could not provide for a reduction of capital unless this was specifically approved in accordance with legislation.

[7.036] Also of particular and ongoing interest are the provisions regarding repudiation of leases which are provided for under ss 544–548 and essentially repeat existing provisions in the previous legislation. The provisions on repudiation of contracts are also repeated in s 525 and the sections on leases must be read in conjunction with this provision.[42]

[7.037] Section 541 adds further provisions regarding the decision of the court in approving proposals. The previous provisions, which are repeated in s 541(4), refer to the requirement that "at least one class of creditors whose interest or claims would be impaired by implementation of the proposals has accepted the proposals"; that the proposals are "fair and equitable"; and that they are not "unfairly prejudicial" to the interests of any interested party.[43] Section 541(5) further clarifies the role of the court in approving proposals from the examiner and provides that without prejudice to the foregoing provisions, the court shall not confirm any proposals in respect of a company to which an examiner has been appointed under s 517 which have the effect of impairing the creditors of that company in such a manner as to "unfairly" favour the interests of the creditors of a company to which it is related.

(d) Liability of third parties for debts of a company in examination

[7.038] The liability of third parties has been clarified in Chapter 4 of this Part. The provisions of s 25A of the Companies (Amendment) Act 1990, as inserted by s 25 of the Companies (Amendment) (No 2) Act 1999, have been divided into relevant sections for the purposes of clarification. The primary issue in this Chapter concerns the positions of guarantors. Most importantly, s 549 concerns the rights of the third party guarantor to vote on proposals for a scheme of arrangement where the creditor proposes to enforce the obligations of that party in relation to a debt.

---

[41] *Re McEnaney Construction Ltd* [2008] IEHC 43.

[42] For a complete discussion of this interesting area of law see Lynch Fannon and Murphy, *Corporate Insolvency and Rescue* (2nd edn, Bloomsbury Professional, 2012) pp 591–599. See further *Re Linen Supply of Ireland Ltd* [2009] IEHC 544; *Re Linen Supply of Ireland Ltd* (Supreme Court, *ex tempore*, 2009) and *Re Linen Supply of Ireland Ltd (No 2)* [2010] IEHC 28.

[43] See *Re SIAC Construction Ltd* [2014] IESC 25 for a consideration of these provisions.

Winding up[44]

[7.039] Part 11 of the Companies Act 2014 dealing with windings up is divided into a number of Chapters as follows:

- Chapter 1: Preliminary and interpretation;
- Chapter 2: Winding up by the court (official liquidations);
- Chapter 3: Members' voluntary winding up;
- Chapter 4: Creditors' voluntary winding up;
- Chapter 5: Conduct of a winding up;
- Chapter 6: Realisation of assets and related matters;
- Chapter 7: Distribution;
- Chapter 8: Liquidators;
- Chapter 9: Contributories;
- Chapter 10: Committees of inspection;
- Chapter 11: Court's powers;
- Chapter 12: Provisions supplemental to conduct of the winding up;
- Chapter 13: General rules as to meetings of members, contributories and creditors of a company in liquidation;
- Chapter 14: Completion of winding up;
- Chapter 15: Provisions related to the Insolvency Regulation;
- Chapter 16: Offences by officers of companies in liquidation, offences of fraudulent trading and certain other offences, referrals to DPP, etc.

[7.040] Many of the changes in relation to windings up are driven by the predominant statutory goal of streamlining provisions regarding the three different kinds of winding up, namely court (sometimes called official or compulsory) windings up, creditors' voluntary and members' voluntary windings up. Some substantive changes are made to achieve this goal, and in addition, provisions which appear in a different sequence in previous legislation have been reordered to achieve a more structured approach.

[7.041] Accordingly, each Chapter from Chapters 2–4 deals with a particular kind of winding up and begins with a general provision which states that the provisions of the particular Chapter apply only to the particular kind of winding up save where otherwise stated.

[7.042] Section 568 states that "save to the extent otherwise expressly provided, Chapter 2 provisions apply only to winding-ups by the court". Similarly, s 579 states that the provisions of Chapter 3 apply only to members' voluntary windings up, and s 586 states that the provisions of Chapter 4 apply only to creditors' voluntary windings up.

---

[44] Lynch Fannon and Murphy, *Corporate Insolvency and Rescue* (2nd edn, Bloomsbury Professional, 2012) Chs 2–5.

[7.043] Chapters 5 to 16 then go on to deal with specific matters pertinent to all windings up unless otherwise stated.

As before, this section will focus on changes to the existing law.

(a) Preliminary and interpretation

[7.044] In the definition provisions, contained in s 559, the definition of "property" now includes the proceeds of any statutory rights conferred on the liquidator or the company by this legislation. Subsections (4) and (5) make important statements regarding the application of the provisions to provisional liquidators.[45]

[7.045] Section 560 states that the Part is generally subject to Chapters I and III of the European Communities (Corporate Insolvency) Regulations 2002 (SI 333/2002), which enact the EU Insolvency Regulation 1346/2000.[46]

[7.046] Section 562, entitled "general statement as to position under Act" aims to clarify the different types of voluntary winding up and where a voluntary winding up can proceed as a members' voluntary winding up. It also aims to clarify the circumstances where a voluntary winding up cannot proceed as a members' voluntary winding up and must proceed as a creditors' voluntary winding up. The legislative structure emphasises the desirability of proceeding through a voluntary winding up and where possible, proceeding as a members' voluntary winding up. However, this inclination depends on the company being able to pay its debts and the necessary procedures reflecting that, being in place. The emphasis on voluntary windings up, and in particular on members' voluntary windings up, must be weighed against the legitimate interests creditors have in controlling a liquidation which will affect their interests.[47]

(b) Court windings up

[7.047] The main changes relating to court liquidations concern the petitioning of the court to commence a winding up. In keeping with the new legislative

---

[45] See paras **[7.078]**–**[7.082]**.

[46] See paras **[7.118]**–**[7.119]** but of course this legislation is subject generally to the provisions of the EU Insolvency Regulation 1346/2000. See further n 11.

[47] It is worth bearing in mind the fundamental principles of insolvency law as described so succinctly by Goode, *Principles of Corporate Insolvency Law* (4th edn, Sweet and Maxwell, 2011) p 58. These are to:

>   (a)   Maximise the return to creditors; b) Establish a fair and equitable system of distribution of remaining assets to creditors; and c) Identify causes of failure and to ensure that where there is mismanagement this is followed by accountability. Achieving a fair and equitable system of distribution relies on a transparent system and whilst this can be balanced against the need for both an effective corporate rescue mechanism and a cheap and effective distribution system where rescue is not possible, all of this requires a balance. (contd..../)

scheme, whereby all liquidations are to be treated similarly (as described above), s 568 provides the saving provision that, save to the extent that it is otherwise expressly provided, each provision of Chapter 2 applies only to court ordered windings up.

[7.048] Section 569 describes the grounds upon which a company may be wound up by the court. This includes the possibility of the company being wound up if the court is "satisfied, on a petition of the Director, that it is in the public interest to do so."

[7.049] Accordingly, under s 569(1)(g), the Director of Corporate Enforcement has been added as a potential petitioner with *locus standi* to petition to wind up a company where the public interest requires this. There is no indication as to what the public interest might mean in this context.

[7.050] Section 571 provides for the *locus standi* of all other petitioners mentioned in previous legislation. Section 571(f) refers to the possibility that a company can be wound up where the company's affairs are being conducted or the powers of the directors are being exercised in an oppressive manner to any member or in disregard of his or her interests as a member, thus repeating existing provisions in the Companies Act 1963.[48] In this case *locus standi* is accorded under s 571(3) to "any person entitled to bring proceedings for an order under s 212".[49]

[7.051] Repeating what is described in this commentary as a legislative emphasis on proceeding if possible through a members' voluntary winding up, s 572(4) provides that the court may order that the company can be wound up as if it were a members' voluntary winding up where the order is made under paras (a), (b), (c), (e) or (f) of s 569(1).

[7.052] Section 569(1)(d) refers to the most usual situation whereby the court is petitioned to wind up a company, namely where the company is unable to pay its

---

[47] (\...contd) Similarly, the "Cork Committee Report" (Insolvency Law and Practice, Report of the Cork Review Committee (Cmnd 8558, 1982) para 198 stated the following:

> ... the aims of a good modern insolvency law are ... to recognise that the effects of insolvency are not limited to the private interests of the insolvent and his creditors, but that other interests of society or other groups in society are vitally affected by the insolvency and its outcome, and to ensure that these public interests are recognised and safeguarded; to provide means for the preservation of viable commercial enterprises capable of making a useful contribution to the economic life of the country.

In the US case of *NLRB v Bildisco & Bildisco* 465 US 513 the court stated that "The fundamental purpose of reorganization is to prevent a debtor from going into liquidation, with an attendant loss of jobs and possible misuse of economic resources."

[48] See generally Courtney, *The Law of Companies* (3rd edn, Bloomsbury Professional, 2012).

[49] This latter section refers to the provisions on oppression. Note that s 569(f) allows for a remedy of winding up even in cases where there are alternative remedies available.

debts. Section 570(a) changes the threshold of indebtedness for creditors. A creditor must now be owed €10,000, which is ten times the existing threshold of €1,269.74. This is a significant change in value. Interestingly, however, s 571(b) allows for two or more creditors representing in aggregate a value of indebtedness of at least €20,000 to bring a petition to liquidate the company.

[7.053] Section 572(2) and 572(3) are inserted to give effect to s 233(4) of the NAMA Act 2009. Section 572(2) provides that the court shall not make an order for the winding up of a company unless the court is satisfied that the company has no obligations in relation to a bank asset that has been transferred to NAMA or a NAMA group entity or where such an obligation exists that a copy of the petition to wind up has been served on NAMA and that that court has heard the agency in relation to the making of that order. Section 572(3) repeats the definition of "bank asset" and "NAMA group entity" which are provided in the NAMA legislation.[50]

(c) Members' voluntary winding up

[7.054] As described above, s 578 provides that save to the extent that a provision in this Chapter expressly provides otherwise the sections of this Chapter apply only to a members' voluntary winding up.

[7.055] The commencement of a voluntary liquidation may be supported by utilisation of the summary approval procedure described above, or the procedure referred to in ss 579(3) and 580. The initiation of a voluntary winding up as a members' voluntary winding up can be displaced (i) where there is a default in the making of the statutory declaration of solvency; (ii) where the court makes an order under s 582(2); or (iii) where a creditors' meeting is held in accordance with s 584.[51]

[7.056] It is also envisaged that a winding up cannot proceed as a members' voluntary winding up where there is a bar to such a winding up or where the procedure under s 586(2) is employed. In such cases the voluntary winding up will be a creditors' voluntary winding up.[52]

[7.057] Section 579 refers to the summary approval procedure referred to in the introductory section in relation to the commencement of a members' voluntary liquidation. The summary approval procedure is described in detail in the legislation in Part 4, Chapter 7 and requires the passing of a special resolution and most importantly, in this context, a declaration of solvency to be sworn by the directors of the company.[53] Section 580, however, envisages an alternative

50 See further National Asset Management Agency Act 2009, s 233.
51 Section 562(1)(a) of the Act.
52 Section 562(1)(b) of the Act. Section 586 applies to the commencement of creditors' voluntary windings up.
53 See para **[7.003]**.

procedure based on the particular circumstances of the company. Thus where a company is formed for a specific duration or purpose as described in s 579(3) then the procedure under s 580 can be utilised involving both a resolution of the company in general meeting and a declaration of solvency from the directors as described therein.

(d) Creditors' voluntary winding up

[7.058] As with the other Chapters, s 585 provides that save where the provision expressly states otherwise, the provisions in Chapter 4 apply only to creditors' voluntary winding up.

[7.059] Section 586 sets out the procedure for the commencement of a creditors' voluntary winding up. Section 586(1) provides that a company may be wound up voluntarily as a creditors' winding up. Section 586(2) goes on to state that where the company is insolvent that company can resolve to wind up at a general meeting where the members must pass a resolution that the company in unable to pay its debts as they fall due.[54]

[7.060] In addition to the situation described above where a voluntary liquidation is commenced *ab initio* as a creditors' voluntary winding up, it is also possible to convert a liquidation which has been commenced as a members' voluntary liquidation into a creditors' voluntary liquidation, with a view to giving the creditors more control over the continuance of the liquidation. Such an eventuality effectively hinges on the question of the solvency of the company.[55]

[7.061] Therefore, s 586(3) clarifies that there are three situations where a voluntary liquidation will become a creditors' voluntary winding up and continue as a creditors' voluntary winding up even where commenced otherwise. These are where:

(a) a creditors' meeting is held in accordance with s 584 whereby this meeting is called where the liquidator in a members' voluntary liquidation forms the view that the company will be unable to pay its debts as they fall due; or

(b) where the court makes an order under s 582(2) following an application by the creditors representing at least one-fifth in number or value of the creditors of the company with the court having formed the opinion that it is unlikely that the company will be able to pay its debts; or

---

54 See further *BNY Corporate Trustee Services v Eurosail-UK* [2013] WLR 1408 on the interpretation of this phrase which is found in the UK Insolvency Act 1986 and a note thereon by Day, "Taking Balance Sheet Insolvency Beyond the Point of No Return" [2013] Cambridge Law Journal 515.

55 See further Lynch Fannon and Murphy, *Corporate Insolvency and Rescue* (2nd edn, Bloomsbury Professional, 2012) Ch 4, pp 120–127.

(c) where the summary approval procedure described in s 202 is purported to be employed or the resolution referred to in s 580, and the procedure therein is purported to be employed[56] and these procedures are not properly made in accordance with the relevant provisions.

(e) Conduct of winding up

[7.062] Certain provisions of Chapter 5 incorporate rules regarding the conduct of the winding up which have hitherto been found in the Rules of the Superior Courts, Ord 74. Thus s 591(1)(b) incorporates a modified version of Ord 74 r 22 regarding the service of an order for winding up or appointment of a liquidator on the company at its registered office as the court might direct. This obligation now rests with the "officer of the court" under s 591(1)(a). Section 594 incorporates a modified version of Ord 74 r 24 regarding the liquidator's entitlement to obtain information further to the making of a statement of affairs as provided for under s 593.

(f) Realisation of assets and related matters

[7.063] Chapter 6 of Part 11 concerns various provisions regarding the collection and realisation of assets in a winding up. The usual provisions are repeated, for example regarding the invalidation of a floating charge under s 597(1) where the charge is created within 12 months of the commencement of the winding up in normal circumstances and two years where the charge is created in favour of a connected person under s 597(4).

[7.064] Section 596(2) is new and is designed to facilitate the recovery of records and assets by liquidators from persons who do not have a right in law to withhold such records and assets from the liquidator. This section now extends to voluntary liquidators but s 596(3) explicitly states that the term "liquidator" in this provision does not include a provisional liquidator. Accordingly, for a provisional liquidator to have similar authority the court order appointing the liquidator would have to expressly refer to this provision.[57]

[7.065] Contribution and pooling provisions which had been provided for in ss 140 and 141 of the 1990 Act, but which have been surprisingly underutilised, are repeated in the new legislation in ss 599 and 600 respectively. The operation of these provisions depends on the "relatedness" of the contributing company to the first company as regards contribution orders and on the "relatedness" of the second company to the first company as regards pooling orders. In relation to

---

[56] See paras **[7.055]**–**[7.057]**.

[57] This new structure regarding provisional liquidators whilst driven by a desire to facilitate a possible rescue of a company, in other words to avoid putting the final nail in the coffin, may in fact be an occasion of abuse unless the specific powers are requested by a provisional liquidator in cases where abuse might be possible. See ss 626 of the Act *ff.*

the latter, the second company must be liquidated before the company's assets can be pooled.[58]

[7.066] Transactional avoidance provisions are contained in s 602, re-enacting ss 255 and 218 of the 1963 Act which are merged into this provision. Section 218 dealt with compulsory liquidations and provided for an avoidance of transactions which were entered into after the commencement of the winding up. Section 255 provided for a similar provision in a voluntary winding up. Now, s 602 provides for avoidance of property dispositions after the commencement of a winding up in exactly the same manner whether the liquidation is voluntary or compulsory.

[7.067] Section 604 repeats the provisions on fraudulent preferences as provided for in s 286 of the 1963 Act but removes the use of the term "fraudulent" to avoid the misunderstanding that fraud is an element of these impugned transactions. The technical term is changed therefore to "unfair preference". Proof of an intention to prefer is still a required element as s 604(2) describes an act "that is done with a view to giving the creditor referred to in subsection (1)(i) ... a preference over the other creditors of the company". Such an act will be deemed to be an "unfair preference". Thus this voidance provision still retains a number of difficulties which have been highlighted by case law and discussed elsewhere.[59] The substitution of "unfair" for fraudulent is repeated in s 605, which is a follow on section concerning the rights of persons who have been unfairly preferred. This may in fact lead to further proof requirements that the transaction is actually unfair to other creditors when in fact it may not be as other creditors may not have any real expectations regarding distribution.[60] The original provision focuses on the intention of the transferor to prefer a particular creditor, in other words to give an advantage to one creditor. The question of whether this is exactly equivalent to a transaction which is unfair is an open one.

[7.068] Whilst there has been some consideration of an over-arching common law anti-deprivation principle in recent case law there is no specific reference to this principle in this legislation.[61]

---

[58] See generally, Lynch Fannon and Murphy, *Corporate Insolvency and Rescue* (2nd edn, Bloomsbury Professional, 2012) Ch 9, pp 385–387.

[59] See generally, Lynch Fannon and Murphy, *Corporate Insolvency and Rescue* (2nd edn, Bloomsbury Professional, 2012) Ch 9, pp 380–385.

[60] Goode makes the helpful distinction between transactions which reduce the value of the entire assets available to creditors (addressed by anti-deprivation provisions) and transactions which allow one creditor to "steal a march" on others without reducing the value of the pie actually available (these infringe the *pari passu* principle). See Goode R, *Principles of Insolvency Law* (4th edn, Sweet and Maxwell, 2011) at p 703.

[61] See generally Goode R, *Principles of Insolvency Law* (4th edn, Sweet and Maxwell, 2011), Ch 7.

[7.069] Section 610 provides for the imposition of civil liability for fraudulent or reckless trading. The criminal offence of fraudulent trading is preserved and enacted in Chapter 16, s 722.

(g) Distribution

[7.070] Chapter 7 of Part 11 provides for the distribution of assets once these are collected in and realised by a liquidator.

[7.071] Section 618 relates to the distribution of property generally and applies the bankruptcy rules to the winding up of insolvent companies as before. Section 618(2) provides for an exception to the *pari passu* principle for subordination agreements.

[7.072] Section 618(3) and 618(4) "re-enact" Article 137 of Table A which concerns the distribution of the property of a company in a members' voluntary winding up on the passing of a special resolution to this effect. The application of these provisions is subject to the general provisions of this Part.[62]

[7.073] The codification, in statutory form, of a provision which was hitherto contained in Table A, repeats a motif of the new Companies Act which replaces most of the provisions contained in Table A and applies them to companies, almost always providing "unless the constitution provides otherwise". In the case of what was Article 137, we see an exception to that general rule as its transposition is mandatory and not subject to the constitution providing otherwise.[63] This removes a discretionary element to this provision and the effect of this statutory codified approach to what were formally Table A provisions *vis-à-vis* any new constitutional provisions of companies registered under the legislative scheme is an issue which will be resolved in different contexts over time.

[7.074] Sections 621 and 622 repeat the provisions regarding preferential status accorded to particular types of creditors. Such preferential creditors include the Revenue Commissioners regarding debts which are enumerated in s 621(2)(i)–(vi). Statutory references have been updated. Although the original provisions conferring preferential status on particular types of creditors are contained in s 285 of the 1963 Act, the categories of creditors to whom preferential status was accorded were added to over time by particular pieces of legislation. In keeping with the possibility that such debts may be added to over time s 621(3) provides that the provisions of subs (2) are "in addition to any other enactment providing for the priority of a particular debt or sum in a winding up".

---

62 This provision allows for the members to pass a special resolution sanctioning the liquidator to "divide among the members, in specie or in kind, the whole or any part of the property of the company".

63 See Ch 2, *Changes in the Basics: Constitutions, Share Capital and Governance* at para **[2.008]**.

[7.075] The accordance of "super-preferential" status under the provisions of the Social Welfare Consolidation Act 2005 is a case in point. Super preferential status means that monies owed to the social insurance fund, for example monies deducted from employees' wages and not paid during the lifetime of the company, are paid in priority to the debts specified as preferential under s 285 of the 1963 Act. These monies are in effect ring-fenced and treated as lying outside the assets available for distribution.[64] Nothing in the legislation detracts from this concept of "super-preferential" debts. Noteworthy is the specific mention in the explanatory memorandum that the preferential status which had hitherto been accorded to claims under the Workers' Compensation Acts 1934–1955 has been abolished.

[7.076] Whilst the Act therefore repeats and re-instates the concept of preferential status for particular kinds of debts, in particular Revenue debts, it is interesting to note that this status has been abolished for Revenue debts in the UK since the passing of the Enterprise Act 2002.[65] There is accordingly a significant divergence between UK and Irish insolvency law in this matter.

(h) Liquidators

[7.077] Chapter 8 of Part 11 deals with liquidators, their powers and duties generally. Section 624 sets out the duties of liquidators in a statutory form.[66] The explanatory memorandum to the legislation describes this as a "new section" and states that s 624(1) and 624(2) codify the duties of a liquidator. These are to "administer the property of the company to which he or she is appointed". Section 624(2) expands on this meaning. Note that in keeping with the overall scheme of the Act regarding provisional liquidators, s 624(3) limits the duties of the provisional liquidator to "those duties provided in the order appointing him or her". This provision is subject to the provisions of s 559(3) to (5) (see below).

[7.078] The definition provisions of Part 11 are contained in s 559. As far as provisional liquidators are concerned, s 559(3) contains a general provision which states that save where there is an express reference made to a provisional liquidator, subss 559(4) and 559(5) apply. Section 559(4) provides that where a provision of Part 11 is applicable in the period prior to the making of a winding up then the phrase "liquidator" in that provision includes a provisional liquidator who might have been appointed prior to an order for winding up. Section 559(5) provides that where the court confers a power on a provisional liquidator which corresponds to a power which is expressly provided for in Part 11 (as applying to

---

[64] See s 19 of the Social Welfare Consolidation Act 2005 for the full range of provisions. See further *Re Coombe Importers Ltd* [1999] 1 IR 492 at 500.

[65] Enterprise Act 2002; see Lynch Fannon and Murphy, *Corporate Insolvency and Rescue* (2nd edn, Bloomsbury Professional, 2012) pp 302–307.

[66] See generally Lynch Fannon and Murphy, *Corporate Insolvency and Rescue* (2nd edn, Bloomsbury Professional, 2012).

liquidators generally) then references in the relevant provision to a liquidator include a provisional liquidator to the extent that the relevant provision is applicable prior to a winding-up order being made. These rather complicated provisions are necessary because the legislation takes a different approach as regards the powers of provisional liquidators compared with the previous position. Effectively, the statutory framework now reverses the traditional position whereby a provisional liquidator appointed by a court would have powers commensurate with a liquidator ordinarily appointed except to the extent that the court expressly limited such powers. Instead, where a provisional liquidator is appointed under this legislation his or her powers are limited to those outlined by the court on his or her appointment.

[7.079] Accordingly, s 627(1) provides that where a provisional liquidator is appointed by the court, then "subject to section 559(3) to (5)", the provisional liquidator has such powers as the court orders. The purpose of limiting the powers of a provisional liquidator in this way is to ensure that it is possible to continue to operate and run the company in as normal a manner as possible prior to the final order to wind up the company being made. Whether this decoupling of the appointment of a provisional liquidator from the ultimate winding up order is realistic is another matter as in the past it was assumed that the appointment of a provisional liquidator preceded the appointment of a liquidator as night follows day. Perhaps in recognition of that more pragmatic approach, the section allows the court to appoint a provisional liquidator with the same powers as an ordinary liquidator with some limitations.

[7.080] This idea is continued in the provisions of s 627(2), which provides that the court may tailor the extent to which the provisional liquidators' powers replace or overlap the powers of officers of the company. In addition, the court has the authority to remove certain powers of the officers of the company, on the appointment of a provisional liquidator, without granting these powers to the liquidator.

[7.081] Both these provisions make the orders made by the court on the appointment of a provisional liquidator potentially quite complicated. It may be the case, however, that the courts will, in most cases, simply grant the same powers to the provisional liquidator as would normally be held by the liquidator generally, to avoid confusion. If this approach is not taken, one can envisage issues arising subsequently regarding the exercise of powers by a provisional liquidator. In particular, complications could arise regarding reliance by third parties on acts of a provisional liquidator where that liquidator is not authorised by the court to so act.

[7.082] Similarly, as described above, s 624(3) states that the duties of a provisional liquidator will be the duties provided for in the court order appointing such a liquidator or provided for in any subsequent order of the court. This provision is stated to be subject to s 559(3)–(5) as described above. The court will therefore be mindful that the duties are adequately described.

(i) Liquidators' powers

[7.083] Section 627 recites the powers of a liquidator.

The powers of the liquidator are set out in a Table, which is in turn divided into a number of sections including the following:

- Legal proceedings, carrying on the company's business, etc;
- Payment of certain creditors, compromise of certain claims, etc;
- Ascertainment of debts and liabilities, sale of property, etc;
- Proving claim in the case of contributory's bankruptcy, etc;
- Obtaining of credit;
- Taking out letters of administration, otherwise obtaining payment from contributory or debtor, etc;
- Security for costs and appointment of agents;
- Custody and control of property and disposal of perishables, etc;
- Residual powers.

[7.084] Paragraphs (1) and (2) of the Table are derived from ss 231(1)(a) to (f) of the Companies Act 1963 but are expanded to allow for the possibility that the business may be recommenced and continue to run, in keeping with the modern focus on corporate rescue. Paragraph (3)(a) is described as being new in the explanatory memorandum and gives power to the liquidator to ascertain the debts and liabilities of the company. Remaining provisions of the Table derive from s 231(2) of the Companies Act 1963 and s 131(3) of the Companies Act 1990.

[7.085] The provisions of s 627 and the following provisions of the Act are designed to provide a uniform set of powers to liquidators in court windings up, and to liquidators in members' and creditors' voluntary windings up replacing separate provisions dealing with these three different kinds of liquidation in previous legislation. Accordingly the powers of the liquidator in all three windings up are now uniform, with the exception of the powers a liquidator has in a creditors' winding up prior to the first meeting of the creditors. The text has already considered the particular different treatment of the provisional liquidator in this legislative scheme.

[7.086] The provision on residual powers is stated at para 10 of s 627 to include the "power to do all such other things as may be necessary for winding up the affairs of the company and distributing its property". This catch-all phrase may be utilised to address situations where particular circumstances might arise.

[7.087] Section 628 provides for the calling of meetings of the company by the liquidator and also provides for the calling of meetings of members, creditors and the committee of inspection as provided for in s 276(1) of the 1963 Act.

[7.088] Section 631 sets out the powers which the liquidator has to apply to the court for determination of issues concerning the exercise of his or her powers. It replaces a combination of ss 231(3) and 280 of the Companies Act 1963.

[7.089] Section 633 represents an important and welcome change in Irish law which has been long awaited. This provision now requires that certain qualifications are necessary for appointment as a liquidator or provisional liquidator. Section 633(1) therefore provides that "subject to ss 635 and 636 a person shall not be qualified for appointment as a liquidator of a company unless he or she falls within a paragraph of the Table to this section".

[7.090] Section 519(1) states that a person "shall not be qualified to be appointed to act as an examiner of a company unless he or she would be qualified to act as its liquidator". However, the section goes on to state that the requirements of s 634 concerning professional indemnity cover are disregarded for this purpose. There is no equivalent provision for receivers.

[7.091] The Table included in s 633 therefore includes individuals who are permitted to act as liquidators or provisional liquidators as follows:

- Members of a prescribed accountancy body;
- Practising solicitors;
- Members of "other professional body recognised by the Supervisory Authority";
- Persons qualified under the laws of another EEA State;
- A "person with practical experience of windings-up and knowledge of relevant law".

[7.092] This last category is described as "limited" and it is envisaged that this individual will make an application to a Supervisory Authority in the prescribed form within two years after the commencement of this section and will have paid a prescribed fee to the Supervisory Authority. This is effectively a "grandfathering" clause allowing for existing insolvency practitioners who may not have actual professional qualifications described above to continue their practice. Section 634(2) allows for such an individual who has applied under this last category to apply for permission to continue to act as a liquidator pending "the determination of that application".

[7.093] Section 634 addresses the requirements of professional indemnity for those practising as liquidators or provisional liquidators. This section gives the Supervisory Authority referred to above an overall supervisory role in relation to professional indemnity matters, regardless of the professional affiliations of particular individuals. The Supervisory Authority referred to here is the

Supervisory Authority described in detail in Part 15 of the Act, which describes in full the functions of the Irish Auditing and Accounting Supervisory Authority.

[7.094] Section 635(6) provides for an offence where an individual acts as a liquidator without qualification.

[7.095] Sections 645–648 deal with matters of importance to the function of the liquidator.

[7.096] Section 645 is a new provision addressing the custody of books and property where a liquidator's office is vacated. The section provides that the former liquidator shall retain books and property until a new liquidator is appointed or is otherwise directed by the court on application by the Director of Corporate Enforcement or former liquidator.

[7.097] Section 646 provides that the remuneration of a provisional liquidator is set by the court.

[7.098] Section 647 describes the procedure for fixing a liquidator's remuneration. Section 647(2) states that such remuneration will be fixed by the creditors or the committee of inspection (for court ordered or creditors' voluntary windings up) or by members (in a members' voluntary winding up). Hitherto, the remuneration of a liquidator in a court winding up was under the direction of the court. The legislation provides for a residual power for the court to set remuneration under this section

[7.099] Section 648 concerns the liquidator's entitlement to receive payment once the remuneration is set as described in s 647. This provides for a two-fold procedure whereby the liquidator must first have the entitlement to remuneration set and then must have any amounts claimed under the entitlement approved prior to taking remuneration.

(j) Contributories

[7.100] By way of introduction and description of this part, it must be noted that s 655 of the legislation restates s 209 of the Companies Act 1990 providing that the liability of a contributory shall create a debt accrued from the time when the liability commenced, but until the call is made the debt does not accrue as due. Any action to recover a debt from a contributory must be brought within 12 years from the date on which the cause of action accrued.

[7.101] Section 659 amends the old s 242, which established a procedure whereby the court would adjust the rights of contributories and distribution of surpluses at the end of the winding-up process. This function has now been transferred to the liquidator.

(k) Committee of inspection

[7.102] In the relatively few sections on the role of the committee of inspection some changes have been made to how liquidations will function or operate in reality. Section 666 is new and provides that the committee of inspection in an official or court ordered liquidation will be established on the initiative of the liquidator or alternatively the liquidator can be directed to do so on the initiative of a minimum proportion of the creditors without court sanction.[67] This replaces s 232 of the Companies Act 1963 and is based in part on s 268 of 1963 Act.

[7.103] Section 667 empowers creditors, without recourse to the court, to appoint a committee of inspection in the case of a creditors' voluntary winding up. It is worth recalling that the purpose of some of these provisions is to align more closely the procedure in creditors' voluntary, members' voluntary and court liquidations. However, fundamental principles of insolvency law require transparency and equity as between parties, and it remains to be seen whether these provisions adequately serve this purpose.

[7.104] Section 668 governs the conduct of meetings of the committee of inspection.

(l) Court's powers

[7.105] This consolidating legislation combines provisions of the 1963 and 1990 Companies Acts with provisions of the Company Law Enforcement Act 2001 giving greater clarity to the enforcement powers of the court in relation to the conduct of liquidations.

[7.106] Section 669 deals generally with the power of the court to annul or stay an order for winding up. New provisions contained in subs (2) are designed to ensure that where such orders are made the public register accurately records the change in the status of a company. Subsection (4) give the court new powers to make orders and directions regarding the retention or disposal of the company's seal, books and papers as the court thinks fit.

[7.107] Section 670 extends the scope of s 246 of the Companies Act 1963 to the conduct of voluntary windings up in keeping with the statutory scheme to align provisions in relation to all three kinds of windings up. Effectively this means that the court can now, on the application of the Director of Corporate Enforcement, a liquidator, or on its own motion, order the attendance of any officer of the company at meetings of creditors, members or contributories or at any meeting of a committee of inspection. This gives significant powers of oversight to the Director of Corporate Enforcement, even in the context of members' voluntary liquidations which would previously have been treated quite differently.

---

[67] Not less than one tenth in value of the creditors of the company.

[7.108] Similarly, s 671 empowers the court to summon persons for examination. This power, which is derived from previous enactments[68] and which originally concerned court liquidations only, is now extended to voluntary windings up, even members' voluntary windings up where there is no insolvency.

[7.109] Section 673 provides for the delivery of property of the company to a liquidator. It re-enacts s 236 of the Companies Act 1963 but is amended so that it now applies to voluntary windings up and to companies to which a provisional liquidator has been appointed.

[7.110] Finally, the court is empowered under s 675 to make an order for arrest and seizure of books, papers and moveable personal property. This power, which was provided in a combination of legislative provisions,[69] has now been extended to all windings up involving a merger of ss 247 and 248D of the Companies Act 1963. The provisions have been amended so that a court order can be made after the filing of a petition to wind up a company or on the passing of a resolution to voluntarily wind up a company.

(m) Supplemental provisions on conduct of winding up

[7.111] To begin with, s 677 applies to all windings up and provides that from the date of the commencement of the winding up the company must cease to carry on its business except insofar as may be required for its beneficial winding up. Section 677(3) provides that on the appointment of a liquidator, other than the appointment of a provisional liquidator,[70] all the powers of the directors of the company shall cease except where the committee of inspection or the creditors sanction the continuance of these powers. This applies in compulsory and creditors' voluntary liquidations. In a members' voluntary winding up, where the members sanction continuance of the powers.

[7.112] Section 679 gives potential control over certain matters in the conduct of windings up to the Office of the Director of Corporate Enforcement. The section provides that the Director of Corporate Enforcement may direct the convening of meetings with a view to ensuring that the provisions of s 680 are operable.

[7.113] Section 680 replaces ss 262, 264 and 272 of the Companies Act 1963. Section 680(1)–(3) apply to members' voluntary windings up and provide for

---

68 CA 1963, s 245, as amended by CA 1990, s 123 and CLEA 2001, s 44.
69 CA 1963, s 247 as amended by CLEA 2001, s 46. See also CA 1963, s 282D as amended by CLEA 2001, s 49.
70 See paras **[7.078]–[7.082]** which discussed the new approach to the appointment of a provisional liquidator, particularly in relation to the reservation of some of the directors' powers for the directors, or indeed the alternative removal of powers from a director but the court now has discretion not to assign those powers to the provisional liquidator.

the convening of a meeting on the yearly anniversary of the commencement of the winding up.

[7.114] Section 680(4)–(7) apply similarly to creditors' voluntary windings-up and to court windings up. The obligation is to call a meeting of the committee of inspection on the anniversary of the commencement of the winding up. If there is no committee of inspection then a meeting of the creditors must be called. The requirement is to call such meetings within 28 days of the anniversary of the commencement of the winding up (in a voluntary winding up) or the order to wind up the company (in a compulsory liquidation). Section 679 refers to the Director exercising control over these meetings also.

[7.115] Section 687 is a new provision, which provides that creditors or contributories may override the wishes of the committee of inspection. It is stated in the explanatory memorandum to parallel s 309 of the Companies Act 1963. Section 687(2) provides that where there is a conflict between the wishes of the committee of inspection and the creditors or contributories, the wishes of the latter will prevail. To this end s 687(3)(a) empowers the liquidator to convene meetings of the creditors and contributories to ascertain their wishes. Section 687(3)(b) goes on to provide that the liquidator must convene meetings of the creditors or contributories where they pass a resolution so directing the liquidator or where such a request is made in writing by not less than one tenth in value of the creditors or not less than one tenth in value of the contributories.

(n) General rules as to meetings of members, contributories and creditors of a company in liquidation

[7.116] Many of the statutory provisions of Chapter 13 replace provisions of the Rules of the Superior Courts, in particular provisions of Ord 74. These relate to the conduct and procedure at meetings of members, contributories and creditors of a company in liquidation. Overall the new legislation does not change these provisions. However, a more general issue is raised: because these are now legislative provisions as distinct from provisions in the Rules of Court there is a different character to the status of these rules. These provisions cannot be as easily changed as Rules of Court (based as they are on a statutory instrument and drafted by the Superior Courts Rules Committee[71]), nor can they be modified as Rules of the Superior Courts may be by a practice direction.[72]

---

[71] The Superior Court Rules Committee is authorised under legislation to enact Rules for the Superior Courts which are then approved by the Minister for Justice as statutory instruments. See the Courts of Justice Act 1924, ss 67 and 68 of the Courts of Justice Act 1936 and the Courts (Supplemental Provisions) Act 1961. Order 74 of the RSC has been most recently amended in SI 121/2012.

[72] See, eg HC55 regarding the presentation of copies of a petition to wind up under Ord 74, r 16 which clarifies an aspect of practice under the Rule.

(o) Completion of a winding up

[7.117] Section 704 is new and deals with the dissolution of a company by the court. The method of dissolution of a company in compulsory liquidation is now the same as that for a company in a creditors' voluntary winding up, unless the court requires the liquidator in the former to return to court at the end of the winding up. The section states the grounds upon which the court may make an order for the dissolution of the company, if it is satisfied that the affairs of the company have been completely wound up.

(p) Provisions related to the Insolvency Regulation

[7.118] Chapter 15 re-enacts various provisions regarding the EU Insolvency Regulation 1346/2000 which have hitherto been contained in the European Communities (Corporate Insolvency) Regulations 2002 (SI 333/2002).

[7.119] The provisions of the EU Insolvency Regulation are currently under review by the EU Commission following various revision reports which have expressed concern regarding uniformity of judicial practice in Member States concerning application of a number of concepts in the legislation, in particular the application of COMI ("centre of main interests"). It is also proposed to codify the decisions of the European Court of Justice on this issue, which would be most welcome. There are other matters which require attention, all of which are described in the Commission's proposals which have been approved by the European Parliament and which are currently being considered by the Council.[73]

(q) Offences by officers of companies in liquidation, offences of fraudulent trading and certain other offences, referrals to DDP, etc

[7.120] The rather cumbersome wording of the heading to Chapter 16 indicates that it is intended to capture a range of matters including very important matters concerning enforcement of company law generally and other less important matters.

[7.121] Section 715(1) states that without prejudice to s 563 (which makes a similar statement in relation to the provisions of the Part generally), ss 716 to 720 in this Part apply to all modes of winding up. Section 715(2) provides that references in any of the following sections to a "relevant person" mean a person "who, at the time of the doing of the act or the making of the omission is or was

---

[73] See n 11. See generally, Lynch Fannon and Murphy, *Corporate Insolvency and Rescue* (2nd edn, Bloomsbury Professional, 2012). Moss, Fletcher and Isaacs, *The EC Regulation on Insolvency Proceedings – A Commentary and Annotated Guide* (2nd edn, Oxford University Press, 2009).

an officer of the company". The section therefore has jurisdictional reach over individuals who may have resigned with a view to avoiding responsibility.

[7.122] Section 720 sets out an additional offence with respect to s 718(c) which relates to the disposal of books and property of a company in winding up. In addition, this provision provides for some additional defences to offences set out in subs (2) of this section relying on the defendant proving to conceal the state of affairs of the company or to defeat the process of law. The onus is on the defendant to prove these defences.

[7.123] Section 722 repeats the offence of fraudulent trading which has been provided for in legislation since 1963, but in this legislation it is decoupled quite dramatically from the civil liability for the same actions, which is described in s 610.

Chapter 8

Compliance and Enforcement

by
Nessa Cahill BL

Introduction

[8.001] Part 14 of the Act addresses compliance with, and enforcement of, the provisions of the Act and of company law. In its nine Chapters, Part 14 covers such topics as the power of the courts to make an order to compel compliance with provisions of the Act;[1] the restriction of directors;[2] disqualification orders;[3] and the categorisation of offences under the Act.[4]

[8.002] This Part of the Act reproduces many pre-existing provisions of the Companies Acts and in particular of the Companies Act 1990 (as amended). There are however three areas of compliance and enforcement to which the Act makes significant changes, which are considered in this chapter:

1. Restriction and disqualifications;
2. Restriction and disqualification undertakings; and
3. Criminal offences.

Restriction and disqualification

[8.003] Here, the following aspects of the substantive law on restriction and disqualification are considered:

    (a) Defences to a restriction application;

    (b) Capitalisation requirements of restricted companies;

    (c) Applications for relief from restriction;

    (d) Automatic disqualification under s 839;

    (e) Application for relief; and

    (f) Security for costs.

---

[1]   Chapter 1, s 797 of the Act.
[2]   Chapter 3 of Part 14 of the Act.
[3]   Chapter 4 of Part 14 of the Act.
[4]   Chapter 7 of Part 14 of the Act.

(a) Defences to a restriction application

(i) Companies Act 1990

[8.004] Under s 150 of the Companies Act 1990 a court was mandated to make a declaration of restriction unless satisfied that the person in respect of whom the declaration was sought acted *honestly and responsibly* in relation to the conduct of the affairs of the company and there was no other reason why it would be just and equitable that he should be subject to a declaration of restriction.[5]

[8.005] The most frequently cited test to determine whether a director acted responsibly for the purpose of restriction proceedings, is the test put forward by Shanley J in *La Moselle Clothing Company Ltd v Soualhi*[6] according to which a court in determining the "responsibility" of a director for the purposes of s 150(2)(a) should have regard to the following:

"(a) The extent to which the director has or has not complied with any obligation imposed on him by the Companies Acts 1963–1990.

(b) The extent to which his conduct could be regarded as so incompetent as to amount to irresponsibility.

(c) The extent of the director's responsibility for the insolvency of the company.

(d) The extent of the director's responsibility for the net deficiency in the assets of the company disclosed at the date of the winding up or thereafter.

(e) The extent to which the director, in his conduct of the affairs of the company, has displayed a lack of commercial probity or want of proper standards."[7]

---

[5]   Companies Act 1990, s 150(1) and 150(2) (as amended). See, generally, Cahill, *Company Law Compliance and Enforcement* (2008), Chs 16, 17, 18 and 19.

[6]   *La Moselle Clothing Company Ltd v Soualhi* [1998] IEHC 66, [1998] 2 ILRM 345. It should be noted that there has been a more recent shift away from applying standardised tests to ascertain a director's responsibility: Fennelly J in Re *Mitek Holdings Ltd* [2010] 3 IR 374 at para 79 cautioned that "I would not be disposed to limit the matters to which regard should be had or to substitute standardised judicial criteria for the general words of the statute. The judgments of Murphy, Shanley, McGuinness and Clarke JJ show that compliance with statutory requirements may be relevant. On the other hand, whether in that respect or in respect of common law duties, it is not every criticism that enables one, in the words of McGuinness J, 'to categorise conduct as irresponsible'."

[7]   *La Moselle Clothing Company Ltd v Soualhi* [1998] IEHC 66, [1998] 2 ILRM 345 at para 11, as approved by the Supreme Court in Re *Squash (Ireland) Ltd* [2001] 3 IR 35 and as followed in a number of High Court cases, such as Re *SPH Ltd, Fennell v Shanahan* [2005] IEHC 152.

[8.006] The courts have also take into account various other matters in assessing a director's conduct in restriction proceedings, of which the following is an example:

- Whether the company continued to trade when the directors are, or ought to be, aware that the company was insolvent;[8]
- Whether there was a failure to prepare or file proper audited accounts;[9]
- Whether the director bore responsibility for the insolvency of the company;[10]
- Whether debts owed to related companies were discharged in preference to other creditors;[11]
- Whether proper books of account were kept;[12]
- Whether annual general meetings were held;[13]
- Whether management accounts were kept;[14]
- Whether annual returns were made to the Companies Registration Office;[15] and
- Whether there was cooperation with the liquidator.[16]

(ii) Companies Act 2014

[8.007] In the Companies Act 2014, the new approach to the defences that are open to directors facing restriction proceedings can be seen in s 819(2). This provides that a court shall make a declaration of restriction unless it is satisfied that the conditions set out in sub-ss 819(2)(a), 819(2)(b) and 819(2)(c) are met.

---

[8]   See *Re Pineroad Distribution Ltd, Stafford v Fleming* [2007] IEHC 55; *Re Verit Hotel and Leisure (Ireland) Ltd, Duignan v Carway* [2002] IEHC 1; *Re Mitek Ltd, Grace v Kachkar* [2010] 3 IR 374; *Re La Moselle Clothing Ltd, La Moselle Clothing Ltd v Soualhi* [1998] 2 ILRM 345.

[9]   *Re Cookes Events Company Ltd, Kavanagh v Cooke* [2005] IEHC 225.

[10] *Re La Moselle Clothing Ltd, La Moselle Clothing Ltd v Soualhi* [1998] 2 ILRM 345; *Re MDN Rochford Construction Ltd, Fennell v Rochford* [2009] IEHC 397.

[11] See *Re Euroking Miracle (Ireland) Ltd, Fennell v Frost* [2003] 3 IR 80.

[12] See, eg, *Re Greenmount Holdings Ltd, Stafford v O'Connor* [2007] IEHC 246, in which McGovern J found that the respondents failed to keep proper books of account contrary to CA 1990, s 202. The court did not however make the restrictions order sought in that case, one of the grounds being that the respondents had made attempts to regularise the situation.

[13] *Re First Class Toy Traders Ltd (in liquidation), Gray v McLoughlin* [2004] IEHC 289 (9 July 2004, unreported), HC, Finlay Geoghegan J, *ex tempore*.

[14] *Re Fergus Haynes (Developments) Ltd, Wallace v Fergus* [2013] IEHC 53, *Re MDN Rochford Construction Ltd, Fennell v Rochford* [2009] IEHC 397.

[15] *Re Lynrowan Enterprises Ltd* [2002] IEHC 90 (31 July 2002, unreported), HC; *Re Newcastle Timber Ltd* [2001] 4 IR 586.

[16] See *Re DCS Ltd, Fitzpatrick v Henley* [2006] IEHC 179 and *Re CMC (Ireland) Ltd, Fennell v Carolan* [2005] IEHC 59.

The mandatory nature of the declaration and the placing of the onus of proof on the director are therefore the same as existed under the Companies Act 1990 (as amended). The change, a potentially significant one, is to the defences enumerated in the legislation. To avoid a declaration of restriction, a director must now prove:

- that he acted honestly and responsibly in relation to the conduct of the affairs of the company, whether before or after it became insolvent;
- that he has, when requested to do so by the liquidator, *"cooperated as far as could reasonably be expected in relation to the conduct of the winding up of the insolvent company"*; and
- that there is no other reason why it would be just and equitable that he or should be subject to a declaration of restriction.

[8.008] It may be noted that the fairness and the constitutionality of the imposition of this burden of proof on a director has been questioned by the Supreme Court. In *Re Tralee Beef and Lamb Ltd*[17] Hardiman J considered the restriction provisions and said that, "the provisions may be regarded as draconian" as "[t]he burden is placed upon the respondent to prove, not only that he has acted responsibly and honestly in relation to the company but to prove the negative proposition '(there is no other reason …)' set out in the last citation from the statute". He went on to make the following comment about this aspect of s 150:

> "I must confess to some doubt as to whether this blanket reversal of the onus of proof, including a requirement to prove a negative proposition, is consistent with fundamental fairness and constitutional justice. It is certainly in stark contrast to the procedures provided in the United Kingdom for the disqualification of directors, and applied in *Re Barings plc (No 5)* [1999] BCLC 433, cited below and much cited in the judgment of the High Court Judge. There, the Secretary of State (the moving party) was compelled to make detailed written charges in advance of the hearing, so that the respondents and the court knew the case that was being made and required to be answered."

[8.009] In light of the adoption of the same language and approach in the Companies Act, the same concerns persist and may be raised by a respondent to an application under s 819.

[8.010] It is relevant to note that the requirement to act honestly and responsibly is now a standalone requirement imposed on directors prospectively by s 228(1) of the Act and not only a standard for analysing *ex post facto* whether the conduct of a director warrants a declaration of restriction. This adoption of the requirement that a director act "honestly and responsibly" as a statutory duty of a director is addressed in Ch 4, *Changes in the Law of Directors' Duties*.[18] This

---

[17]   *Re Tralee Beef and Lamb Ltd, Kavanagh v Delaney* [2008] 3 IR 347 at 355.
[18]   At para **[4.027]**.

change does not alter the statutory requirement to demonstrate that a director acted "honestly and responsibly" in the context of restriction proceedings, but it does render the analysis quite circular: one of the factors that is relevant to determining whether a director acted honestly and responsibly is whether he complied with his obligations under the Companies Acts. Now, a director will have to demonstrate that he acted honestly and responsibly to demonstrate compliance with his statutory obligations, which will then be one of the matters to be weighed in determining whether he acted honestly and responsibly. It may be more sensible to simply state that a director must demonstrate compliance with his obligations under the Companies Act to avoid restriction.

(iii) Obligation to cooperate with liquidator

[8.011] The criterion that a director must prove that he has, when requested to do so by the liquidator, "*cooperated as far as could reasonably be expected in relation to the conduct of the winding up of the insolvent company*" is a new requirement. The court must now be satisfied that the director cooperated with the liquidator. This requirement is subject to three qualifications: first, it only applies to the extent that the liquidator requested the director to so cooperate. Second, it only refers to cooperation in relation to the conduct of the winding up of the company and does not specifically require cooperation in relation to the restriction proceedings. Third, it imposes a requirement to cooperate "as far as could reasonably be expected" rather than an untramelled and unqualified cooperation obligation.

[8.012] While the requirement to prove cooperation within the meaning of s 819(2) is not an absolute one, it is crucial to understand that in placing this criterion in a sub-category of its own, it is no longer only relevant as a factor in assessing whether the director acted responsibly in the conduct of the affairs of the company. In addition to proving that he acted honestly and responsibly, a director must now also show that he cooperated with the liquidator within the meaning of s 819(2)(b), whether or not this has any bearing on the level of his honesty or responsibility in his dealings with the company. Indeed, it may be inferred that the intention of introducing the requirement to prove cooperation is to ensure that cooperation is demonstrated in all cases, even when the liquidator may raise no issue in that regard.

[8.013] As noted above, one of the factors that the courts have often taken into account in assessing whether a director acted honestly and responsibly for the purposes of the restriction regime in place under the Companies Act 1990 (as amended) is the level of cooperation with the liquidator.

[8.014] The courts have assessed the cooperation between a director and a liquidator as a factor that is relevant to restriction applications in two different respects. First, the cooperation or otherwise between a director and a liquidator has been considered as part of the context within which an application must be assessed and a relevant factor to assessing a director's honesty and responsibility. In *Re DCS Ltd*[19] MacMenamin J considered a failure to cooperate which included the "purging" of potentially relevant documents without consultation with the liquidator and an ongoing refusal and failure to assist the liquidator despite numerous requests. This was described by MacMenamin J as part of the "context" of the application, and was a failure to which the court was entitled to have regard in making a declaration of restriction.

[8.015] Second, it is clear from the judgment of Clarke J in *Re CMC (Ireland) Ltd*[20] that the interaction between a director and liquidator may also be relevant to assessing whether it is just and equitable that a declaration of restriction should be made. In that case, Clarke J emphasised:

> "[i]t is axiomatic that the duties of persons who have served as directors include an obligation to be of any assistance which they can to the liquidator in the conduct of the liquidation. The rights of the creditors of a company are likely to be compromised not only by the fact that a company is insolvent and unable to pay its debts as of the date of liquidation but also such rights can be further compromised where, due to inappropriate action or inaction on the part of directors or former directors, the liquidator is prevented from being in a position to effectually get in the assets of the company for the purposes of discharging the liabilities due to the creditors to the greatest extent possible and as soon as possible."

[8.016] The court also took into account in determining that it was just and equitable to restrict the directors in that case, that "the respondent directors failed to cooperate generally with the liquidator and declined, for a considerable period of time, to meet with him".

[8.017] Clarke J concluded:

> "I am satisfied that the failure to cooperate at all with the liquidator is a matter which the court can and should take into account. As was pointed out by counsel for the liquidator anything which places a significant barrier in the way of the efficient conduct of the liquidation is likely to lead to a diminution in the extent to which the creditors of the company will be paid. Even if there is no ultimate failure to recover the assets of the company, delay in their recovery can effect the legitimate interests of the creditors not least because an elongation of the liquidation is likely to mean greater costs which all have to come out of the same pool which ought, properly, be available for the creditors."

[8.018] In that case, it was not until after the initiation of the restriction proceedings, almost one year from the commencement of the liquidation, that the directors first met with the liquidator. This "failure to cooperate at all" was one of the three factors taken into account by the court in making the declaration

---

[19]   *Re DCS Ltd, Fitzpatrick v Henley* [2006] IEHC 179.
[20]   *Re CMC (Ireland) Ltd, Fennell v Carolan* [2005] IEHC 59.

of restriction. It is noteworthy, however, that while there was a clear finding of a total lack of cooperation with the liquidator, the court emphasised that "in my view the actions of both respondent directors, while being sufficiently serious to make it just and equitable to make the order under s 150, nonetheless were on the lower end of the range of seriousness of such actions".

[8.019] One point of interest in predicting how s 819(2)(b) may be applied is that courts have shown a willingness to assess the grounds of an allegation of non-cooperation. In several cases, the courts have weighed the evidence presented and dismissed allegations of non-cooperation as ill-founded or as irrelevant to the application. In *Re Club Tivoli Ltd*[21] MacMenamin J assessed the evidence presented on behalf of the liquidator and the director, with the former alleging that the director was uncooperative and difficult to reach and responded to correspondence through his solicitor rather than directly. The director claimed that there was no failure to cooperate, referring to several meetings with the liquidator including an offer from the director's accountant to the liquidator to assist further, which was not pursued by the liquidator. The court weighed the evidence and rejected the complaints of the liquidator and found, for example, that it was "hardly surprising" that a response to an allegation of failing to act honestly and responsibly was received from the director's solicitor.

[8.020] Similarly, in *Re USIT World plc*[22] there were complaints of non-cooperation with a liquidator which were denied and dealt with in a detailed way by the director. Peart J declined to "examine closely each punch and counter punch in that exchange at this stage" but was satisfied on the basis of the evidence presented that "while the liquidator for whatever reason felt that he was not receiving cooperation, matters required to be dealt with were dealt with". The court was also influenced by the fact that there was an offer of a meeting in the event that the liquidator required anything beyond the information already furnished, which offer was still open and could be availed of if the liquidator so wished. Peart J concluded: "[o]n balance I am satisfied that nothing disclosed under this heading constitutes a reason why a restriction order should be made against these respondents."[23]

---

21   *Re Club Tivoli Ltd Foster v Davies* [2005] IEHC 468.

22   *Re USIT World plc* [2005] IEHC 285.

23   Another example of a case in which the court rejected allegations of non-cooperation is *Re Shellware Ltd, Taite v Breslin* [2014] IEHC 184 per Barrett J: "There is suggestion in the pleadings that there was lack of cooperation with the liquidator. This was not canvassed at length at the hearing of this matter and the court in any event finds that Mr Breslin did substantively cooperate with the liquidator."

[8.021] The most detailed examination of allegations of non-cooperation with liquidators and their relevance to a restriction application can be seen in *Re MK Fuels Ltd*:[24]

"It is clearly of vital importance that directors of any failed company cooperate with the liquidator of such company and the court will not lightly countenance any want of cooperation in this regard. However, the court is mindful that there will often, perhaps invariably, be an element of strain between the former directors of a failed entity and its liquidator, with the directors perhaps fearful that their commercial decisions will lead to proceedings such as those now before the court and the liquidator naturally desirous of discharging his or her duties competently and well. In addition, there may also be something of a 'culture clash' between business-minded directors accustomed to the rough and tumble of commercial life and professionally qualified liquidators who inhabit a world where documentation and detail are of paramount importance."

[8.022] In that case, the issue appears to have been that the directors said they had provided all the information they could, whereas the liquidator claimed he did not receive all the information he needed. Barrett J concluded:

"[i]t may be the case that the directors could have handled their dealings with the liquidator better than they did and, to the extent that this is so, if so, their behaviour is undoubtedly reprehensible. However, the court does not consider that any want of cooperation that the directors may have manifested in this case is of such seriousness as to constitute their behaviour being classified as behaviour that is other than responsible and thus deserving of sanction under s 150."

[8.023] It can be seen from these cases that the courts frequently approach the question of cooperation with liquidators as one of the factors to be weighed in the balance, but rarely as a determinative one, even when serious allegations are made by the liquidator.

[8.024] The introduction of the new requirement that a director must prove that he "cooperated as far as could reasonably be expected in relation to the conduct of the winding up of the insolvent company" does appear to shift the onus firmly onto the directors in relation to this criterion. In previous cases, the liquidators' allegations of non-cooperation were weighed and considered as part of the context or overall circumstances in which the responsibility of the director's conduct was judged or as part of the analysis of whether it is just and equitable to make a declaration of restriction. It remains to be seen how s 819(2)(b) will be interpreted and applied in practice, but it certainly elevates the potential importance of cooperation as a standalone criterion, one which may be valuable in the hands of liquidators. As against this, it may be expected that the courts will continue to assess the factual basis of any allegations of non-cooperation and to adopt a practical view of the cooperation that may "reasonably be expected" from a director.

---

[24] *Re MK Fuels Ltd, Cotter v Gilligan* [2014] IEHC 305 *per* Barrett J.

(b) Capitalisation requirements of restricted companies

[8.025] Under the Companies Act 1990 (as amended) a person who was subject to a declaration of restriction could act as a director or secretary or otherwise take part in the formation or promotion of a company, if the company had an allotted share capital of nominal value of not less than €317,434.52 in the case of a public company and €63,486.90 in the case of any other company, with each allotted share contributing to that aggregate amount to be fully paid up in cash, including the whole of any premium thereon.[25] There was no distinct provision for companies limited by guarantee or investment companies. Three changes are made to these rules.

[8.026] First, there are now specific provisions addressing the capitalisation requirements of companies limited by guarantee and investment companies. In the case of the former, s 819(4) provides that the capitalisation requirements applicable to public and private companies do not apply to companies limited by guarantee. Instead, the company's memorandum of association must specify that the amount of the contribution guaranteed by at least one member of the company is not less than €100,000.[26] With investment companies, the value of the issued share capital must be not less than €100,000[27] and an amount of not less than €100,000 must have been paid in cash in consideration for the allotment of the shares.[28]

[8.027] Second, in the Companies Bill as initiated on 13 December 2012 the requisite level of capitalisation in the case of a public company was rounded up from €317,434.52 to €350,000 and in the case of any other company was rounded up from €63,486.90 to €70,000. In the Bill as amended at Committee Stage on 5–6 November 2013, these capitalisation requirements were again changed: it is now necessary according to s 819(3) that a public company have an allotted share capital of nominal value of not less than €500,000 in value and all other companies have such capital of not less than €100,000 in value, with each allotted share contributing to that aggregate amount to be fully paid up in cash, including the whole of any premium thereon. The reason given for this increase during the Dáil debates at Committee Stage was "to allow for inflation".[29] It also reflects the recommendation of the Company Law Review Group that "the level of capitalisation required for companies with restricted directors should be raised – because such directors have been found to have acted either dishonestly or irresponsibly – but that no change be made to the law

---

25   Section 150(3) of the Companies Act 1990 (as amended).
26   This was proposed as €70,000 in the Bill as originally published on 30 May 2011.
27   This was proposed as €70,000 in the Bill as originally published on 30 May 2011.
28   Section 819(5).
29   Companies Bill 2012: Committee Stage 5 November 2013, *per* Deputy Sean Sherlock.

regarding minimum levels of capital at this time for the generality of companies".[30]

[8.028] Third, the Minister has the power under s 835 to make an order increasing the amounts specified in s 819(3). A similar power existed under the Companies Act 1990 (as amended).[31] However the Companies Act now limits the scope of the ministerial powers in two respects.

[8.029] According to s 835(2), any order shall not effect an increase in relation to declarations of restriction made before the commencement of the order. Therefore, a person who is restricted under the Companies Act before any increase is brought into effect, can be a director of a company (other than a public company) which has paid up share capital of €100,000 and that company does not need to increase its capitalisation to comply with any increased capital requirement subsequently introduced by the Minister. This is in line with s 41 of the Company Law Enforcement Act 2001, which similarly ensured that changes to the capitalisation requirements that were brought in by that Act would not apply to persons who were restricted before its commencement date.

[8.030] Further, s 852(3) introduces the wholly new restriction that the Minister may only make an order increasing the level of capitalisation required of a restricted company if it appears to the Minister that the changes in the value of money that have occurred since the date of the commencement of the Act (or the date of any previous order increasing the thresholds) warrant such an increase "so as to secure the continued effectiveness of section 819". This appears to be designed to ensure that the paid up shares capital requirements imposed on restricted companies are not rendered more prohibitive by means of increases than at the time of commencement of the Act, but rather are maintained at the same level, with adjustments to reflect inflation only as necessary.

(c) Applications for relief from restriction

[8.031] It has always been open to persons who are restricted from acting as directors or secretaries of companies or otherwise from acting in connection with the formation or promotion of a company to apply for relief from such restriction. The Companies Act introduces three changes to these applications.

[8.032] First, under s 152(1) of the Companies Act 1990 (as amended), any application for relief from a declaration of restriction had to be made within one year of the making of that declaration. Section 822 of the Companies Act imposes no such temporal limit on applications for relief.

[8.033] Second, any person who wished to apply for relief from restriction was required to notify the liquidator of the company the insolvency of which gave

---

[30] Report of the Company Law Review Group 2011 at para 5.1.4.
[31] Section 158.

rise to the declaration of restriction of that application. Under s 822(3) a person who intends to apply for relief must now give at least 14 days' notice in writing of this intention to the Director of Corporate Enforcement as well as to the liquidator.

[8.034] Third, the Director of Corporate Enforcement may now appear and give evidence at the application for relief. This is provided for in s 822(5). While no such provision existed under the Companies Act 1990, it was the practice of the courts to allow the Director to become a notice party to applications for relief. In *Re CMC (Ireland) Ltd*[32] Finlay Geoghegan J considered the argument that the legislation excluded the right of the Director to attend and be heard at an application for relief and concluded that, "the Court is not precluded by the terms of s 152(4) of the Act of 1990 from joining the Director as a notice party if it considers it necessary or desirable in the interests of justice to do so on the facts of this application". On the facts of that application, the court ruled that the Director should be joined:

> "It is desirable in our adversarial system of justice that there is a party before the court who is either opposing the application or at minimum has an interest in examining with the benefit of relevant facts and expertise, the validity of the application and making relevant submissions to the court. This is particularly so where, as in an application under s 152, the court is exercising a wide discretion. The Director appears an appropriate person to put before the Court by way of admissible evidence, facts which the Court should take into account and to make relevant submissions.

Finlay Geoghegan J did not purport to decide that such joinder of the Director was appropriate in all cases:

> "In deciding to join the Director in this application I wish to make clear that I am not deciding that he should be joined in all applications under s 152 of the Act of 1990. The Oireachtas has not specified that he is a person to whom notice must be given by the liquidator under s 152(3). Also, the Oireachtas has created a class of persons with an automatic right to appear and give evidence in s 152(4). Whether the Director should be joined in any particular application will depend on the relevant facts and the court determining that it is necessary or in the interests of justice to do so."

[8.035] So, while the Director could be joined as a party to a relief application under the Companies Act 1990, a motion needed to be issued by the Director for this purpose. Under s 822 such a motion is no longer necessary.

(d) Automatic disqualification under s 839

[8.036] Under s 839(1)(a) a person is automatically disqualified if convicted on indictment of "any offence under this Act, or any other enactment as may be

---

[32] *Re CMC (Ireland) Ltd, Cosgrave v Fennell* [2005] IEHC 340.

prescribed, in relation to a company". A person is also automatically disqualified under s 839(1)(b) if convicted on indictment of "any offence involving fraud or dishonesty". Under s 160(1) of the Companies Act 1990 a person convicted on indictment of *"any indictable offence in relation to a company, or involving fraud or dishonesty"* was automatically disqualified.

[8.037] Section 839(1)(a) amends s 160(1) of the Companies Act 1990 by limiting the category of offences which give rise to automatic disqualification. In particular, whereas previously "any indictable offence in relation to a company" was sufficient for automatic disqualification to arise, now the offence must be one that is created under either the Companies Act 2014 or an enactment that is specifically prescribed for that purpose. This change means that there will be certainty and clarity as to the enactments which may give rise to automatic disqualification. Until the Minister makes an order prescribing the legislation that is covered by s 839(1)(a), the only enactment that is relevant is the Companies Act. However, it may be noted that under the Companies Act 1990, persons who are convicted of offences under the Competition Act 1991, for example, were subject to automatic disqualification.[33] It may be expected that the Competition Act will be among those to be prescribed by the Minister. The certainty that will follow from the prescription of the legislation that can give to automatic disqualification can only be welcome.

[8.038] However, there is no definition in the Companies Acts or elsewhere of offences "in relation to a company" or offences "involving fraud or dishonesty", both of which terms remain in the Act, and, furthermore, there is still no requirement in the Act that the offence involving fraud or dishonesty must be an offence in relation to a company or that it must involve the offender's dealings with a company or his position, ability or honesty as a director of a company. While the certainty introduced by s 839(1)(a) is laudable, it is unfortunate that the broad formulation of "any offence involving fraud or dishonesty" remains. Indeed, it is conceivable that conviction on indictment under many legislative enactments *not* prescribed by the Minister under s 839(1)(a) could nonetheless give rise to automatic disqualification under s 839(1)(b).

[8.039] One additional amendment that was introduced to the automatic disqualification provisions of the Companies Act 1990 relates to the duration of such disqualification. Under the Companies Act 1990, s 160(1), a person who

---

33 See Competition Authority, *Annual Report 2006*, at p 9, reporting on the conviction on indictment of JP Lambe to two counts of aiding and abetting price-fixing. In addition to a sentence of six months imprisonment, suspended for a period of 12 months (the first such custodial sentence under the Competition Act) and a fine of €15,000, which the Competition Authority described as "the largest single fine levied by an Irish court on either an undertaking or individual for a competition law offence", he was automatically disqualified and his name was entered on the register of disqualified persons on 2 October 2006, there to remain until 2 October 2011.

was automatically disqualified was disqualified from the date of conviction for five years "or such other period as the court, on the application of the prosecutor and having regard to all the circumstances of the case, may order". A similar provision is contained in the Companies Act but with two notable changes. Section 839(2) provides that:

> "a person disqualified under subsection (1) is disqualified for a period of 5 years after the date of conviction or for such other (shorter or longer) period as the court, on the application of the prosecutor or the defendant, and having regard to all the circumstances of the case, may order."

[8.040] The first change is that the defendant may himself apply for a variation in the period of the disqualification, whereas previously only the prosecutor could do so. Second, it is clarified that the court may order that the period of disqualification be shorter or longer than five years. Under s 160(1), in light of the fact that only the prosecutor could make an application to vary the period of disqualification, it seemed logical that the only revisions would be upwards. Now, however, it is clear that the disqualified person can apply for a reduction in the period of disqualification.

(e) Application for relief

[8.041] Under the Companies Act 1990, s 160(8) it was provided that:

> "Any person who is subject or deemed subject to a disqualification order by virtue of this Part may apply to the court for relief, either in whole or in part, from that disqualification and the court may, if it deems it just and equitable to do so, grant such relief on whatever terms and conditions it sees fit."

[8.042] The procedure applicable to applications for relief from disqualification was not addressed in s 160(8). In *Re Clawhammer Ltd*,[34] Finlay Geoghegan J noted that s 160(8) "would appear to allow a court to grant relief from one aspect of a disqualification order alone, such as the prohibition on involvement in the management of a company". The court then observed that s 160(8) is not subject to the same notice requirements as are contained in s 152, and that it remained to be seen whether a respondent can ask for relief against part of a disqualification order immediately upon the making of that order.

[8.043] Applications for relief from orders of disqualification, and the procedures applicable to them, are now addressed in s 847 and the uncertainties identified in *Re Clawhammer Ltd* are resolved.

[8.044] Section 847(2) provides that an application for relief against a disqualification order must be served on the person who applied for the

---

[34] *Re Clawhammer Ltd, Director of Corporate Enforcement v McDonnell; Re Shinrone Food Market Ltd, Director of Corporate Enforcement v Hoctor; Re Cautious Trading Ltd, Director of Corporate Enforcement v Forristal* (15 March 2005, unreported), HC.

disqualification order and on the Director of Corporate Enforcement. At least 14 days' notice of the intention to make the application must be served on those notice parties. According to s 847(4), if the applicant for the disqualification order was "the liquidator of the company, the insolvency of which gave rise to the application for the disqualification order", on receipt of notice of an application for relief, the liquidator shall as soon as practicable notify the creditors and contributories of which the liquidator is aware. It is a category 3 offence for a liquidator to fail to provide this notice.[35] It may be noted that the same provision is contained in s 822 in respect of relief from restriction, which is logical as declarations of restrictions always arise from insolvent liquidations. It does not however apply so appropriately in the case of disqualification, where there is not necessarily any company "the insolvency of which gave rise to the application for the disqualification order".

[8.045] On the hearing of an application for relief from disqualification the Director of Corporate Enforcement and the person who applied for the disqualification order may appear and be heard. If a liquidator was the applicant, any creditor or contributory may also appear and give evidence.[36]

(f) Security for costs

[8.046] Under the disqualification regime established by the Companies Act 1990, where an application for a disqualification order was made by a member, contributory, employee or creditor of the company, the court could require security for some or all of the costs of the application.[37] According to s 844(5) of the Companies Act:

> "The court may require a person who makes an application under section 842 to provide security for some or all of the costs of the application."

[8.047] This expands greatly the category of persons who may be required to provide security for costs, as the persons who may make an application under s 842 are all the persons listed in s 844 of the Act, namely the Director of Corporate Enforcement; the Director of Public Prosecutions; the Registrar of Companies; a member, contributory, officer, employee, receiver, liquidator, examiner or creditor of the company to which the application relates. Now, any of these persons may in theory be required to provide security for costs. However, it remains a matter within the discretion of the court.

---

[35] Section 847(6).

[36] Section 847(5).

[37] Section 160(4).

Restriction and disqualification undertakings

[8.048] The most significant amendment to the law governing restriction and disqualification is the introduction in Chapter 5 of Part 14 of the Act of restriction and disqualification undertakings.

[8.049] Restriction and disqualification undertakings have been part of the proposed legislation since the publication of the General Scheme of the Companies Consolidation and Reform Bill in 2007.[38] The Company Law Review Group in its Report published in that year noted that:

> "During its preparatory work on the drafting of the General Scheme of the Companies Consolidation and Reform Bill, the Review Group observed that in the UK approximately 80% of disqualifications were now made by way of the undertakings procedure. Furthermore, there was no obvious increase in the numbers being disqualified and the costs involved in disqualifying directors by undertaking were substantially less following the introduction of the procedure. It was considered that the availability of a similar procedure in Ireland would reduce unnecessary use of resources in the making of Court applications. Undertakings also had the potential to restrict or disqualify directors in a more expeditious manner. As a result, the Review Group gave endorsement to a proposed head dealing with undertakings."

[8.050] As somewhat different considerations and schemes apply to each, restriction and disqualification undertakings will now be treated separately.

(a) Restriction undertakings

(i) Features of restriction applications

[8.051] To understand the import and context of the new restriction undertakings it is necessary to emphasise some important features of the restriction regime, as it existed under the Companies Act 1990 and as it continues to exist under the Companies Act.

[8.052] First, if a declaration of restriction is not to be made, the court must be satisfied that the director acted honestly and responsibly and that there is no reason why it is just and equitable that the respondent be restricted.[39] There is an important distinction between restriction and disqualification proceedings in this regard, as highlighted by the High Court in *Re Newcastle Timber (in liq)*:[40] whereas the onus is on liquidators to satisfy the court that the conditions for the making of a disqualification order have been satisfied, under s 150 (and now

---

[38] Head 51, Part A13.

[39] As addressed earlier in this chapter, a director must now also show to the court's satisfaction that he cooperated with the liquidator to avoid restriction.

[40] *Re Newcastle Timber (in liq)* [2001] 4 IR 586.

under s 819): "the Court must make a Restriction Order unless it is satisfied that the person acted honestly and responsibly, and therefore the onus is on the director concerned to satisfy the Court as to his honesty and responsibility." It may be recalled that in *Re Tralee Beef and Lamb Ltd*[41] Hardiman J considered the restriction provisions, noting that: "[t]he burden is placed upon the respondent to prove, not only that he has acted responsibly and honestly in relation to the company but to prove the negative proposition '(there is no other reason …)'." He contrasted the Irish legislation with the position with regard to disqualification in England where the moving party must make detailed written charges before the hearing, so the respondent and the court know the case that is being made.

[8.053] A second feature of restriction proceedings that is relevant to an analysis of restriction undertakings is the unusual non-adversarial nature of such applications. McCracken J in *Re Verit Hotel and Leisure (Ireland) Ltd*[42] acknowledged that "in practice, there are occasions when the liquidator will bring an application under this Section, and will tell the Court that he believes that the directors acted honestly and responsibly". In *Re Dunleckney Ltd*[43] the respondent failed to comply with his statutory duty to file a statement of affairs. The liquidator was satisfied with the cooperation provided by the respondent and expressed the view that the statement of affairs would not have revealed any additional information. The court nonetheless made an order of restriction, noting that, "In my opinion it is not for the Official Liquidator to excuse a director from his statutory obligation".

[8.054] Third, according to s 683(2) and (3) of the Act, unless the Director of Corporate Enforcement has relieved the liquidator of the obligation to do so, the liquidator shall apply under s 819 for a declaration of restriction.[44] A liquidator who fails to comply with this obligation shall be guilty of a category 3 offence.[45]

[8.055] Fourth, if a director does not appear at or present evidence for the purposes of, an application for a declaration of restriction, this person will not automatically be restricted. In *Re USIT World plc*[46] two of the directors against whom restriction orders were sought, neither filed affidavits in, nor were represented at, the proceedings seeking a declaration of restriction. Peart J noted that a court may be satisfied from the information and evidence advanced by a liquidator or from affidavits of other respondents or information otherwise

41 *Re Tralee Beef and Lamb Ltd, Kavanagh v Delaney* [2008] 3 IR 347 at 355.
42 *Re Verit Hotel and Leisure (Ireland) Ltd (In Receivership and in liquidation), Duignan v Carway* [2002] IEHC 1.
43 *Re Dunleckney Ltd* [1999] IEHC 109 (Carroll J).
44 This obligation was previously contained in s 56 of the Company Law Enforcement Act 2001.
45 Section 683(5).
46 *Re USIT World plc* [2005] IEHC 285.

before the court, that an unrepresented director acted honestly and responsibly. There is, according to the court, no presumption that a director against whom an order of restriction is sought acted irresponsibly or dishonestly.[47]

[8.056] Reiterating that there is no burden of proof on a liquidator under s 150, the court determined that:

"... it seems to be contrary to common-sense, if nothing worse, that a Court could be satisfied that the conduct of all the directors was responsible in all the circumstances from its consideration of such a volume of documentation as in this case, as well as perhaps the submissions of other parties, and yet have to decide, in a way which flies in the face of that finding, that a particular director should be restricted because, for whatever reason – perhaps lack of means – he/she had not engaged lawyers to participate in the application."

[8.057] The court referred to the position of directors of insolvent companies and the impact that insolvency may have had on their finances, noting that there may be financial reasons for a director not to be represented on a s 150 application. Peart J expressed a concern over directors conceding that they acted dishonestly or irresponsibly to avoid the expense of court proceedings:

"... For a director to be forced to concede the matter rather than resist, on the basis of it being the lesser of two evils, the greater being perhaps to try and borrow funds to meet the application, cannot be necessary or, more importantly, just and equitable."

[8.058] The conclusion in *Re USIT World plc*[48] is noteworthy:

"In my view, justice requires that the court, even where there is no response by the respondent, should first consider whether it can be satisfied from the facts placed before it by the liquidator that the respondent has acted honestly and responsibly. If it is so satisfied, then it follows that no order should be made, even in the absence of participation by the respondent, as to do otherwise is to presume that an absence of participation gives rise to a presumption of dishonesty and irresponsibility, and the Act provides for no such presumption. It is undesirable that a director should be deemed to have conceded a matter about which the court can be satisfied to the contrary on the documentation before it, especially where the consequences of so doing are penal in nature, if not intent. The effect is to provide protection to the public against someone in respect of

---

47   *Re USIT World plc* [2005] IEHC 285, *per* Peart J: "The section cannot be fairly interpreted, in the absence of express wording to such effect, as meaning that a presumption of dishonesty and irresponsibility is to be inferred where a director takes no step to participate in the application. Such a presumption could fly in the face of matters glaring from the application itself from which the Court is satisfied as to honesty and responsibility. The task of the court is to be satisfied. The section does not confine the Court as to the source of that satisfaction."

48   *Re USIT World plc* [2005] IEHC 285.

whom the public has no need to be protected. That is nonsensical, absurd and unjust."

[8.059] The position is therefore that absent restriction undertakings, a liquidator is required to bring a restriction application unless relieved by the Director of Corporate Enforcement of the obligation to do so. The vast majority of restriction applications are therefore brought by liquidators. In the course of such applications, the court must assess all material presented and may refuse a declaration of restriction, even if the respondent did not participate, and may grant a declaration, even if the applicant did not believe the order to be warranted. The judgments on s 150 highlight that the court's role is not to rubberstamp the application as made by the applicant, but, on the contrary, is to analyse and assess whether the respondent(s) acted honestly or responsibly on the basis of all material before the court. The courts are also mindful of the need for fairness in these applications and of the fact that there is no presumption that a director acted dishonestly or irresponsibly. It is also important to note that the objective of restriction is to protect the public.

[8.060] How these features and procedures of restriction applications will sit with the new restriction undertaking regime is not wholly clear.

(ii) Interaction between liquidators' restriction application and restriction undertakings

[8.061] Restriction is still only available in respect of companies in insolvent liquidation.[49] There will therefore always be, in the first instance, an issue of whether the liquidator is relieved of the obligation to bring restriction proceedings. Presumably (although the Act is silent on this), if the Director intends to propose a restriction undertaking, the Director may relieve the liquidator of the obligation to bring restriction proceedings pursuant to the power conferred by s 683(3) or may postpone making a decision on such relief until a restriction undertaking is given. Neither situation is provided for in the Act. It is therefore unclear how the new restriction undertaking regime will fit within the present regime leading to applications for declarations of restriction.

(iii) Grounds for restriction undertakings

[8.062] The next issue is when and on what basis the Director may decide whether to propose a restriction undertaking. It is necessary to consider the provisions of ss 852 and 853 to cast light on this.

[8.063] According to s 852(2):

"where the Director has reasonable grounds for believing that a person falls within the description of the second-mentioned person in section [819](1),

---

[49] See s 819(1).

namely a person who was a director of an insolvent company within the meaning of Chapter 3 (in this section referred to as the 'person'), the Director may, in his or her discretion, deliver to the person, or to the person's duly authorised agent, [a restriction notice]."

[8.064] The Director must therefore have reasonable grounds for one belief: that the person in question was a director of an insolvent company.[50] If these grounds exist, the Director has a discretion as to whether to serve a restriction notice.

[8.065] The restriction notice is described in s 852(3)(a):

"That notice is a notice in the prescribed form stating – ... the circumstances, facts and allegations that have given rise to that belief of the Director, citing the provisions of section [819](1) and section [818](1) (and also, where appropriate, section [824]) and stating particulars of those facts and allegations (and the circumstances so stated, and those facts and allegations, of which particulars are so stated, are referred to together in this section as the 'underlying facts and circumstances')."

[8.066] Therefore the only information that must be contained in the restriction notice regarding the grounds for restriction are particulars of the "circumstances, facts and allegations" that have given rise to the belief that the individual in question was a director of an insolvent company. This is confirmed by the references to ss 819(1) and 818(1), both of which deal with the directors of insolvent companies. It is very strange in light of the decided cases summarised above, and the criteria for restriction generally, that the Director does not have to state a belief that the director did not act honestly or responsibly; that he failed to cooperate with the liquidator; or that it is just and equitable that he be restricted, or any facts, allegations or circumstances relevant to such belief. On the contrary, a restriction notice under the Act will call on an individual to accept restriction on the bald basis that he was a director of an insolvent company. It almost appears like a presumption that a director of an insolvent company did not act honestly or responsibly, or failed to cooperate with the liquidator or that it is otherwise just and equitable that he be restricted, which is contrary to the clear judicial statements set out above.

(iv) Procedure of restriction undertakings

[8.067] According to s 853(6), the Director shall not issue a restriction notice if he is aware that an application has already been "made" in respect of the same person arising from the same underlying facts and circumstances (ie his being a director of the same insolvent company). This does raise the question of when an application will be deemed to have been "made", although it seems likely that

---

[50] "Director of an insolvent company" is defined in Chapter 3, s 818 as "a person who was a director or shadow director of an insolvent company at the date of, or within 12 months before, the commencement of its winding up."

the application should be deemed to be "made" on the date of issue of a notice of motion in accordance with the Rules of the Superior Courts (as amended).[51]

[8.068] The restriction notice shall specify a date on which the restriction will come into effect (if accepted by the individual) and shall also specify a defined period that will commence at least 21 days from the issue of the notice and expire just before the date of commencement of the restriction, which date may be extended on the application of the individual (referred to as the "notice period").[52] During this period, the individual must notify the Director of his willingness or otherwise to give a restriction undertaking and must return a signed "restriction acceptance document".[53]

[8.069] According to s 852(3)(d), the notice shall state that, during the notice period, "the Director will refrain from making an application in respect of the person under section [819] arising from or in connection with the underlying facts and circumstances." There are two curiosities about this provision. First, it would leave the Director free to commence restriction proceedings in the 21-day period from the issue of the notice prior to the commencement of the notice period (while such an occurrence must be unlikely, the Director is specifically prevented from making an application during the notice period, an equally unlikely occurrence, and a minor anomaly is therefore present). Second, it does not refer to or preclude proceedings being initiated by another person, such as a liquidator or receiver of the insolvent company or its property, both of which have statutory standing to bring such an application under s 820(1). While a person is considering and taking advice as to whether to give a restriction undertaking to the Director, restriction proceedings could be commenced by the liquidator.

[8.070] This is addressed to some extent by s 853(1):

> "Where a notice is delivered under section [852](2), the Director and every person who is aware of the notice shall not, during the notice period, make an application under section [819], arising from or in connection with the underlying facts and circumstances, in respect of the person who is the subject of the notice."

[8.071] The effect of this provision on other applicants for restriction depends on such persons (ie liquidators and receivers) being "aware of the notice", without however specifying how such persons are to be made "aware" of the notice and how such awareness is to be demonstrated. It is easily conceivable that a liquidator could issue restriction proceedings while an individual is considering how to respond to a restriction notice from the Director of

---

[51] See Practice Direction issued by President of the High Court on 24 March 2003.
[52] Sections 852(3)(b) and (c) and 582(5).
[53] Section 852(3)(c).

Corporate Enforcement. The equivocal language of this provision can be contrasted with s 853(4) which states:

"After the expiry of the notice period, neither the Director nor any other person shall make an application under section [819], arising from or in connection with the underlying facts and circumstances, in respect of the person who has given the restriction undertaking."

[8.072] There is therefore no ambiguity but that an individual who gives a restriction undertaking cannot be subject to a restriction application brought by any person arising from being a director of the same insolvent company.

[8.073] A restriction notice does not however state the consequences of non-compliance with a restriction undertaking. While the Minister can introduce regulations under s 854 regarding the restriction acceptance document (which is the document containing the statutory contract[54]) and s 854(2) provides that regulations may be introduced with "consequential and supplemental provisions," this enabling provision does not extend to the content of the restriction notice, which is provided for instead in s 852. It does not therefore appear to be envisaged that regulations may be introduced extending the content of the restriction notice.

(v) Consequences of restriction undertaking

[8.074] When a restriction undertaking has been given, the Director shall as soon as practicable (a) furnish all requisite particulars to the Registrar of Companies for entry in the register of restricted persons; and (b) execute a "restriction acceptance document" and furnish a copy of that document and notify the particulars given to the Registrar to the restricted person.[55]

[8.075] A person who gives a restriction undertaking "shall be deemed, for the purposes of this Act, to be subject to a restriction declaration".[56] However, the restriction notice must state that:

"... if the person gives a restriction undertaking –

  (i) the person may seek to be relieved (whether in whole or in part) from the undertaking only by applying to the court under section [822]; and

  (ii) that, on the making of such an application, the court may grant such relief only if it considers it just and equitable to do so, and then only on the terms and conditions as it sees fit."[57]

[8.076] The Act states that this information must be included in the restriction notice, but there is no provision of the Companies Act confirming that a person

---

[54] See *Report of the Company Law Review Group* 2007 at para 6.1.2.
[55] Section 853(3).
[56] Section 853(5)(b).
[57] Section 852(4)(c).

who gives a restriction undertaking can apply for relief under s 822. Section 822(1) refers to relief in whole or part from a declaration of restriction under s 819(1) or an order under s 821(2)(b), but makes no reference to relief in the case of restriction undertakings under s 853. There may be a lacuna in this regard, although the fact that a person who gives a restriction undertaking is deemed by s 853(5)(b) to be subject to a restriction declaration may be sufficient to fill it.

[8.077] Assuming that a person who is deemed to be restricted can apply for relief, it would appear that such person upon receipt of a restriction notice from the Director stating grounds for believing he was a director of a company in insolvent liquidation, may accept that restriction, and then apply promptly to court for relief against the restriction on the ground it is "just and equitable" for such relief to be granted. The proofs for the restriction undertaking being limited to information about a directorship (as the Act envisages) would seem to make it easier to argue a case for relief under s 822. It seems difficult to imagine a case where it would not make sense to take the restriction undertaking and then apply for relief from same. This is particularly so as a director who does not give an undertaking may be expected to be subject to a restriction application in court (although it is by no means apparent from the Act that a refusal to give a restriction undertaking does have such a consequence). If such an application is made, even if the director in question does not participate in the hearing, he may be restricted and made subject to an order for costs, provided of course the court determines that the criteria for restriction are met and the material presented does not demonstrate that a valid defence to restriction exists.

[8.078] This demonstrates a difficulty with the restriction undertakings as formulated under the Act: the grounds and the information underlying the restriction undertaking are so limited that a director has little means of knowing the basis on which a restriction application may be made; the strength of the grounds that may be relied upon; or the likelihood of a court making a declaration of restriction. It is also not clear from the Act that a refusal to give a restriction undertaking will necessarily result in a court application in that regard. However, it must be assumed to be so and this is supported by the language of s 852(3)(d), for example, which states the "Director will refrain from making an application", suggesting that absent a restriction undertaking the Director would otherwise have made an application in that regard

[8.079] An individual in receipt of a restriction notice must therefore make the decision whether to give a restriction undertaking on the basis of very limited information. As against this, the Act contains no costs implications or other sanctions or consequences of giving or (potentially more importantly) not giving a restriction undertaking. This topic was considered during the work of the Company Law Review Group, but it was ultimately decided that any costs provisions in connection with undertakings would jeopardise the constitutionality of the undertaking regime.[58]

[8.080] If a director has a firm belief in the responsibility of his conduct as a director, he could refuse the undertaking and contest the application. Otherwise, there could be some merit in giving a restriction undertaking on the limited grounds specified under the Act and then relying on all relevant exculpatory material in seeking relief.

[8.081] Another incentive in the Act towards giving an undertaking is in s 583(7):

> "Where the person who has given the restriction undertaking (the 'immediate undertaking') is already restricted by virtue of an earlier restriction undertaking or restriction declaration, the period specified in the immediate undertaking shall run concurrently with the remaining period for which the person is already subject to restriction."

[8.082] Therefore, if a person already stands restricted, there is a good reason to give a restriction undertaking thereby avoiding both (a) the risk of a costs order in a contested application under s 820(2) and (b) the possible prolonging of the period of restriction.

(b) Disqualification undertakings

(i) Background

[8.083] On an application under s 842 of the Act as under s 160(2) of the Companies Act 1990, the court enjoys full discretion in determining whether to make an order of disqualification and the appropriate period of disqualification. The Supreme Court held in *Re CB Readymix Ltd*:[59]

> "The onus does fall on the applicant to establish the allegations on which he relies and, even where a case is made out, the use of the word 'may' in s 160(2) confers a discretion on the court whether or not to make the order as was pointed out in *Re Newcastle Timber Ltd (in liquidation)* [2001] 4 IR 586."[60]

[8.084] A court may therefore refuse to make an order of disqualification, even if satisfied that the grounds for making such an order have been fully established. This demonstrates the breadth of the discretion enjoyed.

[8.085] The High Court has however noted the absence of a procedure under s 160 for a respondent to furnish an undertaking not to be involved in companies in the manner prohibited by disqualification orders. In *Re National Irish Bank*

---

58 See *Report of the Company Law Review Group* 2007 at pp 73–75.
59 *Re CB Readymix Concrete Ltd, Cahill v Grimes* [2002] 1 IR 372.
60 *Re CB Readymix Concrete Ltd, Cahill v Grimes* [2002] 1 IR 372 at 381, *per* Murphy J.

Ltd, Director of Corporate Enforcement v D'Arcy[61] the respondent did not contest the disqualification application, as Kelly J recorded:

"I am satisfied that Mr. D'Arcy should be given credit for the approach which he has taken to the Director's complaints. He is entitled to allowance for the fact that he indicated from the outset that he would not contest this application and, in fact, consented to the disqualification order being made.

He went somewhat further than that because even before these proceedings were commenced his solicitors wrote, on his instructions, tendering his resignation with immediate effect from the two companies of which he is a director. He also indicated a willingness to give an undertaking in writing to the Director that he would not act as director, promoter, officer or involve himself in any way in the formation or management of both those companies or any company whatsoever."[62]

[8.086] Kelly J concluded that the approach taken by the respondent was a mitigating factor and reduced the period of disqualification by two years to reflect this fact.

[8.087] In *Director of Corporate Enforcement v Curran*,[63] Mr Curran submitted that the Director did not contact him to seek information regarding his future plans or inviting an undertaking as to the level of responsibility he would take in any business in which he might be involved before initiating the disqualification proceedings.[64] Murphy J made the following observation:

"The question arises whether the legislation should be amended with a view to compelling the Director to require an undertaking from such a director/officer. There would appear to be no provision whereby such undertaking could be a matter of public record. It could be noted by the Director of Corporate Enforcement and/or by the Company Registration Office. It would be an immediate remedy and a saving in court time and of costs."[65]

[8.088] A similar proposal was made by the ODCE, but was not enacted in the IFCMPA 2006:

"... the introduction of 'consent' procedures for disqualification and restriction in recognition of the fact that many such Court proceedings were not contested. These consent undertakings would have a similar legal status to the present Court

61 *Re National Irish Bank Ltd, Director of Corporate Enforcement v D'Arcy* [2006] 2 IR 163.
62 *Re National Irish Bank Ltd, Director of Corporate Enforcement v D'Arcy* [2006] 2 IR 163 at 180.
63 *Re National Irish Bank Ltd, Director of Corporate Enforcement v Curran* [2007] IEHC 181.
64 *Re National Irish Bank Ltd, Director of Corporate Enforcement v Curran* [2007] IEHC 181 at para 9.13.
65 *Re National Irish Bank Ltd, Director of Corporate Enforcement v Curran* [2007] IEHC 181 at para 9.13.

orders and would therefore save the associated legal costs of proceeding to Court. In relevant cases, this would benefit the liquidation and make more funds available for distribution to the company's creditors."[66]

[8.089] In England, it has been possible since 2001 for a person to give an undertaking in the terms of a disqualification order for such period between two and fifteen years as may be agreed.[67] As reported by the Department of Trade and Industry:

"On 2 April 2001, amendments to s 6 of [Directors Disqualification Act 1986] made by the Insolvency Act 2000 came into force. Amongst other things, this allows directors, whom the Secretary of State considers to have exhibited unfit conduct, to avoid the need for a court hearing by offering a Disqualification Undertaking acceptable to the Secretary of State. A Disqualification Undertaking has exactly the same legal effect as a Disqualification Order made by the court and usually includes a Schedule identifying the unfit conduct upon which it was accepted. The consequences of breaching a Disqualification Undertaking are the same as those for breaching a Disqualification Order. This undertaking is enforceable in the same manner as an order of disqualification."[68]

[8.090] The need for disqualifications by consent without the necessity of contested court proceedings has therefore been well-flagged in the Irish courts. Chapter 5 of Part 14 of the Companies Act now introduces disqualification undertakings into Irish company law. The provisions are similar to those that apply to restriction undertakings, but differ in some significant respects.

(ii) Grounds for disqualification undertakings

[8.091] According to s 850(2), where the Director has "reasonable grounds for believing that one or more of the circumstances specified in section [842](a) to (i) applies to a person" the Director may, in his or her discretion, deliver to the person a disqualification notice.

[8.092] The grounds that are specified in s 842(a) to 842(i) are the grounds on which an order of disqualification may be made.[69] If the Director has reasonable grounds for believing one of those grounds to exist, he must set out in the disqualification notice which of the grounds he believes to apply and particulars

---

[66] ODCE, *Annual Report 2006* at p 9.

[67] See DTI, "Fast Track Disqualifications results in Record Bans" (2 January 2002).

[68] DTI, "Fast Track Disqualifications results in Record Bans" (2 January 2002). The Department also reports that: "Under the new rules directors can give an undertaking not to act as a director for an agreed period between 2 and 15 years. The undertakings are made to The Insolvency Service and registered at Companies House. They are accessible by public search and if contravened will constitute criminal offence. Today's figures show that of the 935 disqualifications recorded in the half year period (Q2&3), 57 per cent were on the basis of undertakings given to and accepted by The Insolvency Service."

[69] See Cahill, *Company Law Compliance and Enforcement* (2008), Ch 22.

-of the facts and allegations that give rise to that belief. The notice must also state the period of disqualification. It is important to note that the Director cannot send a disqualification notice, if he believes that a period of disqualification of more than five years is warranted.[70]

(iii) Disqualification notice

[8.093] The disqualification notice shall state that, for a period commencing at least 21 days after the date of the notice and ending on the date on which the disqualification period would commence,[71] the person in question may notify the Director of his willingness to give the undertaking and return an executed "disqualification acceptance document".[72]

[8.094] According to s 850(3)(e), the disqualification notice shall state that, during the notice period, "the Director will refrain from making an application in respect of the person under section [842] arising from or in connection with the underlying facts and circumstances". There are two things to observe here. First, it would leave the Director free to commence disqualification proceedings in the 21-day period from the issue of the notice (although this is of course highly unlikely). Second, it does not refer to or preclude proceedings being initiated by another person, such as a liquidator, receiver, member, contributory, examiner, creditor, officer, employee, or indeed the Director of Public Prosecutions or Registrar of Companies, all of whom have statutory standing to bring such an application under s 844. While a person is considering and taking advice as to whether to give a disqualification undertaking to the Director, disqualification proceedings could be commenced by any one of these individuals. What should happen in that circumstance is not clear from the Act, although it is difficult to see how the issue of a disqualification notice could trump the issue of court proceedings by a person who has standing under the Act to issue such proceedings.

[8.095] This is addressed to some extent by s 851(1):

> "Where a notice is delivered under section [850](2), the Director and every person who is aware of the notice shall not, during the notice period, make an application under section [842], arising from or in connection with the underlying facts and circumstances, in respect of the person who is the subject of the notice."

[8.096] The effect of this provision on other applicants for disqualification depends on such persons being "aware of the notice", without, however, specifying how such persons are to be made "aware" of the notice and how such

---

70   See s 851(6).
71   This period may be extended on the application of the person in receipt of the notice. See s 850(5).
72   Section 850(3).

awareness is to be demonstrated. It is easily conceivable that a member/director/ liquidator could issue proceedings while an individual is considering how to respond to a disqualification notice from the Director. A further issue that arises in the context of disqualifications is that the legislature has chosen to give standing to a wide category of persons to bring disqualification proceedings. While in practice the vast majority of such applications are brought by the Director, a person who has standing under the Act could find that standing supplanted by the potentially arbitrary fact of being "aware of" a notice issued by the Director. The operation of this provision may be problematic for such persons who wish, for example, to seek disqualification in conjunction with other reliefs in civil proceedings.

[8.097] The equivocal language of this provision can be contrasted with s 851(4) which states:

> "After the expiry of the notice period, neither the Director nor any other person shall make an application under section [842], arising from or in connection with the underlying facts and circumstances, in respect of the person who has given the restriction undertaking."

[8.098] There is therefore no ambiguity but that an individual who gives a disqualification undertaking cannot be subject to a disqualification application brought by any person arising from the same grounds and facts that gave rise to the undertaking.

(iv) Consequences of a disqualification undertaking

[8.099] When a disqualification undertaking has been given, the Director shall as soon as practicable (a) furnish all requisite particulars to the Registrar of Companies for entry in the register of disqualified persons; and (b) execute a "disqualification acceptance document" and furnish a copy of that document and notify the particulars given to the Registrar to the disqualified person.[73]

[8.100] A person who gives a disqualification undertaking "shall be deemed, for the purposes of this Act, to be subject to a disqualification order".[74] It may be noted that the disqualification notice must state that:

> "... if the person gives a disqualification undertaking –
>
> (i)   the person may seek to be relieved (whether in whole or in part) from the undertaking only by applying to the court under section [847]; and
>
> (ii) that, on the making of such an application, the court may grant such relief only if it considers it just and equitable to do so, and then only on the terms and conditions as it sees fit."[75]

---

[73]   Section 851(3).
[74]   Section 851(5)(b).
[75]   Section 850(4)(c).

[8.101] The Act states that this information must be included in the disqualification notice, but there is no provision of the Companies Act confirming that a person who gives a disqualification undertaking can apply for relief under s 847. However, s 847(1) does state that the court may "on the application by a person who is subject to a disqualification order" grant relief from such disqualification in whole or part, without limiting the grounds on which or the means by which that person may have been disqualified. The fact that a person who gives a disqualification undertaking is deemed by s 851(5)(b) to be subject to a disqualification order appears to bring a person who gives such an undertaking within s 847.

[8.102] If a person is already subject to disqualification, the period of the disqualification undertaking shall run concurrently with the unexpired portion of that prior period of disqualification.[76]

(c) Enforcement of restriction and disqualification undertakings

[8.103] The enforcement of restriction and disqualification undertakings is not addressed specifically by the Act. According to s 851(5)(b), a person who gives a disqualification undertaking "shall be deemed, for the purposes of this Act, to be subject to a disqualification order." Section 853(5)(b) similarly provides that a person who gives a restriction undertaking "shall be deemed, for the purposes of this Act, to be subject to a restriction declaration".

However, it seems a big step to apply the enforcement provisions and sanctions of Chapter 6 of Part 14 of the Act to persons who were not the subject of court proceedings of any form. This is particularly so when one considers that a person could face criminal prosecution and liability for the debts of the company if found to have contravened a restriction declaration or disqualification order. As against this, if the same enforcement provisions that apply to restriction declarations and disqualification orders are not applied in the case of restriction and disqualification undertakings, the latter will be deprived of any weight.

In this regard, it seems that the provisions of Chapter 6 are not specifically adapted to dealing with restriction and disqualification undertakings. First, some of the provisions dealing with enforcement refer specifically to orders made under s 819 or 842, which does not seem broad enough to encompass an undertaking under s 851 or 853.[77] However, it may be that a person being "deemed to be" subject to a restriction declaration or disqualification order "for the purposes of this Act" will be interpreted so as to allow a court to find that such person is in fact deemed to be subject to an order under a specific provision of the Act, namely s 819 or 842.

---

[76] Section 851(7).
[77] See eg ss 858 and 855(1)(b).

Second, s 855(5) which deals with enforcement does contain certain technical provisions regarding the use of words "deemed to be subject to" for the purposes of Chapter 6. However, it is reasonably clear that these words do not apply to restriction and disqualification undertakings. The opening line of s 855(5) confirms that the interpretation set out in s 855(5)(b) of the words being "deemed to be subject to" a disqualification order apply to that section and subsequent provisions of Chapter 6. The same clarification appears in s 855(6) in relation to restriction. The fact that there are particular provisions in Chapter 6 dealing with the wording of persons being "deemed to be subject to" restriction or disqualification, which relate only to the use of those words in Chapter 6, only serves to highlight the fact that the status of restriction and disqualification undertakings which are not the product of orders under s 819 or 842 are not addressed by that Chapter. The enforcement of such undertakings is not therefore provided for in clear or explicit terms by the Act at present. However, as against this, a court may find that the effect of s 851(5)(b) and s 853(5)(b) is that a person is already deemed to be subject to restriction or disqualification and is not solely so deemed under Chapter 6. The consequence would be that there is no need to apply s 855 to such a person. Therefore it may be that the technical application of Chapter 6 to restriction and disqualification undertakings is capable of resolution. However, there is then a more fundamental question to consider.

[8.104] In introducing the regime for restriction and disqualification undertakings the Company Law Review Group was very mindful of potential constitutional issues. As the 2007 Report records:

> "The first issue is whether, as a matter of constitutional law, it was appropriate to have a system of consent orders under which a non-judicial personage (the Director of Corporate Enforcement) would be conferred with a function of accepting undertakings which would have the effect of deeming a person to be restricted or disqualified. Is such an act executive or administrative (and accordingly, one that can properly be vested in the Director) or does it represent an exercise of a judicial power (and, accordingly, one which Article 34.1 of Bunreacht na hÉireann vests exclusively in the Courts, subject only to the right of the Oireachtas to confer limited judicial powers on non-judicial personages in non-criminal cases in the manner contemplated by Article 37.1 of the Constitution)? ... In the light of these concerns, the Review Group considered and concluded that —
>
> (a) the powers presently vested in the High Court under section 150 and section 160 of the 1990 Act are judicial in nature;
>
> (b) given that the effect of such a disqualification order or even a restriction order is to restrict the director in question from following a particular vocation, trade or career and further impacts adversely on his or her reputation, these powers could not be regarded as being 'limited' for the purposes of Article 37.1 of the Constitution;

(c) it follows that these powers could not be exercised in contested cases by a non-judicial personage such as the Director of Corporate Enforcement, and legislation which proposed to transfer such functions to the Director in respect of such cases could be found to be unconstitutional; and

(d) while the issue of whether the Director could be vested with such a jurisdiction in consent cases is far less clear-cut than in the case of contested applications, the Review Group remained of the view that it could not safely be concluded that this jurisdiction in such cases could be so transferred. This is in part due to the fact that the making of these orders – even by consent – concerns issues of status and operate in rem.

A court would, for example, have a jurisdiction to decline to make such orders (even where the making of such an order was by consent), where it considered that, for example, the director was not properly advised or there was duress.

The Review Group considers that a potential solution to this problem, which would not require or involve the court process, would be to offer the director or other person the opportunity of submitting to a disqualification or restriction pursuant to a statutory contract, the effect of which would be that the person would be disqualified or restricted from holding a directorship in the manner akin to the present section 150 or section 160. It might further be provided that an agreement of this kind would have the same status as an actual order made pursuant to section 150 or section 160." [78]

[8.105] The CLRG concluded:

"The main advantage here would be that the Director of Corporate Enforcement would not make the restriction or disqualification, but rather the director or other person would elect to submit to a restriction or disqualification through the mechanism of an enforceable and binding statutory contract. In other words, the election by the affected individual to submit to a binding statutory contract rather than face Court proceedings, would be a voluntary decision which he or she would not be able to contest as against the Director at a later date."

[8.106] This background and insight into the nature of restriction and disqualification undertakings is important. If the true nature of an undertaking is a "binding statutory contract", and not the product of a judicial or quasi-judicial process, it is difficult to see how a breach of the undertaking can be a criminal offence without engaging some of the constitutional issues outlined by the Review Group in 2007.

Criminal offences

[8.107] The Companies Acts specified various sanctions for offences and defaults under the Acts, ranging from fines, terms of imprisonment, daily

---

[78] *Report of the Company Law Review Group* 2007 at para 6.1.2.

default fines,[79] to orders of personal liability for the debts of a company, among others.[80] The sanction applicable to an offence was typically specified in the legislative provision that created the offence. Certain provisions of the Acts did not however stipulate any sanction for the offence created. In respect of those provisions, s 240 of the Companies Act 1990 provided that, in respect of summary convictions for which no penalty is specified in the Acts, the rule is that the maximum fine shall be €1,904.61 or, at the discretion of the court, a maximum sentence of imprisonment of 12 months, or both. The monetary fine was amended to a Class C fine (up to €2,500) by s 6 of the Fines Act 2010. When a person was convicted on indictment of an offence for which no penalty was specified in the Acts, the maximum fine was €22,220.42[81] or, at the discretion of the court, a maximum sentence of imprisonment of five years, or both.[82]

[8.108] The Companies Acts 1963 to 2013 contained approximately 138 offences that could be prosecuted on indictment.[83] These offences could also generally be tried summarily. Further, every offence which was punishable by a Class C fine or a term of imprisonment not exceeding 12 months, or both, could be prosecuted summarily.[84]

[8.109] This area of company law has now changed considerably. The Companies Act contains a novel provision categorising offences under the Companies Acts into category 1, category 2, category 3, and category 4 offences. The Company Law Review Group proposed that this categorisation of offences would apply to all offences under the Companies Acts, subject to some narrow exceptions involving the most serious offences, such as fraudulent

---

[79] Note that, in respect of default fines, CA 1990, s 240(6), provides: "Where, in relation to a contravention of any provision of the Companies Acts, it is provided that for continued contravention a person shall be liable to a daily default fine, he shall be guilty of contravening the provision on every day on which the contravention continues after conviction of the original contravention and for each such offence he shall be liable to a fine not exceeding the amount specified in the provision, instead of the penalty specified for the original contravention." The effect of this is that liability to pay the daily default fine only arises after the person has been convicted of the default in question, and when the default is ongoing, the daily default fine shall be substituted for the penalty which he would otherwise face.

[80] For a table of indictable offences under CA 1963–2005 (as the Acts were at that time) see appendix to ODCE, Revised Guidance on the Duty of Auditors to Report Suspected Indictable Offences to the Director of Corporate Enforcement, Decision Notice, D/2006/2, available at www.odce.ie.

[81] As amended by s 9 of the Fines Act 2010.

[82] CA 1990, s 240(1), as amended by CLEA 2001, s 104.

[83] See ODCE, List of Indictable Offences pursuant to the Companies Acts 1963–2005, available at www.odce.ie.

[84] CA 1990, s 240(3), as amended by CLEA 2001, s 104.

trading and market abuse.[85] The CLRG described the manner in which these categories have been compiled as follows:

> "This four-fold system will allow for an appropriately graduated system of penalties as between different offence provisions. In preparing these Heads, the CLRG has undertaken a comprehensive exercise, in conjunction with ODCE officials, of classifying the offences on what is thought to be the appropriate basis. In addition, it leads to the law being more easily understood because in each of the many provisions throughout the Bill creating offences, it is now possible to simply add a phrase along the lines of 'which will be a Category 2 offence'."[86]

[8.110] The CLRG described this approach as a "new initiative"[87] and as a "root and branch review of all criminal offences arising under the Companies Acts".[88]

[8.111] The proposal of the CLRG has been adopted and according to this new approach there are now four categories of offences:

(a) A "Category 1" offence is punishable, on summary conviction, by a Class A fine or imprisonment for a term not exceeding 12 months, or both.

On conviction on indictment, a "Category 1" offence is punishable by a maximum fine of €500,000 or a maximum term of imprisonment of 10 years, or both.[89]

(b) A "Category 2" offence is punishable, on summary conviction, by a Class A fine or maximum sentence of imprisonment of 12 months, or both.

On conviction on indictment, a "Category 2" offence is punishable by a maximum fine of €50,000, or a maximum sentence of imprisonment of 5 years, or both.[90]

---

85 See CLRG, *Report on the General Scheme of the Draft Companies Consolidation and Reform Bill 2007*, at p 68. It may be noted that Pt A13, Head 57(2) envisaged only four categories of indictable offences: category 1 and 2 offences; offences under the Market Abuse Regulations; and offences under the Prospectus Regulations.

86 CLRG, *Report on the General Scheme of the Draft Companies Consolidation and Reform Bill 2007*, at p 68, available at www.clrg.org.

87 CLRG, *Report on the General Scheme of the Draft Companies Consolidation and Reform Bill 2007*, at p 68.

88 CLRG, *Report on the General Scheme of the Draft Companies Consolidation and Reform Bill 2007*, at p 3.

89 Section 871(1).

90 Section 871(2).

(c) A "Category 3" offence is punishable, on summary conviction to a Class A fine or a maximum term of imprisonment of 6 months, or both.[91]

(d) A "Category 4" offence is punishable, on summary conviction to a Class A fine.[92]

[8.112] There is no provision for convictions on indictment in respect of category 3 and category 4 offences, and category 4 offences are subject to the sanction of a fine only.

[8.113] The exceptions to this categorisation are the three "super offences", as so described by the CLRG.[93]

A serious market abuse offence under s 1368:

> "A person who is guilty of an offence created by Irish market abuse law (being an offence expressed by that law to be an offence to which this section applies) shall, without prejudice to any penalties provided by that law in respect of a summary conviction for the offence, be liable, on conviction on indictment, to a fine not exceeding €10,000,000 or imprisonment for a term not exceeding 10 years or both."

A serious prospectus offence under s 1356(1) of which provides:

> "A person who is guilty of an offence created by Irish prospectus law (being an offence expressed by that law to be an offence to which this section applies) shall, without prejudice to any penalties provided by that law in respect of a summary conviction for the offence, be liable, on conviction on indictment, to a fine not exceeding €1,000,000 or imprisonment for a term not exceeding 5 years or both."

A serious transparency offence under s 1382:

> "A person who is guilty of an offence created by transparency (regulated markets) law (being an offence expressed by that law to be an offence to which this section applies) shall, without prejudice to any penalties provided by that law in respect of a summary conviction for the offence, be liable, on conviction on indictment, to a fine not exceeding €1,000,000 or imprisonment for a term not exceeding 5 years or both."

[8.114] Applying the new categorisation of offences throughout the Act as Category 1, 2, 3 of 4 offences, provisions which create criminal offences do not state the sanction applicable to that offence, but instead specify the category of offence that is created. This will make the legislation more clear and will also make the severity of the offence more readily apparent. It will also assist in the identification of indictable offences, which is particularly relevant for the

---

[91] Section 871(3).
[92] Section 871(4).
[93] *Company Law Review Group Report 2011* at para 5.5.1.

discharge by auditors of their obligation to report the suspected commission of indictable offences. The CLRG issued the following guidelines to be applied in the categorisation of any new offences that may be created in the future:

- "Proportionality between the commission of an offence and the consequence of committing an offence is key. Proportionality between the consequences for committing the new offence and other offences in the Bill should also be taken into account.

- It is unlikely that additional new 'super offences' would be introduced. Indeed, there is a case for their consolidation into the new scheme as Category 1 offences.

- New offences introduced should be reviewed to see whether they should be classified as 'technical' or 'filing' offences, in which case they should be classified as a Category 4 offence, or in the case of technical or filing offences which are likely to have a wider impact, possible as a Category 3 offence.

- Category 1 and 2 offences although capable of being prosecuted summarily, are also capable of prosecution on indictment and it is considered that only the more serious offences where there is a public policy reason for classifying the offence as indictable, should be classified in this way. In determining the respective merits of a Category 2 or 3 classification, account should be taken of the exceptional case of misconduct and the need to facilitate a Court in imposing a proportionate penalty in such a case.

- In assessing the potential deterrent effect of classifying a default in complying with a Companies Act requirement as an offence, regard should be had to the potential impact which the commission of such an offence would have on all relevant stakeholders, including without limitation, the company, its shareholders and creditors. Wider policy considerations such as the importance of the maintenance of accessible public records in respect of companies incorporated in Ireland might also be considered."[94]

[8.115] A further new provision that is relevant in the context of criminal convictions is s 872 which provides:

"The Court in which a conviction for an offence under this Act is recorded or affirmed may order that the person convicted should remedy the breach of this Act in respect of which that person was convicted."

[8.116] A person may potentially face a three-fold sanction: a fine, imprisonment and an order to remedy the breach.

[8.117] Certain other changes have been made to the enforcement provisions of the Companies Acts. It should be noted, for example, that the enforcement powers of the Registrar of Companies have been curtailed.[95] The offences which

---

94   *Report of the Company Law Review Group 2011* at para 5.5.2.

can be prosecuted summarily by the Registrar are now only those which can be prosecuted on the basis of evidence available on CRO records or through access to court orders. The explanatory memorandum to the Companies Bill explains this change as follows:

"The CRO does not have an investigative function and, accordingly, it is not considered appropriate to continue to vest the Registrar with a capacity to prosecute offences which require that evidence be adduced which can be obtained only following a more comprehensive investigation. Such offences will, however, remain prosecutable by the Director of Corporate Enforcement."[96]

---

95   See s 865 of the Act.
96   Explanatory memorandum to the Companies Bill 2012 at p 287.

Index

Note: references are to *paragraph* number